Dear J.D.

What to Do with Your Law Degree

Nelson P. Miller

Dear J.D.: What to Do with Your Law Degree.

Miller, Nelson P.

Published by:

Crown Management, LLC – July 2014
1527 Pineridge Drive
Grand Haven, MI 49417
USA

ISBN: 978-0-9905553-1-5

All Rights Reserved
© 2014 Nelson P. Miller / Crown Management, LLC

To Boo ... yes, you!

Table of Contents

Foreword vii

Part 1: Character

1 Conversation 1
2 Care 4
3 Question 6
4 Stress 9
5 Intrinsic Value 11
6 Rule of Law 13
7 Economics 15
8 Effectiveness 18
9 Master or Servant? 20
10 Constraints 23
11 Choices 26
12 Good Decisions 29
13 Happiness 32
14 Direct Pursuit 34
15 Virtue 37
16 Affinities 39
17 Meaning 42
18 Philosophy 45
19 Persons 48
20 Faith 50

21 Calling 52
22 Legacy 55
23 Courage 58
24 Listening 61

Part 2: Structure

25 Licensure 63
26 Making a Living 66
27 Employment or Practice 68
28 Full Time 71
29 Part Time 74
30 Personal Finances 77
31 Skill Building 80
32 Confrontation 84
33 Choosing Sides 87
34 Forums 90
35 Firm Size 92
36 Large Firms 95
37 Mid-Size Firms 97
38 Small Firms 100
39 Solo Practice 103
40 Management 106
41 Rainmaking 109
42 Firm Finances 112
43 Practice Fields 115
44 Practice Mix 118
45 General Practice 121

46 Specializing 125
47 Boutique Practice 127
48 Transactions or Litigation 130
49 Transactional Practice 133
50 Litigation 136
51 Dispute Resolution 139
52 Criminal or Civil 142

Part 3: Practice

53 Criminal Justice 145
54 Criminal Defense 148
55 Drunk-Driving Defense 152
56 Federal Defense 155
57 White-Collar Defense 159
58 License Defense 162
59 Civil Litigation 165
60 Commercial Litigation 169
61 Federal Litigation 172
62 Class Actions 175
63 Appellate Advocacy 178
64 Personal Injury 182
65 Insurance Defense 186
66 Worker's Compensation 189
67 Social Security Disability 193
68 Malpractice 196
69 Civil Rights 200
70 Family Law 203

71 Juvenile Law 206
72 School Law 209
73 Employment Law 212
74 Labor Law 215
75 Bankruptcy 218
76 Collections 222
77 Estate Planning 225
78 Probate Practice 228
79 Business Planning 231
80 Securities Law 235
81 Intellectual Property Law 238
82 Taxation 242
83 Real Property 245
84 Natural Resources Law 249
85 Insurance Law 252
86 Health Law 255
87 Municipal Law 259
88 Administrative Law 262
89 Immigration Law 266

Part 4: Employment

90 Prosecution 270
91 Public Defender 274
92 Public Interest 277
93 Legislative Work 280
94 Judicial Positions 283
95 Corporate Counsel 286

96 Judge Advocate General Corps	289
97 Legal Education	293
98 Human Resources	296
99 Business Management	298
100 Risk Management	301
Conclusion	304
About the Author	306
Bibliography	307
Index	313

Dear J.D.

Foreword

The author acknowledges the support of Thomas M. Cooley Law School, its board, and its President and Dean Don LeDuc. The law school has practice preparation as its mission. The school carries out that mission through a dedicated full-time and adjunct faculty comprised of skilled and experienced practitioners. The school also offers practice-preparation courses in management, development, technology, and finance. The author also thanks the head librarian of the school's Grand Rapids campus Aletha Honsowitz and her staff members including Amy Ash and Matthew Sherman for research support.

The school's support led to development of the Practice Series of books supporting the everyday work of lawyers. The first of those books *A Law Graduate's Guide: Navigating Law School's Hidden Professional-Development Curriculum* helps law students and recent graduates connect their law studies and co-curricular and extra-curricular activities with law-practice opportunities. The second of those books *Lawyers as Economic*

Drivers: The Business Case for Legal Services helps lawyers see and project their work for the generative value-add that it is. One must first know the value of what one does to get others to rely on it. The third Practice Series book *Building Your Practice with Pro Bono for Lawyers* helps lawyers reach the underserved so as to expand the ordering and generative benefits of law services. The fourth Practice Series book *Entrepreneurial Practice: Enterprise Skills for Lawyers Serving Emerging Client Populations* helps lawyers develop reliable packaging, pricing, and delivery models so as to extend the reach and positive influence of their law services. The fifth Practice Series book *Lawyer Finances: Principles and Practices for Personal and Professional Financial Success* helps lawyers develop and deploy sustainable financial practices to ensure the continued availability of their services.

This sixth Practice Series book *Dear J.D.: Deciding What to Do with Your Law Degree* helps law students and lawyers identify and commit to a particular law practice among the hundreds of possible choices. Liberty depends on the rule of law, which depends on the frequent, discrete, and minute services of lawyers on behalf of individual, corporate, nonprofit, and public clients. Lawyers must be able to form and manage an effective enterprise to provide those critical services. The first step in doing so involves choosing that enterprise's mission, strategies, location, clientele, and services. This book *Dear J.D.* offers a conversational study of how to go about making that important decision of law practices.

The book begins with several short studies on the character of lawyers and law practice. You must first have the right attitude, put some fundamentals in place, or, as we say, *get your head on straight* before you can think clearly about what to do with your law degree. The book's second part offers several more short studies on the structure of law practices. You should know something of how lawyers deliver law services so that you can see how the structure of those delivery forms and mechanisms affect your preferred position. The book's third part offers many short studies of specific practice areas that lawyers pursue within private for-profit law firms. Private practice within firms is the primary delivery vehicle for law services, the heart of the profession. Each such section lists related practice areas to help you see the overlap, mix, and relationship of practice areas. The book's fourth and last part studies employment opportunities. While most lawyers practice in private law firms, many other lawyers are employees of government and nonprofit agencies, often performing the same or similar services as lawyers in private practice but doing so under different work conditions.

To simplify and guide your reading, the main reading in each short section of the book ends with a one-sentence takeaway and then a short response that you may adopt—a proposed answer to what you will do with your law degree. To guide and engage you more fully, each short section also offers reflection questions and engagement exercises. To help you envision actual lawyer models for practice, many of the short sections also offer practitioner profiles and snapshots of illustrative exchanges between lawyers in those practice areas. Best wishes in choosing a meaningful, engaging, sustainable, and effective law practice.

Dear J.D.

Part 1

Character

1 Conversation

May we talk? You've been looking stressed lately, not fully yourself, as if something has been weighing you down more than that something should. I think that I know what *that something* is, having to do with your career choice and job search, about which you seem so unsure. Yet first, remember who I am. I am your lawyer father, or if you prefer (because who wants to listen to a father?), then maybe your kindly lawyer uncle or aunt, or if they're all crazy like my aunts and uncles are crazy, then that lawyer friend of your family who inspired you to go to law school. Yes, that's it. When you are having a rough day like you seem to be having today, blame law school on me. I am fine with that. Sometimes you need someone to blame, even though at the same time you really want to thank them rather than blame them. You just need to let them know how hard things seem to have gotten when they shouldn't be so hard. "The process of job- or career-transition is not linear in nature. … [T]he key to a successful transition is flexibility and persistence." ARRON, WHAT CAN YOU DO WITH A LAW DEGREE? at 228.

So let's talk, and not just right now, but whenever you have a few minutes, here and there, over the next few weeks and months. I want to see that lightness return to your step and that smile grace your face once again. Sometimes you need to stop to remind yourself that you are doing something so special. The job and career will come. "Here is the good news: Almost all of you will find work. Some will do it sooner than others; some will get more money than others; some will find jobs with more prestige than others; some will be happier with where they land than others. But you *will* find a job." MUNNEKE, THE LEGAL CAREER GUIDE, at 4.

Takeaway: **Talk with trusted advisors about what you plan to do.**

Response: "I do not know yet what law I want to practice but am speaking with knowledgeable career advisors who are helping me and am confident of soon getting a better sense of my direction."

Reflect: How have you been feeling about law school? Have you found yourself frustrated or confused over your choice to pursue a law degree, or down and maybe even depressed at times? If so, then what do you think is the source? Also, who inspired you to attend law school? Who has supported you the most? Have you spoken with them lately about your progress? Consider doing so.

Engage: On a scale of 1 to 10, from least to most, rate your confidence in the value of pursuing a law degree. If your answer is anything less than a 9, then commit to taking the steps that this book recommends to improve your confidence.

If your answer is a 9 or 10, then commit to helping other law students increase their confidence.

Snapshot: "You know, don't you, that you are an insurance-defense lawyer?" the law professor joked with the law student in a private meeting that the student had sought over career choices. "What do you mean?" the student replied, not having given litigation, no less insurance defense, any particular thought. Just to make the point, the student added in jest, "I thought I'd be some kind of office lawyer drafting obscure documents." The law professor explained that the student's outstanding success in college athletics as the focal point of her teams had proven both her leadership and performance skills, even if that pursuit had been physical rather than intellectual. "You have the courage, presence, and command of a trial lawyer," the law professor summarized, adding, "but with a judge in your family, you also have a discerning spirit that helps you see through things. Those, my friend, are the skills and attributes of an insurance-defense lawyer." Two years later, immediately after graduation, the student had joined a leading statewide insurance defense firm. A year later, the law professor saw the student at an insurance-law conference, with all of the confidence and command of a star collegiate athlete, only now completely at ease in her insurance-defense role.

2   Care

Please trust me (although I hope that you know better than to trust anyone else who tells you to trust them). You know that I care about you. You should also realize that others who care about you just as much as I do surround and support you here at your law school. Sometimes, we care more about you than we care about ourselves, which is actually quite rare and hard to do. Yet we do care about you. We so badly want to see you flourish and prosper. "My purpose is to inform you about the choices that you will face in pursuing a legal profession, the importance of having well-informed choices—made by you and for you. In the end, it is all about choices and the limitations of some career paths and the opportunities of others." BLAKELY, BEST FRIENDS AT THE BAR, at 5.

We know this profound truth that every soul has infinite worth no matter its circumstance or condition. Your professors have discovered that law school of all places allows us to pursue that truth through serving and supporting you in your learning and development. On our very best days we might even hope to have inspired you, although much more often you are our inspiration. See how deeply we care? You should care so much about you! "[E]ach of us must take on the quest of finding work that we care about, and caring about the way we work." ARRON, WHAT CAN YOU DO WITH A LAW DEGREE?, at 261.

Takeaway: **Find people and professionals who care about you, and listen to them.**

Response: "While I am still unsure of what law to practice, I am finding that senior lawyers care about and mentor new lawyers."

Reflect: To what degree have your law professors supported your learning? How well have they supported your career exploration? Have you sought them out for career advice? Have you met regularly with your school's career and professional-development staff? Do you know and use the resources that your school's career office offers?

Engage: On a scale of 1 to 10, from least to most, rate the support of your law professors and career advisors. If your answer is anything less than an 8, then commit to meeting with the placement dean, student dean, faculty dean, or campus dean to find stronger career-advising support. If your answer is an 8, 9, or 10, then plan to help other students find strong career support.

3 Question

So here it is, *that something* that has been weighing on you. You know, like every other law student knows, what polite friends and family members routinely ask law students by way of greeting: "So, have you decided what kind of law you want to practice?" *The question* has been weighing on you, hasn't it? The funny thing is that as much as law school helps you prepare to practice law, it does not always help you answer *the question*. Think of it: has anyone offered you a well-developed framework within which to explore your own answer to *the question*? "[A] unique and idiosyncratic mix of factors ... affect your universe of options. What you will be able to attain is affected by such things as your core competencies or skills, your career goals, the current market, your personality, workplaces that are busy enough to hire, how you handle an interview, your motivation, and many other variables. There is no master list of workplaces that have jobs that are right for you. This is a frustrating situation. There is inadequate information for you to rely on as you begin your search." NIELSEN, JOB QUEST FOR LAWYERS, at 1.

Oh sure, you've heard our personal stories, maybe even some sage advice, but what about a really well-thought-out approach to that most-important question? Law school professionalism programs introduce you to model lawyers. Law school clinical and pro bono programs give you actual law-practice experiences. Yet for all of that help in exploring practice areas, we may not be helping you with thoughtful frameworks within which to address *the question*. So again, maybe we should talk. "The first step toward a balanced and healthy practice is to figure out what you want to get from it. Once you have a clear picture of your personal goals for your legal career and your life, it becomes easier to sift through the things you must accept and the things you accept responsibility to change. So take a second to think about your goals. What do you really want?" HOUCHIN, FUEL THE SPARK: 5 GUIDING VALUES FOR SUCCESS IN LAW AND LIFE, at 6.

Takeaway: **You may be unsure of what to do with your degree and may not yet have found the framework within which to evaluate that question.**

Response: "I have been looking for a sound framework within which to explore the issue of my choice of practice area."

Reflect: Who has asked you recently what kind of law you wish to practice? Make a list of all of the persons who have asked you that question since you started law school. Include in your list not only family members and friends but law students, law professors, and lawyers.

Engage: On a scale of 1 to 10, from least to most, rate the career insight, whether about yourself or about law fields, that each of the persons you listed who asked you *the question* could offer you. Keep those persons whom you rated 8, 9, or 10 in mind as you think about getting advice on what law field or career would be best for you.

Snapshot: The law professor had gotten used to having his own child attending his law school. Nothing was particularly unusual about it. Several faculty members had children attend, just as many lawyers have children who follow them into law practice, even joining them in their firms. The experience, though, had given the law professor a refreshing reminder of that one big question that most law students face, a question that he heard family and friends repeatedly ask his daughter, "So, what kind of law are you going to practice?" Listening to his daughter's various replies, he also realized how difficult the answer could be when law students have no particular way to go about developing a sound answer.

4 Stress

No doubt, students suffer real anxiety over *the question*. Some students seem to fall apart emotionally, psychologically, or spiritually just near the end of law school. Their sudden decline at the end rather than at the beginning or in the middle surprises both them and us. The challenge of law school should be getting in and through it, not getting out of and beyond it. For a lot of us lawyers, life *after* law school is bliss compared to life *during* law school. Sure, accumulating financial obligations, uncertainty over job prospects, and the looming bar examination unnerve students in their third year. Any one of those factors would naturally produce some level of stress. "[Lawyers] tend to be skeptical, cynical, judgmental, questioning, argumentative, and self-protective. This skepticism characteristic serves us well when dealing with our adversaries, but doesn't serve us well ... when designing our lives and careers." VOGT, PREPARING FOR REENTRY, at 9.

The question of what to do with your law degree compounds each of those challenges. *The question* undermines a student's commitment to facing and overcoming those other challenges, which after all are quite manageable. Yes, you can pass the bar exam. Yes, you will find a job, probably just soon enough. And yes, you will pay off your student loans, probably earlier than you expected. What, though, will you do with that law degree? You still need to answer that question. "Some students simply avoid dealing with career issues because the stress involved in job hunting makes it easy to procrastinate. Perhaps because of the numerous demands placed upon their time, many law students have a tendency to deal only with problems that need immediate attention. These students often look for jobs only when they absolutely, positively have to do it. If you act on information in a timely manner throughout your law school career, not just when you are approaching graduation, you will maximize your options." MUNNEKE, THE LEGAL CAREER GUIDE, at 45.

Takeaway: **Not knowing what career to pursue can stress you.**

Response: "While not knowing what I plan to do with my law degree stresses me some, I am committed to exploring options intentionally until I have a clear answer."

Reflect: How sure are you of what you will do with your law degree? If you are reasonably sure, then how would you explain to another why you are so sure? If you are mostly unsure, then think of law student friends or acquaintances who seem sure. What made them so? Commit to asking some of those acquaintances.

Engage: On a scale of 1 to 10, from least to most, rate where you stand when it comes to knowing what to do with your law degree. If my answer is anything less than a 6, then I commit to exploring specific options through the steps this book suggests until I can state a more-probable-than-not answer about what I plan to do with my law degree.

5 Intrinsic Value

One good response to *the question* is that completely apart from what kind of law you plan to practice, education in law has intrinsic value. We have few better ways to learn and grow than to study the organization, disruption, and detritus of social interaction, that care for one another, promise to one another, provision for ourselves, and constitution of social regulation that comprise the subjects of law school. How effectively and ineffectively do we organize, govern, and relate pursuing everything from feeding ourselves to creative works, indeed, to reproducing and raising children? "After law school, you will always be a lawyer, no matter where you are or what you do." MUNNEKE, NONLEGAL CAREERS at 14.

Law school forces the inwardly turned college graduate to turn around and face outward. That fundamental act of maturing has its own value that we see the world through the collective experiences of others. What price do you put on living a fuller life through a deeper understanding of its social responsibilities and possibilities?

Takeaway: **Careers aside, value your law learning in itself.**

Response: "Although I have not yet decided what law to practice, I am enjoying learning law and am confident that my learning has value."

Reflect: Has your view of the world and its workings expanded since starting law school? If you left law school today, then would you have nonetheless gained a clearer view of how people organize and interact likely to influence your actions deep into the future? Would the world be a better place if everyone had at least a little more understanding of law?

Engage: If you had one opportunity to consult an oracle about a decision you had to make that was going to affect you, your family, and many others for a long time, then would you rather that the oracle have been trained as an (a) theologian, (b) neurosurgeon, (c) psychiatrist, (d) economist, (e) engineer, (f) cosmologist, (g) astrologist, (h) philosopher, or (i) lawyer?

Snapshot: The question had never seemed that important to him. While other law students stressed about what might be their future practice field, he was confident alone in the value of his learning. He had been a military chaplain. He had been in the middle of battles without a weapon to defend himself, there only to support and comfort, and guide the conscience of, his unit's members. He could distinguish the important questions, the fundamental questions, from the practical questions. Yes, he would soon begin to use his law training. Yet until then he learned as broadly and deeply, and grew intellectually and spiritually, as much as he possibly could. After graduation, he joined a close friend in a general law practice but continued to accept deployments as a military chaplain. Oddly, both law practice and military chaplaincy placed him frequently in places of intimate trust and confidence, exactly as he sought and for what his nature best fitted him.

6 Rule of Law

When facing *the question* of what to do with your law degree, the significance of law, or more properly of the *rule* of law, hardly seems like a satisfying answer. Yet get this part of your answer right, and you will go a longer way than you might think in ensuring a meaningful career. The rule of law is hugely important, something so precious that you can hardly underestimate it. By *rule of law*, I do not mean a thicket of regulation or a veritable rule of lawyers. Just the opposite. I mean that least bit of social control that most ensures the greatest liberty of the greatest number. "Lawyer-Altruists expect to practice law graciously, the way they remember Gregory Peck portrayed Atticus Finch in the film version of *To Kill a Mockingbird*. They want to uplift the downtrodden, be an advocate for the oppressed, and bring peace to the lives of those in great turmoil, confusion and pain. Lawyer-Altruists are neither unusual nor delusional." ARRON, RUNNING FROM THE LAW, at 58-59.

You see, that lightness of touch on the wheel (so to speak) is exactly the hardest part of the whole practice of this magnificent profession. People are so doggone ambitious and accomplished that you must give them their liberty and then stand back to watch the incredible things that they will accomplish. Yet people are also so doggone corrupt, every one of us, that we better not stand back too far, or we will see the most unbelievable evil destroy our relations in epic reign. Do not miss it: this thing *law* is tremendously precious and special.

Takeaway: **The rule of law has enormous value to us all.**

Response: "While I cannot yet say exactly what law I will practice, I am looking forward to any practice area in which I can see that my work contributes to the rule of law, which has such great social and democratic value."

Reflect: Have you any familiarity with a lawless society? Have you had your personal security threatened? Have you had substantial property stolen or deliberately destroyed? Do you grieve with the mourner and hurt with the victim? Do you have a passion to address and end injustice? If you could end one destructive practice that people commit against one another, then what would that practice be?

Engage: On a scale of 1 to 10, from least to most, to what extent do you believe that the world fills with deliberate and senseless injustices that lawyers could help redress. If your answer is anything less than an 8, then commit to following local, national, and international news more regularly to identify injustices that lawyers could redress. If your answer is 8 or higher, then commit to identifying one such injustice that your law practice could at least in part redress.

Snapshot: After nearly a decade abroad with his family, he was returning to the United States to practice law. The decade in Central and Eastern Europe, the Middle East, and Western Asia working for intergovernmental agencies on rule-of-law, international-trade, and peace initiatives had been an exciting one, exactly what he had sought as a law student and then as a new lawyer, only more so. Sometimes, the law work had been a little too exciting, such as twice when he briefly got caught in mortar and gun fire between warring factions. Mostly, though, he had enjoyed negotiating basic trade agreements and supporting nascent democracy initiatives in some of the oldest and most famous cities in the world. With his children maturing, though, it was time to get back, and time to join a law firm and establish a private law practice.

7 Economics

The rule of law means everything to personal security and liberty. It also means a lot to economic prosperity. Most of those who ask *the question* will not appreciate all that lawyers do to help businesses, markets, economies, governments, and even families work peacefully and efficiently enough to produce and sustain a modicum of prosperity. Want to form a business? Call a lawyer. Need to stop a consumer scam or investment swindle? Call a lawyer. Want to pass wealth onto the most-responsible rather than least-responsible members of the next generation? Call a lawyer. Need to negotiate a labor agreement to get striking bus drivers back to work? Call a lawyer. Need to bond-finance a new arena, bridge, or public hospital? Call a lawyer. Want to get a disabled worker back to work with accommodations? Call a lawyer. "Research confirms that the best lawyers, those who are high value-added individuals or difficult to replace, are also the happiest lawyers and often the most financially solvent." VOGT, PREPARING FOR REENTRY, at 41.

Need to form two productive households out of one non-productive one (such as in divorce involving domestic violence)? Call a lawyer. Try answering *the question* in those terms that you just want to make more people more productive so that the living standards of all rise. Know and communicate the economic value of what lawyers do. While we do not quite have King Midas' touch, we add value to our clients' matters as a matter of course in whatever we do. Know, rely on, and communicate your economic value. Build on that confidence.

Takeaway: **Your law services will generate prosperity.**

Response: "I am looking forward to practicing any area of law that contributes substantially and directly to our material prosperity. I want to see standards of living rise as my clients become more secure, creative, and productive through my law services."

Reflect: Do you value economic prosperity? Do you like it when people are working and providing for themselves and others? Where do you think your services as a lawyer would most increase the economic welfare of your community? Can you identify a renewal project underway in your community, whether of neighborhoods, commercial districts, or vocational opportunity?

Engage: Place in order of your preference one through five each of the following legal-service opportunities, to: (a) as a bond lawyer, help arrange financing for a new community hospital; (b) as a deal lawyer, help a local manufacturer acquire a competitor; (c) as an intellectual-property lawyer, help a local inventor patent a break-through technology; (d) as a legal-aid lawyer, establish new precedent for the accommodation of disabled workers; or (e) as a criminal-defense lawyer, arrange a plea deal that saves the job of a father of five young children.

Snapshot: The senior lawyer laughed at her interviewee's flip answer that the only practice that the interviewee was not interested in was something boring like a *bond lawyer*. Apparently, the interviewee had not read the bios of all of the firm's lawyers. "Do you know my practice specialty?" the senior lawyer asked politely. "No," the interviewee replied, suddenly looking worried and adding with a nervous giggle, "You aren't a bond lawyer, are you?" The senior lawyer nodded, giggling back to relax the interviewee, whom she liked. "Come here," the senior lawyer motioned as she rose from behind her desk and walked to the 20th-floor window. "See that bridge? See that stadium? See that hospital?" the senior lawyer asked as she swept her hand across the great city's panorama while identifying other landmarks, before declaring, "I built those. Now, I like you, and you're hired if you want to be a bond lawyer." A dozen years later, the two were still working together as law partners and among the nation's best bond lawyers.

8 Effectiveness

Thus the best response to "what kind of law do you want to practice?" may be that the friend or family member has asked precisely the wrong question. *Your* desire within a hardened self-conception is no longer the focus. Your focus should be outward, not inward. Maybe you will do *this*, and maybe you will do *that*, but soon the needs of others, drawn both from their pursuit of flourishing and equal pursuit of evil, will do your deciding for you. Perhaps you should instead be thinking about gaining enough skill, confidence, and experience to be useful for what your clients want and need you to do. "For a job to be satisfying and a career path to be highly successful for you, it helps if your work can utilize your strong suits. If you are innately good at what you do, you will be more likely to be satisfied and successful at work." NIELSEN, JOB QUEST FOR LAWYERS, at 140.

Once you turn outward from what *you* want to do to what *they need you to do* for them, the choice gets a lot easier. The choice becomes an edict to prepare the best you can prepare to be of the broadest and most effective service. What kind of lawyer do you and I want to be? Maybe we want to be effective ones who end and redress injustices, and promote the economic prosperity of our communities, in whatever ways that our clients require.

Takeaway: **Prepare to be *effective* in your law career, whatever clients ask of you.**

Response: "I want to be able to do well whatever clients ask most of me, which means I am going to make myself as skilled as possible to serve as broadly as possible."

Reflect: How effective do you think you could be with the law knowledge and skills that you have so far acquired? What are you missing to be a more effective lawyer? What course, program, event, or opportunity would increase your effectiveness?

Engage: On a scale of 1 to 10 from least to most, rate how effective you could be today providing each of the following services a client asked of you: (a) license an invention; (b) obtain a divorce; (c) close the sale of a home; (d) discharge debts in bankruptcy; (e) resolve a neighbor's boundary dispute; (f) negotiate a partner's buyout; (g) form a professional corporation; (h) draft a standard consumer contract; (i) renegotiate a commercial lease; (j) collect rent from a deadbeat tenant; (k) copyright a novel; (l) make a health insurer pay for an experimental service; (m) negotiate a better education plan for a disabled student; (n) get a driver's license restored; and (o) defend a charge of minor-in-possession of alcohol. Then, on a scale of 1 to 10, from least to most, rate how effective of a lawyer you could be today if you could choose your client and client's matter, in the field in which you would be most effective. What field did you choose? Why?

9   Master or Servant?

See, law practice, at least in a general, all-comers practice of the kind that is so wonderfully satisfying, is a lot like that. *You* think you will draft and file a divorce complaint today because you drafted and filed one last week. *They* think you should instead sue their neighbor for building a deck on their beachfront property. *You* think that you will form a limited-liability company today because you formed two of them last week. *They* think that you should instead document the complex terms of a swift buy-out of their dishonest joint venturer. *You* think that you will depose the plaintiff in preparation for trial. *They* think that you will draft and forward a settlement agreement including a confidentiality provision. Thus the right approach to answering *the question* may be to decide whom you would most like to serve. "We lawyers are analytical, cognitive and, some would say, detached. Too often we forget to take a step back to ponder our careers. Aspirations are fine, but alone they're not enough; good intentions are central, yet they, too, only get us so far." MORRIS, ASK THE CAREER COUNSELORS, at 3.

Lawyers are not masters of their work because they are not masters but servants, albeit generally well-paid and mostly voluntary servants. In that sense, choosing a law career is like choosing a master. If you start disliking your clients, then you will have an unhappy career. In law practice, you work for them as much as or more than you work for yourself. Choose masters whom you value and who value you.

Takeaway: **Clients will tell you what they want you to do.**

Response: "While I do not yet have a clear view of any specific client or matter, I so look forward to the compelling work that I expect innovative and needful clients will bring to me."

Reflect: For whom have you worked in the past? What was their character and the character of their conduct? What difference to your work did their character make? Did they appreciate, value, respect, and reward your work?

Engage: List in order of your preference the legal service you would most wish to provide, helping: (a) professional couples adopt foreign orphans; (b) world visionaries form charitable nonprofits; (c) billionaire philanthropists establish foundations; (d) charismatic political operatives organize action committees; (e) ace investigators obtain cold-case warrants; (f) disaster victims obtain welfare relief; (g) museum directors license masterworks; (h) master educators charter urban magnet schools; (i) private entrepreneurs accomplish space travel; and (j) utility companies generate green electricity.

Snapshot: She kept her general practice in a small strip mall along the main highway just a few blocks from the small-town courthouse. The strip-mall location, she knew, was not traditional for a law office, but her clients found it highly convenient. And besides, she owned the strip mall, which meant that she had no rent check to cut each month. She could also move her office up and down the strip mall anytime a new tenant wanted her old space. Without realizing it immediately, she had long ago developed the reputation across the rural county and into adjacent counties as a fast-acting, flexible, and creative problem-solving lawyer. Her representation was affordable and effective, meaning she never had a lack for work, was never bored, and was constantly acquiring new skills as she took on whatever her rural clients needed most. While the few other lawyers in the area maintained traditional law practices in estate planning, criminal defense, and divorces, she handled all of those areas and everything else. She managed through diligent research and a network of niche practitioners she had developed in the distant metropolitan area through bar events. Her one passion was simply to be effective for her rural clients, whom, it occurred to her one day, she just simply loved, despite all of their problems and peculiarities.

10 Constraints

Notice, though, that the kind of effectiveness that lawyers can honestly and consistently possess is a *constrained* effectiveness. Lawyers hold only a little authority that non-lawyers do not hold, such as to represent another in a court proceeding including in some systems the right to issue a subpoena ordering attendance at those proceedings. Judges have the power to jail or free, fine or forgive. Lawyers do not. Most of what lawyers do, they do out of skill rather than out of power and privilege. Individual parties can even represent themselves in court but often do not do so because of their ineffectiveness in so regulated, challenging, and important of a forum. Yet whether a lawyer acts out of privilege, such as the privilege to issue a subpoena, or acts out of skill, such as when retained by an individual party to advocate at a trial or hearing, the lawyer must act in a manner consistent with law, rule, and authority, or the lawyer will in most cases act unsuccessfully.

Lawyers do not get away with things. They accomplish things for clients because they know what is consistent with the lawful, equitable, just, and right. "[I]ndividuals tend to like doing things in which they succeed, and ... they will succeed in the future in activities similar to those in which they have succeeded in the past. The connecting thread between past, present, and future success is the skill set that helps the person to be successful." MUNNEKE, THE LEGAL CAREER GUIDE, at 28. We are not tools, or if we are tools, then we are not sharp tools but blunt tools capable only of nudging client matters closer to what they should be even as we pursue what our clients want them to be. Do not hesitate to work for scoundrels in need of your reform. The clients whose conduct you would most despise and condemn may also be the clients whom you could most help change their ways. Yet work only in ways that are within the law and thus possible honorably to succeed.

Takeaway: **You have only so much you can do for clients.**

Response: "I expect to have clients who, not knowing any better, will ask of me things that I cannot lawfully or do, and that I will not do. One of the things I most look forward to in practice is helping clients distinguish right from wrong."

Reflect: Has anyone ever asked you to do something illegal to assist them? Do ends justify means? Are you a good influence on people? Do you believe that people can have a major change of heart? Would you rather carry out the commands of a saint or work to save a sinner?

Engage: List in order of your preference the three of these ten clients whom you would most wish to represent—or least object to representing: (a) indigent defendants charged with crime; (b) employers alleged to have violated workplace-safety rules; (c) chemical makers alleged to have violated environmental rules; (d) manufacturers alleged to have made defective products; (e) hospital administrators alleged to have participated in illegal kickback schemes; (f) physicians alleged to have committed malpractice; (g) taxpayers alleged to have underpaid taxes; (h) parents alleged to have neglected their children; (i) children charged with juvenile delinquency; and (j) homeless persons alleged to have trespassed.

Snapshot: "Yeah, that's right, it's a fake," the medical-records clerk confirmed for the personal-injury lawyer, "The doc signed a slip for four days, not four months. I'll fax you a copy of the original." A new client had just handed the lawyer an off-work slip that said "4 months" when the lawyer had never seen any such doctor's excuse for more than a few days and so had called the clerk to check on its accuracy. The lawyer promptly called the client back into the office. "I am not representing you," the lawyer told the client firmly but politely as soon as the client walked in and before he could sit down. Still standing at the office door with the client, the lawyer explained calmly that he had to assume that the client had altered the off-work slip, explaining further that it would be a fraudulent and even criminal act if presented to an insurer by wire or mail for wage-loss compensation. "I love representing honest clients who need my services," the lawyer concluded, "and I am not losing my license, reputation, income, soul, and freedom to help a client defraud an insurer. Go home, think about what you have done, and don't ever do it again." The client turned silently without changing his expression and left the office. The lawyer sat down and calmly resumed his work on other matters.

11 Choices

Ah, but if you satisfy yourself with any of the above assertions about effectiveness, then your friends and family members will just smile at your non-answers to *the question*, believing that you are merely philosophizing. And in one respect, they will be right that you must still choose *something*. The law school curriculum requires choices. The rich law school co-curriculum and extra-curricular options demand more choosing. If you had gone to dental school, then you would know that you would very probably be examining your patients' teeth someday soon. Yet you chose law school. "It is all about informed choices: choices as part of a career plan, choices to make you happy, choices to make you proud, and choices to give you power. Your choices. Choices to make you *you*. Choose well and often, if necessary." BLAKELY, FRIENDS AT THE BAR, at 219.

You might someday soon be charging others with crime, or forming businesses, or negotiating public-bond deals, or disputing child custody, each pursuit reflecting its own unique set of concerns and interests. Dentists have few choices. You have many choices. Public defender or prosecutor? Family law or estate planning? In-house or private practice? Litigation or transactional work? Real estate or administrative law? Nonprofits or for-profits? Plaintiff's lawyer or defense counsel? Large firm, small firm, or solo? Your problem is your opportunity, that (to repeat a very old and curious saying) the world is your oyster. "Once you accept the notion that law is not just one career, but encompasses many different careers, it is a short step to the conclusion that you must make choices during law school regarding options available to graduates. You cannot simply wait for the right thing to come along, or postpone critical career decisions until after graduation." MUNNEKE, THE LEGAL CAREER GUIDE, at 29.

Takeaway: **Law school gives you many options.**

Response: "I have been surprised and at times even overwhelmed at the large number of options that a law degree gives me, but I am also coming to value and appreciate many of those options."

Reflect: How well do you process choice? Do decisions frustrate, confuse, or scare you? Do you have a hard time choosing what to wear, where to eat, what movie to see, or when to get your suit dry-cleaned? Or is it only the big decisions that concern you? Whom do you know that you respect as an effective decision-maker? List three such persons, recalling why you judge them to be so effective.

Engage: On a scale of 1 to 10, from least to most, rate how confident, decisive, and effective you are as a decision-maker. If you rate yourself anything less than a 6, then commit to getting the advice of one of the effective decision-makers you listed above.

Snapshot: He had always had a plan but at the same time always kept his options open. Civil rights had first interested him in law when he was in grade school. Yet by the time he entered law school, the plan had been to prepare for a law practice supporting real-estate development, drawing on personal experience and family connections. He had even gotten a job offer with a big real-estate firm in a hot metropolitan market, after completing elective coursework in property law and real-estate finance. Yet once again, just before graduation, that plan changed when the real-estate market in that region had collapsed. His family hadn't wanted him to move there, anyway. So he just stayed on at the small local law firm at which he had worked throughout law school. He realized then that while law school was preparing him for a field that he would not pursue, his work as a law clerk at the firm had prepared him for a civil-litigation field that he would pursue. Over the next decade and a half, his civil litigation in personal injury and commercial disputes gradually evolved to include civil-rights work. The journey had taken that long, but he was finally doing that which had first attracted him to law way back in grade school.

12 Good Decisions

Good decisions usually require a lot of thought. Do not misunderstand me. Most good decisions do not really seem like decisions. You think about them a lot, get a lot of counsel, and then the right things just sort of happen. Yet the thinking was probably critical to the good and orderly things that happened. Without your thought, they would not have happened in the proper order and with the necessary design that they did. A philosopher much too discredited to identify, once said that we give too little thought to things, that the world just has too little thinking. I agree. We should think more often, more clearly, and more deeply about the matters that most affect us. "[R]esponsibility for creating a satisfying career lies solidly with the individual lawyer. ... [W]e should embrace the responsibility because we can then create the careers we desire rather than being forced into square holes for which we are often ill-suited round pegs. Speaking from experience, I can say unequivocally that well-satisfied lawyers are those who feel they have control over their lives and their careers." VOGT, PREPARING FOR REENTRY, at 5.

Only when you get to the root of things, the kind of root that only deep reflection can discern, do you get good decisions. So think deeply about *the question*. Listen to wise counselors, while eschewing the counsel of fools. Then think about that counsel. Process it. Mull it. Examine it. Something good happens to our intentions and actions when they have the right thought behind them, whether or not that thought leads to a discernible decision. Deep reflection over lifelong courses of action may be the single surest way to improve the quality, meaning, and impact of a life. Examine historical figures who stood above the challenges of their time, and you will uniformly find that their thinking set them apart. "There is a natural impulse to shortcut the process of making career choices, not only because it is uncomfortable to ask hard questions about life choices, but also because most law students do not understand how to manage effectively the career choice process. Just because you made a career choice in deciding to come to law school does not mean that you will not make other choices during law school or after graduation, for that matter." MUNNEKE, THE LEGAL CAREER GUIDE, at 29. "Making good career decisions has never been more important. Today's attorney is highly likely to have multiple jobs during his or her career. The era of graduating from law school, going to work for a law firm, and retiring with a gold watch 40 years later is long gone." MUNNEKE, MANAGING YOUR LEGAL CAREER, at 7.

Takeaway: **Think deeply and often about what you want to do.**

Response: "I have thought often and deeply about that very question without yet coming to a clear answer, but I expect to go on thinking, researching, talking, and listening until I can make the best decision. What advice do you have?"

Reflect: What do you think about most often and most deeply? How do your deep thoughts affect your mood and motivation? Can you recall an instance of seeing things differently after having given a subject considerable study, research, and reflection?

Engage: On a scale of 1 to 10, from least to most, rate the depth of thought and consideration that you have so far given to your choice of a law career. If you chose anything less than a 7, then schedule time now to reflect, research, and write about career choice.

13 Happiness

Appreciate one of your biggest challenges, really more like an obstacle, in answering *the question*. People expect you to pursue your own happiness, especially in a career choice. How many times have you heard to just do what makes you happy, and things will work out alright? The first problem with that approach to answering *the question* is knowing what will make you or anyone happy. Who knows wherein happiness lies? "By all accounts, we lawyers have it all. Perhaps no other field offers a comparable combination of monetary rewards, prestige, and potential satisfaction as does the law. Certainly, no other career offers as wide an array of options. Why, then, are we not happy?" MUNNEKE, THE LEGAL CAREER GUIDE, at 8.

Some of us happen to land in circumstances that seem ideal only to find anything but happiness. Others of us land in circumstances that sound difficult but turn out to suit us so perfectly that we find happiness just where we thought we would not. And anyway, lawyers have a particularly hard time equating any specialty or role within their profession with happiness. As a tour director at Disney World, yes, you could see yourself happy, or if you prefer, then as a hunting or fishing guide. Yet, probably no one, particularly a law student, thinks of law practice as fertile ground for happiness. Students choose law studies for some reason other than pursuing happiness. For the law profession, happiness is an uncertain guide. "Another approach is to use personal inventories (e.g., the Myers-Briggs Type Indicator, or MBTI) to test how well an employee will fit into a given work environment. These tests have the advantage of relying on a scientific method in their development and validation. When properly employed, they can provide valuable insights about the individuals tested."

MUNNEKE, THE LEGAL CAREER GUIDE, at 33. "In order to find true work satisfaction,... you have to do more than simply avoid an unpleasant work environment. What is needed is a thorough understanding of how your own personality fits key aspects of the job you select. The better the fit between your personality and your job, the greater the likelihood that you will experience job satisfaction." STAUDENMAIER, CHANGING JOBS: A HANDBOOK FOR LAWYERS, at 18.

Takeaway: **Be careful thinking you should make yourself happy.**

Response: "I am not sure that law practice is so much about my choosing something that will make me happy, so I have instead been exploring what are the deeper commitments that led me to law studies."

Reflect: How happy are you? How happy do you wish to be? What one pursuit would make you most happy in the short term? In the long term? Can you think of a happy lawyer? If so, then what can you learn from that lawyer about career choice?

Engage: Select from the following trades and professions the three most likely to make you happy if you pursued them for a living: (a) doctor; (b) lawyer; (c) accountant; (d) police officer; (e) firefighter; (f) banker; (g) baker; (h) decorator; (i) event planner; (j) carpenter; (k) plumber; (l) bricklayer; (m) salesperson; (n) photographer; (o) programmer; and (p) artist.

14 Direct Pursuit

Another problem with pursuing your own happiness in a career choice is that we generally do not attain happiness by its direct pursuit. Have you ever? Some of the hardest times to have a good time are when you pursue a good time. The good times instead seem to come when you are pursuing something else. We seem to enjoy life most when not particularly trying to enjoy life but instead to live life as we should. The pursuit of happiness we find a modern burden in itself, even believing that we ought to change careers, change spouses, or at least medicate ourselves when not sufficiently happy. The difference is a bit like examining your spouse or best friend closely on one hand, when they can sometimes seem to come up a bit short, versus just embracing them to the fullest on the other hand, when looking back they always seem to have exceeded your best dreams. Perhaps thankfully, hewing too closely toward happiness tends to make us sad. "The ABA conducted a study a few years ago, and found from surveying your lawyers all over the country that the number one factor in determining job satisfaction was intellectual challenge." WALTON, AMERICA'S GREATEST PLACES TO WORK WITH A LAW DEGREE, at 14.

The saddest laugh is the one made artificially with nitrous oxide (laughing gas). To force a laugh is painful. To fake happiness hurts worse than simply being sad. We end up feeling the worst about ourselves when, like the substance abuser, we pursue feeling good too ambitiously for the very short term. Happiness is the ephemeral product of things other than its own pursuit, things like the sense of growing with the work that we do and facing and overcoming challenges. "Many lawyers do find happiness in their careers. They use the law as a vehicle to develop and sustain the lifestyle they have chosen. Most lawyers would not give up their jobs to do something else." MUNNEKE, THE LEGAL CAREER GUIDE, at 8.

Takeaway: **Better to lead a decent life in service of others if you want happiness.**

Response: "One of my challenges is thinking that I should choose to make myself happy, when my happiness probably depends on my choosing something else."

Reflect: Can you recall an instance when you should have been most happy but were instead most sad? What things do you do to make yourself happy in the short term? In other words, what cheers you up? What things have you planned to help yourself be happy in the long term? What is the difference between the two—short-term and long-term happiness?

Engage: On a scale of 1 to 10, from least to most, how happy are you, and then again on the same scale, how happy do you think you ought to be? If the difference between the two measures is any greater than two points, then re-examine your assumptions about happiness. Talk to the happiest and least-happy professionals you know, to see what you can find out.

Snapshot: "Wow, you must have taken *two* of your happy pills this morning," plaintiff's counsel grumbled good-naturedly at insurance defense counsel after the deposition concluded. "And you, *two* of your grumpy pills," the beaming defense counsel laughed back at him. She had always had what her mother called a "sunny disposition." She had been glad to discover that she could maintain that happy outlook in law practice, even insurance defense. While her role was to challenge all claims, undermining exaggerations and destroying the few bold liars to the extent that she could, she found no reason to be mean or unhappy about the work. To the contrary, she just put her sunny disposition to the best effect, charming overreaching plaintiffs into appropriate admissions while building strong positive relationships with the plaintiff's lawyers. When those good professional relationships did not result in settlements on terms her insurers found reasonable, then she just charmed the judges and jurors. "Happy, happy, happy," she used to think to herself, long before the expression became popular.

15 Virtue

Of course, the ancients would say that the kind of happiness we ought to pursue is their kind of happiness, the Greek *eudemonia* generally translated as virtue, flourishing, excellence, or good. We live in a therapeutic age where we see, judge, and pursue things through the lens of how things make us feel. We have thus distorted the meaning of happiness into a therapeutic pursuit involving how things make us feel rather than recognizing that happiness involves a standard that is external, hard, and real. Now, we should all be in favor of pursuing excellence in all things. We moderns make far too little of virtue. "What distinguishes Lawyer-Integrators from other practitioners is that they choose to reject the hectic legal lifestyle for one that is slower-paced, and that integrates work and play, family and career, and home and community." ARRON, RUNNING FROM THE LAW, at 49.

In truth, good lives bring happiness in abundance. Yet our literature and culture pretend that they do not—pretend that a life of balance and beauty, service and sensibility choke rather than satisfy our passions. Our therapeutic focus then gives us plenty of fodder to find unhappiness in the best of circumstances. Rather, we should pursue a virtuous career because in the nobility of our law services we would most likely find happiness even if the secure kind of happiness that the ancients valued. "Above everything else, whatever your specialty or wherever you decide to practice, you must be an excellent lawyer. Being an excellent lawyer means more than just working hard, staying abreast of recent developments in your specialty that will benefit your clients, and providing excellent client service. In addition to working hard, being an excellent lawyer also means working smart. " BLAKELY, FRIENDS AT THE BAR, at 117.

Takeaway: **Consider pursing a virtuous career as a way to ensure your satisfaction and success. Plan and prepare to do the right thing.**

Response: "My greater concern than which practice area to choose is that I act nobly in whatever I do as a lawyer. Of all things that I hope to accomplish in my law practice, I want others to know me as a sound person and professional who always does the right thing."

Reflect: How do you define happiness? What alternative definitions would make the most sense when considering law careers? Does happiness have a definition that fits with what you might attain through a rewarding law career?

Engage: Rank the following attributes in order of their importance to you as a professional: (a) happiness; (b) virtue; (c) nobility; (d) courage; (e) balance; (f) reliability; (g) loyalty; (h) effectiveness; (i) willingness; (j) sensitivity; (k) compassion; (l) excellence; (m) trustworthiness; (n) discernment; (o) gravitas; and (p) vitality.

16 Affinities

We do find other reliable guides for a happy career in addition to the strategy of pursing a noble one. Effective law practice means engagement in one's community, whichever community that law practice serves. You could do worse than to think of the community of which you wish to be a part and then to choose the law field and practice that best serve that community's members. Have you always held a fascination for how people live and thrive within dense metropolitan areas? Then discover the services that lawyers offer, whether landlord-tenant law, lease and other contract negotiations, business or tech startup work, or securities work, to serve those urban denizens. "Defining yourself is especially important for law students as they look forward to choosing a practice after law school. It is a temptation to look at a job description, view it with intrigue and excitement, and allow it to influence your decision about a situation that might not be right for you. Remember to define yourself and stay true to your objectives." BLAKELY, FRIENDS AT THE BAR, at 31.

Do you feel best about the world when around members of the arts community? Then prepare for an intellectual-property, licensing, and nonprofit-law practice. If you like farmers, then study agricultural law with all of its sales, business, financing, and real-property law concerns. For doctors study health law, engineers patents and products liability, auto-workers labor law, sailors maritime law, the elderly estate and Medicare planning, and children school or abuse-and-neglect law. For the poor study street law, for the rich study foundations. Find your community, your people, your folk and affinity, to get engaged and involved. Above all, work for people whom you respect and, better yet, whom you like. Doing so is the surest way to have a busy, long, successful, and enjoyable career. "[M]ost of us can do a better job of making decisions about our lives. We may not be able to eliminate the risk of making a bad choice, but we can reduce it. And while we may not be able to guarantee our future happiness, we can improve our chances of finding it." MUNNEKE, THE LEGAL CAREER GUIDE, at 283.

Takeaway: **Pick work for clients with whom you have an affinity.**

Response: "As you know, I have always felt a bond for the urban poor of our community whom I now expect to serve in new ways with my new law skills."

Reflect: Which community invigorates you the most? Which community do you invigorate? Who attracts you, and whom do you attract? If you found yourself wrecked upon a deserted island, then which group would you take with you?

Engage: Pick the top three client populations with which you would most like to interact on a day-to-day basis: (a) 65-year-old chief executives managing multinational corporations; (b) 60-year-old real-estate magnates redeveloping urban districts; (c) 55-year-old farmers protecting farmlands; (d) 50-year-old ranchers preserving grazing rights; (e) 45-year-old union workers increasing wages; (f) 40-year-old retailers managing shops; (g) 35-year-old filmmakers producing movies; (h) 30-year-old single parents keeping households together; (d) 25-year-old tenants dealing with landlords; (g) 20-year-old minors charged with alcohol offenses.

Snapshot: Her path and its outcome had been odd but also peculiarly appropriate. She was the child of migrant laborers, barely finishing her grade schooling as she and her parents picked crops in two different states on opposite sides of the country in the winter and summer seasons. She and her parents wanted more for her than a life of migrant labor, yet she did not want to abandon her migrant community. Once she married her immigrant husband and had children, she began working as a secretary for a solo practitioner whose clientele included many migrant laborers and other immigrants. The work was everything she had hoped, still helping her people but now in a semi-professional role. Yet she still wanted more. So she attended a law school with night and weekend classes until she earned her degree. Her first job was with a big firm where she learned tons, had outstanding mentors, and loved the pay—but was no longer working for her migrant community. So after a short while, she moved to an assistant prosecutor's job in her local community, the first immigrant prosecutor in that region. The role gave her real influence and authority over the most important of matters affecting the members of her migrant community. In retrospect, she now knew she had her dream job, even though she had not originally imagined it.

17 Meaning

Another helpful guide in addition to pursuing excellence in service of those for whom you have the greatest affinity, is to pursue meaning. Now admittedly, pursuing meaning sounds too conceptual and far-fetched to be of much use in answering *the question*. Yet think of your challenge this way. Pretend that you are coming home from a day's work, where you meet the wisest and most-caring listener you know, who asks you what you did today. If you truly want to flourish in your work, then you must be able to make solid sense, solid meaning out of what you do at work each day. "[W]hen you inquire about making your career more meaningful, I have to suggest that you may be overlooking the subtle opportunities simply to mean something special to others, to be a trusted advisor, to do or say something they cannot do or say for themselves. You'd be surprised at the way something so small can make such a big difference, how much more meaning you can find in your day when you approach your work with the goal of working meaningfully." MORRIS, ASK THE CAREER COUNSELORS, at 4.

If all you can say is that you answered a bunch of email, or pushed paper around all day, then you have failed to draw meaning from your work. On the other hand, if you can say that you got your community one step closer to bringing hospital services locally, or protected a battered spouse, or got guardian services for a mentally ill client living under a bridge because drug dealers were stealing the client's disability money, then you will have found meaning in your law work. Tell your family and friends that your law degree is going to help you gain asylum for refugees, patents for inventors, housing for the homeless, or access for the disabled, and they will understand. Be sure your answer makes sense to you, whether or not to them, because life is a lot about making meaning.

Takeaway: **Pick work the rich meaning of which you can articulate.**

Response: "I just want to be able to come home from work each day saying that my services that day made the small businesses that are so critical to our community a little stronger, securer, more responsible, and more productive."

Reflect: Dream for a moment. What would you most like to say that you do each day? What work would you be most pleased to describe to the person who cares the most about you each day? What work would the person who cares the most about you want to be able to tell others that you do?

Engage: Choose the top three legal services from which you would draw the most meaning, representing: (a) sports stars in contract negotiations; (b) film stars in product-endorsement deals; (c) military leaders in battle-truce negotiations; (d) government leaders in trade-treaty negotiations; (e) corporate leaders in regulatory negotiations; (f) union leaders in contract negotiations; (g) securities traders in compliance investigations; (h) African-American workers in discrimination claims; (i) migrant workers in wage claims; (j) female workers in harassment claims; or (k) injured workers in compensation hearings.

Snapshot: The brief representation had, in retrospect, been among the most satisfying of his career. He had met the client only once for an hour at a pro bono site in the basement of her church. The young working single mother of two infants (one of whom she had brought with her to the pro bono clinic) had briefly fallen behind in her mortgage payments. She now had the money to make up her payments, but the local bank, which still held the mortgage, was refusing. The lawyer patiently explained the bank's right to declare default and foreclose the mortgage but her corollary right to redeem and remain in the home provided that she could find other financing. The lawyer knew, though, that the client's best option was to convince the bank to give her another chance, which the lawyer believed the bank just might do if the bank understood that she now had the assistance and representation of a committed lawyer. Back at the office, the lawyer faxed the bank a letter of representation and got his legal assistant to confirm by telephone the precise amount the client owed. The plan worked. With the lawyer quietly advocating the client's merits, the bank forgave the default and reinstated the mortgage loan, even waiving some fees in the process. Sometimes, the simple things bring the greatest satisfaction and meaning.

18 Philosophy

Here, though, we may be dealing largely with formulas and philosophizing, when instead we should be dealing with the practical and real. It is hard to make a good life out of formulas and philosophies. They can help you see some things, even pursue some things. Formulas and philosophies can mostly affirm or contradict things that you have already chosen and done. Yet formulas are lifeless in themselves, abstractions from which we find it hard to draw direction. Exhortation toward things is fine as far as it goes, that we should agree about what is good, better, or best, but exhortation tends not to be particularly effective at changing behavior. It is hard to get the spirit of a mere concept, even ones so powerful as *virtue, engagement,* and *meaning*, inside one's heart, mind, and motivation. "New lawyers experience the greatest levels of dissatisfaction in the first one to two years of practice, but satisfaction increases over time, as they gain experience." MUNNEKE, NONLEGAL CAREERS, at 14.

Rather, we take those things when present as evidence of commitments that we have already made or when not present as evidence of commitments we have forgone or lost. Let us speak of nobility in our profession once we have approached and maybe even possessed it, not necessarily as a practical guide for what field we should choose. Nobility, affinity, engagement, and meaning may be things discovered rather than pursued. "The lawyers we interviewed spoke openly about their passion for their practice. What a joy it is to talk to professionals that find great satisfaction in their work! They told us, at length, about how much they like the daily rhythms of their work, how much they enjoy the intellectual challenge of their work, and how much pride they take in their relationships with their clients." ABRAMS, THE OFFICIAL GUIDE TO LEGAL SPECIALTIES, at xvi.

Takeaway: **When it comes to career choices, philosophical musings only go so far. Better to do it than say it.**

Response: "I do not have any magic words or formulas for success in my law practice but instead have a passion to get into practice to see what special attributes it develops in me."

Reflect: What proverb, adage, or saying can you remember your mother, father, or other close caretaker repeating as a confirmation or guide to behavior? Do you have shared sayings, things that others also say, that you take as reliable folk wisdom? Have you ever sought them out?

Engage: Which of the following proverbs would you rely on the most? "Laziness brings poverty while diligence brings wealth." "The wise accept direction while fools ignore it and come to ruin." "Hate stirs conflict while love covers all wrongs." "Fools multiply words while the prudent hold their tongues." "Storms sweep the wicked away while the righteous stand firm." "Pride leads to disgrace, while humility strengthens." "Better righteousness than wealth." "Gossips betray, so trust instead those who keep secrets." "Kindness brings honor, ruthlessness only wealth." "Give freely to gain more, for stinginess leads to poverty." "Better to be nobody with food than to pretend to be someone while starving." "Work for food rather than chase fantasies." "Fools are always right in their own mind, while the wise listen to others."

Snapshot: Nothing had distinguished her in law school, not academics, competitions, writing, student leadership, or any other curricular, co-curricular, or extra-curricular success. Her resume claimed barely more than that her grades had been just good enough to graduate. Yet her law recall and analytic skill were also just strong enough to pass the bar on her first try. She had no ambition for pursuing any particular field and no illusion about special practice opportunities but instead had one faint family connection with a solo practitioner back in her rural hometown, which she had used to wangle an internship. Now, he had offered to help her get started in practice as the only other lawyer in that town. She jumped at her only option, and it worked. She was in practice, when some of her more-successful classmates were still not. And now that she was in practice, her very ordinariness, that one attribute that had so handicapped her in law school, had become her greatest strength. She walked, talked, and thought just like the clients whom she now served so effectively, except that she had the basic competence and necessary licensure of a lawyer. Her clients had the inestimable gift of having a lawyer just as ordinary as they were but nonetheless peculiarly effective for exactly that singular reason. And those law professors who had gotten to know her best knew that someday she would be one of those award-winning practitioners whose career of service elevated them above the gifted.

19 Persons

So then again, perhaps we ought not to be pursuing any*thing* in our choice of what to do with a law degree but rather be pursuing some*one*. We have plenty of laudable personages to pursue. The classical model for education involves just that, to see our work not as something disembodied but rather as embodied in the ones from whom we learn. So go ahead, look around you at the lawyers and law professors, and the non-lawyer community leaders, from whom you learn. Whom might you wish in some degree to emulate? "Unfortunately, when many law students begin thinking about their job search, they tend to focus on the wrong issues. They'll ask, "What are my options?" or "What's out there?" The problem is that before you can effectively look for a job you need to ask yourself what you want in one." SCHNEIDER, SHOULD YOU REALLY BE A LAWYER? at 139.

Beyond those whom you know, what famous figure, present or past, might you wish in some degree to emulate? You can put on a person's character, wear their personality, easier than you can put on or wear a concept or thing. Your answer to *the question* could easily be that the kind of lawyer you wish to be is the kind that someone else whom you know or know of has already been. I have sometimes wished for a moment that I had the articulation of this lawyer, command of that lawyer, and insight, warmth, or humor of another one. Yet do not think that I envy anyone. Know only that I recognize and respect the various superior skills and uniquely effective personalities of my fellow lawyers and to a small degree would if I could emulate some of them. Do you?

Takeaway: **Find lawyers to respect, model, and emulate.**

Dear J.D.

Response: "I do not know my field of law yet but met two mentor lawyers who have already opened my eyes to the kind of lawyer whom I hope to be someday. Let me tell you about them."

Reflect: Do you personally know local lawyers whose knowledge, skill, articulation, warmth, or personality you especially respect and admire? Who would you tell a friend is your favorite lawyer?

Engage: Rank the following lawyers in order of those whom you would most wish to emulate: (a) Abraham Lincoln; (b) Thurgood Marshall; (c) Mary Ann Glendon; (d) Johnnie Cochran; (e) Sandra Day O'Connor; (f) Melvin Belli; (g) Ruth Bader Ginsburg; (h) Antonin Scalia; (i) Clarence Darrow; (j) Clarence Thomas; (k) Geraldo Rivera; (l) Nelson Mandela; (m) Bill Clinton; (n) Hillary Clinton; (o) Barack Obama; (n) Michelle Obama; (o) Mohandas Gandhi; (p) Robert Louis Stevenson; (q) John Knox; (r) Charles Albert Finney; (s) Sonia Sotomayor; (t) Gloria Allred; (u) Mohammed Ali Jinnah; (v) Alan Dershowitz; (w) Thomas More; (x) Willie E. Gary; (y) Preet Bharara; or (z) Fatou Bensouda.

20 Faith

Of course, you and I reach far deeper than wishing to emulate others. We accept the spirit and image of the one whom our faith calls us to pursue. We make our first and last commitment to him, knowing that he who formed our personality so uniquely will also make us into the unique professionals he wants us to be. He offers us rich meaning, engagement, and prosperity, asking only that we seek his will rather than our own. For the right law career, we must bring our faith along with us into the profession rather than leaving it at the office door. A law practice without such a foundation is a risky and uncertain proposition, even potentially dangerous to others and one's self. "[T]he concept of "The Right Choice" is a bit problematic. It continues to imply that there is but one job out there that's right for you. It suggests that you need to identify, before you even begin to look, exactly where you are going to go. It also conveys an underlying concern about making a mistake that will doom your career." MORRIS, ASK THE CAREER COUNSELORS, at 30.

We could have no better answer to *the question* than to seek and serve him rather than ourselves, for in him we have our only satisfaction, especially insofar as he made the law and justice that we practice. He gave us both the capacity and the purpose. We should trust him to show us where he wishes us to serve, even as we pursue each opportunity exactly as if he had done so. You have permission to pursue your faith in your professional practice. You have need of it as much in your career as anywhere else.

Takeaway: **Connect your faith to your law career.**

Response: "The special thing that I have discovered is that law practice will enable me to pursue my Lord's will, letting him work among the poor and troubled through me."

Reflect: How have you reflected your faith in your career pursuit so far? How might your faith be influencing your choice of what to do with your law degree? What connects your faith to your work? What evidence of your faith do others see in your work?

Engage: On a scale of 1 to 10, from least to most, rate the degree to which you could articulate your faith to a client or to a lawyer who asked you to do so for their benefit. If you rated your ability at 6 or less, then consider whether you should improve your articulation, and determine who or what would help you do so.

Snapshot: The law professor was a little surprised at the student's question but should not have been. The student, still in his first term, had come to the professor's office to ask whether the student could continue to practice his faith even while he learned and qualified to practice law. "My friends at church think that law school and the profession of law will change me," he ended. "If you hold firm to true faith, then law studies will *equip* and *position* you," the professor corrected thoughtfully, "but not *change* you except to deepen your faith." They then discussed the many ways that lawyers of traditional and profound belief live and carry out their faith through law practice, sometimes explicitly but always implicitly in the sacrificial service work that they do. A decade later, the student was doing estate planning as a partner in a mid-size law firm, leading a faith-based charitable organization, and daily living out his deep faith while held in higher esteem than ever by his same church friends.

21 Calling

If we want the most out of our career, then we should at all times maintain that sense of our career as involving a *calling*. The concept of a calling is a profound and powerful one. Consider its literal meaning. We do not so much create our own career as instead our career, made and fitted in advance for us, calls us to it. We do not so much see our future, but our future knows what it has for us and so draws us to it. Do you see, then, how freeing is the concept of a calling, that we need not manufacture our future but instead only discover and accept it? Faith is precisely that, to believe with confidence in good things to come when we have no particular evidence of them. We must first believe in the opportunity of a profound career, and only then are we able to receive it. "Once we cross this philosophical rubicon—that is, once we affirm law as a calling that transcends client or self-interest—the remaining points logically fall into place. From the basic idea of lawyers striving to serve the common good, it is an easy next step to affirm the traditional understanding of lawyers as 'counselors,' as 'officers of the court,' and as 'peacemakers.'" HORN, LAWYERLIFE: FINDING A LIFE AND A HIGHER CALLING IN THE PRACTICE OF LAW, at 18.

By engaging so broad and challenging of a curriculum, and by doing so with such vigor, you have acted in faith that your pursuit will produce for you and others a valuable harvest of some kind. We need not know our destination precisely, when the knowledge and skills that we acquire have such value to so many. When we prepare for our calling with such diligence, it becomes more and more evident to us. The choice of a career involves an act of faith. When we least see the answer to *the question*, we most trust that the answer lies within our grasp.

Faith fosters hope, while hope fosters action, and action seizes opportunity. "When you share your dream, goal, or objective, and you use clear prototypes and enough detail to create an image for them, you help your contact not only identify places and people who could advance your search, but identify personally with your vision." NIELSEN, JOB QUEST FOR LAWYERS, at 98. "[T]he concept of law as a public service "calling" led prior generations of lawyers to volunteer countless hours to their communities, to worthy organizations and causes, and to clients unable to pay their fees. Not surprisingly, public respect for lawyers and professional "fulfillment" followed what began essentially as an idea, or a series of ideas, about what it meant to be a lawyer." HORN, LAWYERLIFE: FINDING A LIFE AND A HIGHER CALLING IN THE PRACTICE OF LAW, at 78.

Takeaway: **Treat your law career as a calling.**

Response: "While the exact path is not yet clear to me, I already sense a strong call for law practice, which is why I am so determinedly pursuing my studies so that I will be most prepared for practice and most able to answer that call effectively."

Reflect: Think of someone close to you, whether a family member, friend, or acquaintance, who exhibits a sense of calling in their life or vocation. What do you know, or what can you find out, about their experience of that calling? Have you ever had the sense of pursuing a calling? Do you wish to do so?

Engage: On a scale of 1 to 10, from least to most, rate the degree to which you see your law career as involving a calling. If you rated that degree anything less than an 8, then examine thoughtfully the relationship of your faith to your law studies. Consult your career advisors and faith advisors until you increase your confidence that your law career can be and should be a calling.

22 Legacy

As you connect deep and profound things with your career exploration, consider also how your career should look to you and others when it is over. A professional legacy is a career's residue that informs, guides, directs, and enriches others. Lawyers leave valuable legacies. We know the rich legacies of the statesmen lawyers like Lincoln, Gandhi, and Mandela, and groundbreaking lawyer-justices like Thurgood Marshall and Sandra Day O'Connor. Yet everyday lawyers, small-town lawyers, general-practice and boutique-practice lawyers, and solo practitioners also leave rich if most-often unheralded legacies. You will leave a legacy, whether for better or for worse. Why not think of it now? "If you are working in a place where you are valued and listened to, your opinion matters, and you have developed some expertise, you are probably becoming more confident not only as a lawyer, but as a person in general in the world outside of work." NIELSEN, JOB QUEST FOR LAWYERS, at 148.

Many who do leave rich legacies think of those legacies, even plan for those legacies, long before they develop, indeed when first choosing a career. The opportunity to shape a legacy is greatest at the beginning of a career, not at its end. Choices that you make at the start of a career, and then one year into the career, and then two years in and five years in, have greater influence over your legacy than choices you make in the last one, two, or five years. Thinking about how you want your career to end can help you think about how to begin it. "Lovely old words: wisdom, virtue, character. Hardly ones that come immediately to mind when the contemporary lawyer is considered, but good words or ideals from which much else good in the practice of law once flowed. Among them: the ideal of the seasoned lawyer as a wise counselor...." HORN, LAWYERLIFE: FINDING A LIFE AND A HIGHER CALLING IN THE PRACTICE OF LAW, at 118.

Takeaway: **Choose a field in which you can leave a legacy.**

Response: "Whatever field I end up pursuing in practice, I want it to be one that leaves my children, grandchildren, and community a legacy on which they can draw and build far into the future."

Reflect: Think of an older acquaintance of yours, perhaps a friend or family member, who seems most likely to leave a strong legacy. How does that person act differently to distinguish that legacy? What choices has that person made that appear to be making for a strong legacy? Can you articulate the legacy that your acquaintance seems to be leaving?

Engage: Select the top two legacies you would like to earn by the end of your law career, that you were: (a) "always willing to serve when anyone needed you"; (b) "always prepared to listen with compassion"; (c) "so astute and insightful as to be a constant inspiration"; (d) "a consummate peacemaker able to bring the worst enemies together"; (e) "the most reliable provider for firm and family"; (f) "a constant generator of new ideas, work, and relationships"; (g) "a people person able to connect with anyone"; (h) "the most discerning member of any group of which you were a part"; (i) "the most generous giver to all causes that came to your attention"; (j) "always thinking of what others needed to do better"; (k) "a lawyer's lawyer to whom everyone turned for wisdom"; or (l) "everyone's friend and confidante, especially in times of trouble."

Snapshot: The gruff old lawyer was collecting yet another bar-association award among many previous honors and recognitions for his pro bono, law reform, and bar leadership work. His acceptance speech was typically brief, gracious, and entirely humble, giving no real clue to his motivation or inspiration. Only a few close observers of the old lawyer's career, those who knew him best, understood what set him apart from nearly every other lawyer in the room. His distinction was not a saint-like spirit, a servant's heart, or natural charisma or brilliance. To the contrary, he seemed just about as rough around the edges as any other person including other lawyers. No, what set him apart was that he thought often and deeply about his legacy. He acted each day as if his career would be over before he knew it, leaving only a memory of the quality of his actions.

23 Courage

We should admit that part of your challenge in choosing a law career lies in the fear you must overcome that you will fail in pursuing it. Courage faces fear. Feeling no fear is foolhardiness, not courage. Courage means embracing and overcoming your fear, not avoiding it. Nearly any field of law has its challenges. Many people fear public speaking, but nearly all trial lawyers speak in public constantly, some of them overcoming significant nervousness and even fear to do so. Many people fear losing, but even the better trial lawyers lose at least occasionally, while nearly all of them loathe losing. Many people fear high-stakes negotiation, but deal lawyers negotiate for high stakes constantly, many of them feeling significant stress while doing so. Many people would dread writing a 20-page thesis paper, but lawyers write lengthy analyses constantly, many overcoming significant reluctance to do so. " 'I was never so intimidated in an academic setting as I was in law school. But I graduated and have been in practice five years now. I'm glad I persevered because my legal education enriched my view of the world and empowered me on behalf of my clients and in support of worthy causes.' — Samantha, public interest lawyer." SCHNEIDER, SHOULD YOU REALLY BE A LAWYER? at 138.

Many people fear confrontation, but judges, arbitrators, and mediators confront others constantly, many feeling significant stress to do so. Many people fear violent criminals, but prosecutors and public defenders deal with them constantly, many facing their own fears to do so. Many people fear complexity and ambiguity, but transactional lawyers deal constantly with both, often feeling challenged in doing so.

Lawyers exhibit courage because someone must do so. You can, too.

Takeaway: **Expect fear, but have the courage of your convictions.**

Response: "I am actually apprehensive about law practice, which is what makes it so attractive to me that I know I will be stretching myself to face and overcome my fears about things like confronting wrongdoers, correcting the powerful, and standing up for what is right."

Reflect: Recall an instance when you faced and overcame your fear. What fears do you face in being a lawyer? How do other lawyers deal with fear? Identify a courageous lawyer. How do you think that lawyer feels when pursuing matters that require such courage?

Engage: Which of the following actions would make you feel both the greatest fear and sense of accomplishment: (a) jury-trying an easy should-win major case, to a winning verdict; (b) jury-trying a hard will-lose major case that no one else would try, to a losing verdict; (c) negotiating a ten-figure bet-the-company corporate acquisition; (d) probating a nine-figure estate to closure; (e) prosecuting a child-sex-abuser to conviction; (f) prosecuting an alleged but possibly innocent sex-abuser to not-guilty verdict; (g) filing a patent application for a major company's only product; (h) negotiating a labor deal for 20,000 workers; (i) acting as emergency manager for a city of 100,000; (j) handling the bankruptcy reorganization for an employer of 50,000; (k) suing the president of the United States; (l) defending the governor of your state in civil litigation; (m) documenting a five-party deal to finance a $500 million manufacturing plant.

Snapshot: Even as it was happening, the trial lawyer sensed that it would be a defining moment in her career. The two-week federal civil jury trial would start tomorrow. The judge had just excoriated her, unduly she was still sure, for her having even thought of offering certain evidence that, though controversial, was certainly relevant, as the judge's ruling barring the evidence had acknowledged. Yet the judge had gone well beyond simply ruling the evidence out to the point of attacking the trial lawyer's intelligence, decency, and fitness to practice law. The trial lawyer knew the judge's stern reputation but had not quite borne the full brunt of it as on this occasion. She wanted to crawl into a hole and not come out until her career was over. Instead, though, she knew that she had nothing to do but soldier on. She even guessed that the judge was just trying to bully her into recommending to her clients an unsatisfactory settlement. Two weeks later, the trial lawyer had a winning verdict in hand. After the verdict, the judge brought her and opposing counsel into chambers to say how much he had appreciated their skill. The trial lawyer construed it as the stern judge's way of apologizing for his pretrial outburst, her defining moment. She would never again fear a judge or anyone else in the profession. She soon came to forgive and even like the judge because rather than in spite of his outburst.

24 Listening

Do not miss that *the question* actually presents a good opportunity for you to see what others think fits you best in the way of a career choice. Sometimes, others know us better than we know ourselves. When you get *the question*, do not hesitate to venture an answer, as crazy as it may sound to you. Yet listen to the reaction. The important thing may be to give the friend or family member who asked you *the question* an opportunity to react, to say what is on their own mind about where your personality, character, and passions lie. If you get affirmation to your answer, then consider it so. You might be on track to a fitting career. If you get surprise, then re-examine your answer. "How do you learn what's out there? You need to commit to the quest, to learning, to listening, to being willing to look like you don't have all the answers—something lawyers are reluctant to do. Browse online and in bookstores in the careers section, spend time in the library, read trade journals, talk to people who are happy in their work who may practice law for a living... ." MORRIS, ASK THE CAREER COUNSELORS, at 42.

Ask your listener why they think your choice might make a good or bad fit. Your listener may know nothing about the field or specialty that you mentioned and may have made a poor supposition. Or they might know you better than you think and may have had some intuition or insight. Ask them to share it with you. Answer *the question* with your own question, "What do you think I should do?" You may just have some fun with it. You may also just learn something about yourself that you never knew. "Friends, family, and co-workers will all be ready to tell you what you can and ought to do with your talents. ... It is very likely that the assessments of those who know you will coincide with your analysis of yourself. If their perceptions of you do not seem to be accurate, you might ask yourself, 'Why?' Either they are not getting a clear picture of you from things you tell them or you have not been totally honest with yourself in the evaluation." MUNNEKE, THE LEGAL CAREER GUIDE, at 54.

Takeaway: Listen to what fields others think you should choose.

Response: "Great question, the answer to which I don't have any clear idea yet. You know me as well as anyone. What do you see me doing?"

Reflect: Vow now to answer *the question* next time with a specific field, while asking your questioner what they think you should do. Journal your answer and their answer. Then try it again with a different answer and different person. Seek out three persons to tell your ideas for a career, then asking each what they think you should do, journaling their answers.

Engage: Select from this list the two best persons to tell what career you plan and to ask what field they think you should choose: (a) career advisor; (b) favorite professor; (c) least-favorite professor; (d) law school dean; (e) dean's secretary; (f) partner with whom you are interviewing; (g) lawyer mentor; (h) local bar president; (i) local judge; (j) smartest classmate academically; (k) most street-smart classmate; (l) pastor; (m) psychiatrist or therapist; (n) barber/hair-stylist; (o) bank teller; (p) tailor; (q) former grade-school teacher; (r) barista at the drive-through window; (s) mother or father; (t) sister or brother; or (u) niece or nephew.

Part 2

Structure

25 Licensure

One of the easier things some new lawyers can decide is the state in which they will work. Lawyers license state by state. You may not know what kind of law you will practice but you must choose a bar to which to apply and then prepare to take its bar exam because you cannot practice without being a member of a bar. So consider choosing a state bar first, meaning to choose a state first. You may have several good reasons to choose a state without thinking of the field in which you will practice there. Family may make a difference. Weather may make a difference. Cost of living, the economy, recreational opportunities, healthcare, and other quality-of-life factors may make differences. "You are much more likely to see the inside of a courtroom much sooner in your career in the country than you will in the big city. You will also find that civility among opposing counsel still largely exists, if only because they see each other in court and across the negotiating table much more frequently, so there is a premium in acting mature, restrained and civil." HERMANN, FROM LEMONS TO LEMONADE IN THE NEW LEGAL JOB MARKET, at 76.

Also, do not overlook that states can have different kinds of legal work. Yes, most states will have criminal-law, family-law, and estate-planning practices. But some states can have either a lot of work or no work in other fields. New York is good for finance and securities law but not so much for mining and ranching law. Iowa is good for municipal law and agriculture law but not so good for maritime law. Texas is great for oil-and-gas law but not so great for labor law. Get to know the major law fields in your home state or likely destination state. They might help you choose a vital field. "You can do ... 'locational analysis' for virtually any practice area. Doing so is not only important to your initial decision about what to practice and where to practice it, but also for your long-term economic and career 'health.'" HERMANN, FROM LEMONS TO LEMONADE IN THE NEW LEGAL JOB MARKET, at 113. "Geographic location matters for several reasons. First, you want to live in a place where you envision yourself thriving. For some, this can mean a city where you have existing connections. For others, it can be a part of the country that speaks to you because of its natural beauty or vibrant cultural life." GERSON, CHOOSING SMALL, CHOOSING SMART, at 25.

Takeaway: **Let the state you choose for licensure guide your choice of law fields.**

Response: "I plan to take the bar exam in my home state of Louisiana where we have a lot of oil-and-gas companies and related businesses, and my father managed a refinery, and so I plan to specialize in energy law."

Dear J.D.

Reflect: What do the lawyers do most of in your home state or destination state? Look at some law-firm websites, both in major metropolitan areas and in suburban and rural areas to see what kind of law in which they specialize.

Engage: List in descending order the five states in which you would most like to practice law. Then list in descending order the five states in which you think you are most likely to practice law. Add the rankings on the two lists to see which state is both the most desirable and most likely.

26   Making a Living

You should make a living at your law practice. Probably, you must make a living because no one else is handing it to you. Most of us have to make a living, which is a healthy obligation for us, by the way. Living off of someone else is often not living to the fullest. Necessity is indeed the mother of invention. The fundamental commitment to first provide for ourselves and then if able for our families has probably created more character, fostered more maturity, and driven more innovation than anything else. The point is to balance career choice with financial responsibility. "[T]hink about your financial needs, compare them to your financial wants, factor in the life you'd like to have while you earn a living, and proceed as an individual, rather than a statistic in a category, or a dollar amount on a list. After all is said and done, your worth as a person means far more than any price tag ever could." MORRIS, ASK THE CAREER COUNSELORS, at 11.

Choosing the field of law in which you want to practice is fine as far as it goes, but your choice needs to be sustainable financially. Law offers many fascinating fields like aviation law, maritime law, entertainment law, law of philanthropy, art law, animal law, military law, and human-rights law. Lawyers can make a good living in all of those fields. Yet many specialized or boutique fields require years of experience and networking beyond law school to enter profitably. Get into the profession gainfully employed, so that your heart and passion can gradually attract the clients you want, offering the matters you wish to pursue. You may start out at what seems like a dead-end job, but when it provides healthcare benefits and pays the bill, that dead end can look pretty attractive. For some of us, a fair answer to *the question* about what kind of law we want to practice is "anything legal that pays."

Takeaway: **Choose a law field that will earn you a living.**

Response: "I don't much care what kind of law that I practice so long as it makes me a decent living on which I can support myself and my family. Lawyers make a decent living in many different fields, and I plan to pursue the first one that gives me the opportunity."

Reflect: What responsibility do you have currently to support yourself financially? If you are not supporting yourself now, then will you be soon? Should you be soon? Do you have other dependents? If not, then may you soon have others who depend on you financially? How does your need for income affect your vision for law practice? Have you investigated what lawyers make in different fields?

Engage: Choose the minimum annual salary that you need to make ends meet: (a) $20,000; (b) $25,000; (c) $30,000; (d) $35,000; (e) $40,000; (f) $45,000; (g) $50,000; (h) $55,000; (i) $60,000; (j) $65,000; (k) $70,000; (l) $80,000; (m) $90,000; (n) $100,000; (o) $125,000; (p) $150,000; (q) $175,000. Now get the lawyer-income survey from the state bar you plan to join, to see what work would pay you at least that minimum annual salary.

27 Employment or Practice

One distinction that you must appreciate is the difference between private law practice (either as a solo practitioner or with other lawyers in a for-profit law firm) and other employment through which lawyers provide law services. As the book's foreword mentions, lawyers deliver the bulk of law services through private practice in firms. Other lawyers take employment with courts, prosecutor's offices, regulatory agencies, or other government or nonprofit agencies, or work directly as in-house counsel for insurance companies or as corporate counsel for other non-law businesses. "[N]onlegal careers have a special appeal to people who are trained in the law and have other areas of experience. If you are one of these people, your legal training expands your career potential dramatically because you now offer special skills that have dozens of applications in your chosen field." MUNNEKE, NONLEGAL CAREERS, at 6.

For the new lawyer, joining a law firm may seem pretty much the same as working as an employee of an agency or other entity besides a law firm. In both cases, you still have an employer and get a paycheck. The major difference has to do with clients. Lawyers in law firms need them. Lawyers working for agencies or other entities don't need them. Either in a literal or figurative sense, their employer *is* their client. That major difference of the private-practice lawyer needing and directly serving clients affects nearly everything else having to do with the lawyer's employment. While the law firm cuts the paycheck, the lawyer's professional duty is to the client. Indeed, the lawyer's loyalty may also be to the client. Maybe not initially when the firm first hires them, but soon enough most lawyers within firms need to gain and retain clients to justify their continuation with the firm. This responsibility makes law practice market-based and entrepreneurial in ways that direct employment is not. For these and other reasons, this book treats practices first and separately from employment. Appreciate how significant is this difference.

Takeaway: **Lawyers practicing in private for-profits firms deliver most of the nation's law services, although many other lawyers pursue law careers as employees of agencies and entities without private clients.**

Response: "My goal has always been to practice privately in a law firm where I can use my entrepreneurial skills, although I continue to explore alternative employment with government agencies and nonprofits in which I would still be doing law work."

Reflect: Does entrepreneurial activity, in which you give thought and action to the financial success of your private enterprise within a market for its services, interest you? Are you, in other words, a productive, innovative, responsible, disciplined, and creative go-getter, while expecting the reward for being so? Or do you prefer to work in a non-market enterprise, each to his own, where paychecks (yours and those with whom you work) depend less directly on creativity and labor?

Engage: Choose one or the other attribute in each pair, the first representing a common condition of private law practice and the second of non-private-practice employment: (a) competitive versus collaborative; (b) for-profit or nonprofit; (c) reward versus compensation; (d) innovative versus sustaining; (e) entrepreneurial versus institutional; (f) value based versus status based; (g) accountable versus loyal; (h) clients or employer; (i) delegated versus supervised; (j) capital versus labor. Consider focusing on either one in which you counted eight or more.

Snapshot: His ambition had always been to serve as in-house counsel. While he appreciated private practice and would not have minded continuing in it, he knew that he would prefer contributing long-term to the welfare of his own employer. His preference might have had to do with his father's career or just have been his loyal nature, but whatever the source, he knew that he was, in the old parlance, a *company man*. While most jobs advertised that they required a minimum of five years of experience, he developed a strategy that netted him an associate-corporate-counsel job in just three years. The role was everything that he had hoped it would be. He soon established himself not only as a consistent and loyal worker but also as an expert in the law fields most affecting his employer. Before much longer, he was training and supervising the employer's newer lawyers, on his way no doubt to a long and prosperous career as corporate counsel for one of the region's largest and most respected employers.

28 Full Time

To make that living, many lawyers work full time rather than part time. Like other professionals, lawyers in different fields and at different points of their careers can work a spectrum of hours, from barely part time to more than full time, not just 40 hours a week but 50, 60, 70, or 80 hours. Some practice areas tend to require full-time practice because of intense and unpredictable demands. Litigation can be an example, where the court and opposing side control your schedule as much as you do. Yet mergers and acquisitions, development work, corporate-counsel work, and other areas can also require full devotion to practice demands. Lawyers in those practice areas may in late career have the illusion that they can slowly withdraw from practice, working seasonally or part time, but they often find themselves constantly on call and pulled back into practice.

Part of that allure is the identity and satisfaction that lawyers draw from practice. We say that we cannot get away, but truth is that we do not want to get away. We are not who we have become unless we are practicing. "A full-time law practice as an attorney-mother presents many challenges. On the one hand, some partners and supervising lawyers might try to lighten the load on working mothers as a form of protection that generally translates to less attractive and less interesting work assignments. As a result, that protection can become limiting to the working mother who wants the opportunity for good and meaningful work and believes that it is her place, not the firm's, to determine whether she is up to the challenge." BLAKELY, FRIENDS AT THE BAR, at 31.

Still, law practice has its demands. If we build a practice to the point that we have a reasonable number of corporate or individual clients relying on our services, then we find it hard to tell them when they need those services or get them. They tell us. Circumstances arise. They call. We answer, or they will have to call someone else unfamiliar with their matters. In some practices, taking vacations can even be a challenge. Lawyers must arrange backup assistance either from other lawyers in the firm or, if a solo, then from a network of lawyers in other firms. Consider whether you are prepared for full-time practice or want to devote less than full time.

Takeaway: **Consider whether you are prepared for full-time law practice or need or want to devote less than full time.**

Response: "I am ready to take on full-time law practice from the moment that I graduate and pass the bar. I want to gain as much experience as quickly as possible to ensure that I have the greatest opportunities later in my career—and the income from full-time practice will certainly help."

Reflect: Can you see yourself devoting full 40-hour weeks or more to law practice? What would you have to give up to do so? Can you see yourself not devoting full time to law practice? What practice opportunities and career opportunities might you miss? What would your earning range be in full-time practice? How would that contrast with part-time practice?

Engage: Rate each statement with +1 (agree), 0 (neutral), or -1 (disagree): (a) I need to work full time for the income; (b) I want to work full time for the experience; (c) I need to work full time because of my chosen practice field; (d) I want to work full time because I have nothing better to do; (e) my family needs or expects me to work full time; (f) my friends expect me to work full time; (g) I like to stay busy most of the time; (h) part-time practice would leave me feeling left out; (i) part-time practice would leave me with too much time on my hands; (j) I wouldn't know what to do with myself if I only had a part-time practice. If your plusses and minuses total five or more, then consider full-time practice. If your plusses and minuses are zero or less, then consider part-time practice.

29 Part Time

While law practice can be so engaging as to shape your identity and consume your full time, plenty of lawyers nonetheless practice only part time. Some of those lawyers practice in firms, whether of large or small size. They are often senior partners who contribute substantial client-development work to the firm. Indeed, when they are not working, their social time may be contributing importantly to their networking and client development. While the trend is certainly not true of all firms, many law firms are also allowing newer lawyers to work in flexible schedules including part time. They may particularly do so to retain talented newer lawyers in whom the firm has already invested heavily but who have new (and perhaps temporary) child-rearing or other family obligations. "Alternative employment arrangements are evolving to meet the needs of those attorneys who enjoy the work, but who don't enjoy the way it tyrannizes their lives. Contract employment and part-time practice are two popular options." ARRON, RUNNING FROM THE LAW, at 122-123.

Lawyers may also practice part time to pursue other interests, like policy or public-interest work, that contribute to their professional development, bring clients to the firm, and increase the firm's reputation. Lawyers who work part time often do so in law partnerships that ensure that others in the firm are available full time. Part-time lawyers also rely on family partnerships where together, working family members provide sufficient income for family needs. A lawyer may work from home part time, perhaps doing contract work without primary responsibility for any files, while caring for children or other dependents, while the lawyer's spouse works full time. Part-time practices and home-based practices are increasingly possible, particularly with the increasing use of communication technologies. Your answer to *the question* may be part time.

Takeaway: **Consider part-time law practice if you have other substantial obligations or want to pursue other interests that contribute to your professional development, and if you do not need full-time income.**

Response: "I plan to practice law part time in a law partnership with a lawyer who practices full time and can cover matters at any time. I expect to have family obligations and to pursue other professional interests while practicing law part time."

Reflect: Do you have other substantial obligations that require that you practice law only part time? If so, then do those other obligations permit you to practice part time, and if so, then in what field? What would you do with your other time if you chose to practice law only part time? Would those other activities contribute to your professional development as a lawyer and to your law practice? Would your law firm value those other activities?

Engage: To which if any of the following activities would you be so interested in devoting substantial time that you would practice law only part time to do so? (a) Writing books for publication. (b) Taking a major pro bono case. (c) Leading a charitable non-profit. (d) Maintaining a blog. (e) Participating in community theater. (f) Raising and training animals. (g) Farming, gardening, or other horticulture. (h) Caring for a disabled family member. (i) Having and caring for children. (j) Building or keeping a home for other working family members.

Snapshot: She had not gone to law school thinking that she would be a part-time lawyer, but then life intervened. Her first job out of law school was doing pretrial civil-litigation work full-time with a major law firm. When she and her husband, also a professional, had their first two children, each time she had quickly returned to full-time work. Then they had their third child while also learning that their second child had special needs. So ended her full-time work for the firm. Yet the firm valued her research and drafting, and kept sending her assignments that she could handle from home. A decade later, she was still working part-time from home in what had turned out to be a highly satisfying, financially rewarding, and yet balanced and flexible career.

30 Personal Finances

Make financial goals and planning part of your career planning. Finances are like anything else, that if you do not plan them, then someone else will do so for you—someone like Amazon, Citibank, Macy's, Neiman Marcus, and any number of other powerful and perceptive marketers. Careers and finances intersect, particularly although not solely at the outset. If you have managed your finances well through law school, then you should have more career choices. If you have managed your finances poorly, then you may well have fewer career choices. Lawyers can earn lots of money. Lawyers head around 10% of the nation's millionaire households. Law, though, like any other profession, is no license to print money. Lawyers generally need to be just as wise, indeed often wiser, about money as other professionals. "You might need to pay off your student loans by going to a large firm and working extremely long hours for a period of time, but your long-term plan could include a move to a small town or a government job after a few years of practice; both of those tend to have somewhat more reasonable hours and often, but not always, less stressful settings." NIELSEN, JOB QUEST FOR LAWYERS, at 145.

As you develop clearer career plans, also develop clearer financial plans. The two work well hand in hand. You may need to start with a firm doing work that you do not particularly enjoy but that pays well, and yet with strong financial management soon be able to create and sustain your own satisfying law practice. Or you may need to start on your own doing work that you do not particularly enjoy but pays well, and yet with strong financial management soon be able to join a public-interest firm or legal-aid office doing the work you always wanted to do. When you think of careers in law, think also of finances. Plan for both. "Persist toward your financial goals. Evaluate your progress periodically and adjust your spending habits as you go." ARRON, WHAT CAN YOU DO WITH A LAW DEGREE?, at 125. "Living *beneath* your means is the path to financial freedom, the path of maximum options... and paradoxically perhaps, even the way to maximize our material pleasures. By controlling our expenses and saving a substantial part of what we make, when we *are* able to afford the nicer car or go on a great vacation... the pleasure will not be compromised by the stress inherent in being overextended financially." HORN, LAWYERLIFE: FINDING A LIFE AND A HIGHER CALLING IN THE PRACTICE OF LAW, at 97.

Takeaway: **Maintain a financial plan to increase career choice.**

Response: "I am not sure what I will practice yet, but I have been managing my finances wisely, and so I plan to try a couple of different fields until I am confident that I have found the right one out of which to make a career."

Reflect: What financial planning do you do regularly? Do you have a budget? Do you have a balance sheet? Do you know your net worth?

Engage: Give yourself one point for each "yes" answer to the following questions: (a) do you keep a personal budget?; (b) do you maintain a personal balance sheet?; (c) do you know your net worth?; (d) do you know the total debt that you owe?; (e) do you pay all credit cards to zero balance every month?; (f) do you have $1,000 in cash on hand for emergencies?; (g) do you have enough savings to pay your living expenses for six months?; (h) do you have life insurance?; (i) have you given any thought to funding your children's education?; (j) have you

Dear J.D.

given any thought to funding your retirement? If you scored yourself 5 points or less, then seek financial counsel.

31 Skill Building

Do not underestimate the value of what may seem to you like worthless experience at the beginning of your career. The work that you do out of necessity at the beginning of your career, so far from your career choice, may give you exactly the experience you need to enter your preferred field. "What skills do you most enjoy using? By skills we mean the day-to-day activities that you do on the job—the way you spend your day at work. You know what lawyering skills are: writing (briefs and other legal documents), researching (legal issues), interviewing (clients, witnesses, experts), advising (clients and colleagues) and negotiating with others (opposing counsel). But you might not be aware of the extent to which different types of attorneys utilize different skills." SCHNEIDER, SHOULD YOU REALLY BE A LAWYER? at 153-154.

Lawyer skills are complex. They build on one another. Much of the preferred work requires layers of skills and experience that lawyers develop over time, maybe short time but sometimes long time. View every job, every assignment, as adding to your skill and experience. Seek work that stretches and challenges you. "Did you know that the average person has seven different careers in their lifetime? Your first job out of law school, no matter how happy it makes you, is unlikely to be your last.... Happy law school graduates tend to feel that the experience they're getting now will be valuable to them down the road." WALTON, AMERICA'S GREATEST PLACES TO WORK WITH A LAW DEGREE, at 24.

Accept work that exposes you to fields that you may not pursue later but that will inform you when practicing within your preferred field. Law overlaps. Commercial litigators need to know bankruptcy law and bankruptcy lawyers commercial litigation. Divorce lawyers need to know tax law and tax lawyers divorce law. Poverty lawyers need to know administrative law. Sports lawyers need to know insurance law. Take as much as a few years paying the bills while building your skill and knowledge base. Lawyers learn so much in their first few years. Respect the concept of earning your own keep, as a guide to building valued knowledge and skills. "Most of us have little experience at identifying skills. Because we seldom identify skills, we cannot articulate them when we need to in the job search process.... This stumbling block is the single biggest impediment most law students have to effective job hunting. It can now be revealed: Skills are things one can do." MUNNEKE, THE LEGAL CAREER GUIDE, at 49.

Takeaway: **Let earning your keep be a reliable guide for building important skills.**

Response: "My plan is to take the first job that gets me fully into practice doing the most challenging work so that I can hone my skills for the career that I really want to pursue later, about which I am still unsure."

Reflect: Think of your favorite field of law, and then list other fields that touch on it. Can you discern a path through those other fields to your preferred field? Ask two or three lawyers what professional path took them to the work that they do today. Also, ask them what experience outside of their current field made the most difference to their skill within their current field.

Engage: Choose three of the following experiences that, though well outside your choice of career work, would nonetheless stretch and build your knowledge, network, and skill, by accepting a judge's appointment to: (a) defend an indigent person charged with homicide; (b) represent a prisoner in a claim for medical treatment; (c) mediate an insurance dispute over abuse claims at a daycare center; (d) lead a task force on establishing a business court; (e) serve as guardian ad litem for a severely autistic child seeking education services; (f) plan a judicial conference on Native-American law; (g) present a research paper updating developments in welfare laws; (h) co-chair a committee to improve bench-bar relations; (i) investigate harassment allegations in the clerk's office; (j) serve as board chair for the local legal self-help center; (k) be the practitioner representative on the court's technology committee; (l) mentor judicial clerks in relationships with the local bench and bar; (m) review, edit, update, and revise the local court rules; (n) write a protocol for evaluating pro per litigation for docket management; (o) represent the assigned-counsel list in negotiating new assignment compensation and terms.

Snapshot: She had thought at first that her solo practice back in her home state and then the work that she started doing with another solo practitioner were dead ends or at least sharp detours from her dream in-house job. She wanted to work for a major corporation, maybe practicing international law. Instead, she was handling administrative deportation hearings, one after another, for mostly poor individual clients, about as far from major corporate work as she could imagine. Yet after three years, she heard about a corporate opening back where she had gone to law school, for a job one of her adjunct favorite adjunct professors had held. After she interviewed and got the job, they told her that her administrative-hearing work was the distinguishing factor. She was now to supervise retained counsel on two continents for a multinational corporation, her dream job by a route she thought involved dead-end work.

32 Confrontation

One of the things that you soon realize in law practice is that many fields have two distinct sides to them, where one side in some respect confronts the other. Lawyers in those fields practice either on one side or on the other side, rarely if ever switching sides on different matters. Criminal-law practices are an example. You are either a prosecutor or a defender, not both. Labor law tends to be another example, that you either represent management or the unions, not both. In personal-injury practice, you tend to represent either the claimants or the insurers, not both. In collection practices, you represent creditors or debtors, not both. In malpractice, you either sue or defend physicians and hospitals, not both. In rental disputes, you either represent landlords or tenants, not both. In sports and entertainment practices, you either represent the organizations or the talent. Sides can matter to us, depending on our commitments, experiences, and perceptions. "An[] area worth exploring involves work values. Values are subjective attitudes you hold concerning work that will affect your perceptions of any job you take. They reflect how you feel about yourself, your colleagues, and your work environment. When you work at a place where the institution is consistent with your work values, you are likely to feel positively about what you are doing." MUNNEKE, THE LEGAL CAREER GUIDE, at 52.

So many practice areas have their sides, with lawyers tending to choose one side or the other. In employment law, you either represent employers or employees. In administrative law, you either represent the regulators or the regulated. In municipal law, you either represent the government or the public. In school law, you either represent the schools or families and their children, or in labor negotiations the school boards or the teachers. In securities law, you either represent issuers or investors. The list goes on. Other practice areas, like business startups, estate planning, and intellectual-property work, tend to be more collaborative and less confrontational. Consider whether you want to practice in a field that divides itself between two differently situated sides in some level of confrontation.

Takeaway: **Lawyers practice on only one side in many areas.**

Response: "I don't want to practice in any of the fields where lawyers take sides, like criminal prosecution or defense and insurance claims or defense. I want to practice in a more-collaborative field like estate planning or real-estate development."

Reflect: Do you like to take sides? Do you readily develop affinities for people, seeing their side of things through their perspective? Or instead, do you tend to stay on the proverbial fence, seeing things from both sides? Do you draw people to you for your advocacy? Or instead, do people seek you out for the balance of your views? Do you think you would feel more comfortable in a one-sided practice always on the same side, or in a balanced practice where sides are less important?

Engage: In each pair of words, quickly choose the word that first attracts you: (a) hot or cold; (b) advocate or mediate; (c) passionate or dispassionate; (d) befriend or advise; (e) loyal or aloof; (f) subjective or objective; (g) compassion or discernment; (h) commit or reserve; (i) choose or defer; (j) battle or truce; (k) challenge or conform; (l) represent or mediate. Count the times you chose the first word over the second word. If your count is 6 or higher, then you may prefer taking sides over not taking sides.

33 Choosing Sides

Choosing sides wisely can be important. Even within the same practice field, the work can be quite different depending on the side you choose. You may have strong affinities for the people or the cause on one side or the other. For example, you might like working with detectives and police officers as a prosecutor on one hand or with confused and fearful indigent clients as a public defender on the other hand. In regulatory work, you might have a passion for advocating for environmental protection on one hand, and thus representing the regulators, or for property rights and liberty on the other hand, thus representing the landowners and users. The important thing is to know that the side you choose can make a huge difference to your career satisfaction and success. "[S]tarting out on the management side [of labor law] and then switching over to the labor side is a rare career move. When considering a career in the field of traditional labor law, this polarization should be kept in mind. It is important to spend some time thinking about which side of this divide your personal philosophy and politics fall." GRUBB, VAULT GUIDE TO LABOR AND EMPLOYMENT LAW CAREERS, at 21.

The finances for each side can also be starkly different. In personal-injury work, you might love the high-risk and high-reward of plaintiff's contingency-fee practice on one hand or much prefer the steady hourly compensation insurers pay for defense work on the other hand. In criminal-law work, you might love earning fixed up-front fees from private clients or prefer a prosecutor's steady salary. The level of supervision and degree of teamwork can differ significantly on each side. One side may draft and document, while the other side investigates and negotiates. The sides within a practice area can be as different as night and day. Lawyers might switch sides at some point in a career, but switching can be difficult, often meaning leaving behind a law firm, network of contacts, skill set, perspective, and disposition. Choose sides thoughtfully. "Law students often tell us they don't have time to explore different legal jobs. So they do nothing at all. But doing even one thing a day toward your career search—even spending an hour a week—is better than blowing it off entirely. If you devote as much time to career exploration as you do on one course outline, you would make infinitely better job decisions." SCHNEIDER, SHOULD YOU REALLY BE A LAWYER? at 111.

Takeaway: **Choose with care the side on which you wish to practice.**

Response: "While I am not sure yet of the practice area, I know that I want to represent individuals rather than government or corporations. I have always had an affinity for the little guy, sort of like David against Goliath."

Reflect: Choose just one of the practice areas mentioned in this section and the prior section. Picture yourself first on one side of that practice. Then picture yourself on the other side of that practice area. For which side do you have the greater affinity? How stark is the difference? Would you be happy and satisfied with your career on either side or just one side? Now try the same exercise with a different practice area.

Engage: In each pair, thoughtfully choose the work condition that most attracts you: (a) teamwork or independence; (b) supervision or delegation; (c) risk/reward or guarantee; (d) professional colleagues or public clients; (e) document or negotiate; (f) irregular or regular hours; (g) travel or no travel; (h) fees or salary; (i) corporate or individual clients; (j) substantial financial resources or few resources; (k) sophisticated or unsophisticated clients; (l) predictable or unpredictable work; (m) many clients or few clients; (n) many matters or few matters. Compile your choices into a preferred-work profile. Use the profile to evaluate career opportunities.

Snapshot: For nearly two decades, the small firm had done almost exclusively insurance-defense work. Then two major insurers consolidated their assignment lists, dropping the small firm in favor of major statewide firms. Two other of the small firm's insurers stopped underwriting in the state, closing their claims offices. The firm still had other insurers, but those insurers were holding down hourly rates while imposing budgets and requiring litigation plans and approvals. In response, one of the partners started taking plaintiff's cases, doing so well that the firm's plaintiff's practice quickly burgeoned. Yet conflicts arose, requiring that the firm reject potential large cases. The firm's partners soon agreed that practicing on both sides just would not work. The firm accordingly split, surprising everyone except the partners.

34 Forums

You should recognize that law-practice fields in some respects involve forums within which you act. The courtroom is one obvious forum, a place where lawyers may or may not feel comfortable, to which they may or may not be drawn. Some lawyers in some fields practice almost solely in their own offices, where they are most effective and most at home. Other lawyers spend significant time at their clients' corporate offices, where they may feel most energized, interested, and engaged. For lawyers engaged primarily in pretrial practice, depositions, whether at an expert's office or at the office of opposing counsel, are the key forum where they perform and are most in command. Consider these different forums when you think of where you might work best. "In an ideal world, you would get multiple jobs in multiple settings so you could make the best evaluation. But we're not dreamers. Even one job on the support staff of a diversified law firm will help clarify what you really want to do with a law degree, if anything—by giving you a realistic picture of what different practice areas involve." SCHNEIDER, SHOULD YOU REALLY BE A LAWYER? at 92.

The practices of other lawyers may take them to hospitals, through workplaces, or to worksites, where their skills are most critical and in demand. For some lawyers, just getting to certain destinations to investigate or observe, wherever that key place may be, can be the core of what they accomplish. Law practices have places for them, movements to them, and physicality about them that distinguish them from one another.

Takeaway: **Discern the forum where you are at ease and engaged.**

Response: "Although many fields interest me, I know that I want to practice in a field where I move freely about in a collaborative forum, like mergers and acquisitions or public-bond work. I do not want to be tied to a desk or thrown into a confrontational forum."

Reflect: In what forum are you most at home? In what forum are you most effective? In what forum are you most energized and engaged? Make a mental list of the forums in which you have seen lawyers at work. In which of those forums can you picture yourself working?

Engage: Choose your preferred forum from each pair: (a) federal or state; (b) office or courtroom; (c) rural or urban; (d) stationary or traveling; (e) your own or someone else's; (f) investigation or resolution; (g) solitary or communal; (h) formal or informal; (i) personal or impersonal; (j) busy or staid; (k) quiet or loud; (l) creative or conforming; (m) regulated or unregulated; (n) procedural or freewheeling. Then compile your choices into a forum profile with which you can evaluate career opportunities.

35 Firm Size

The size of the law firm you join, assuming you join a firm, can have a lot to do with how effective and engaged you are, and how successful you become, in a career. Law firms range in size from as small as one lawyer to as large as over 1,700 lawyers. The 14 largest U.S. law firms each have over 1,000 lawyers. The United States has about 400 law firms each having more than 100 lawyers. Yet about half of all lawyers practice solo or in very small firms. And of course, you find law firms of every size in between large and small. The size of a firm alone does not dictate success. While equity partners at the largest firms average higher income, some solo practitioners have higher incomes even than that. While larger firms tend to have more resources, smaller firms draw on special resource networks of their own. While larger firms may assign mentors to new lawyers, new solo lawyers can find mentors through the local bar. The primary differences you find among firms of different size, then, tend to involve institutional dynamics that affect how you go about your job. "If you are a person who thrives on lots of responsibility and independence, possesses an entrepreneurial spirit, manifests a strong interest in client service, and combines all of that with a passion for learning and succeeding in the business of law, then small firm practice may be a good path to pursue." GERSON, CHOOSING SMALL, CHOOSING SMART, at 25.

Generally, large employers must have more structure and administration than small employers. Organizational policies, politics, behavior, and culture generally matter more as the size of the organization increases. Some of us prosper within organizations, the bigger the better, while others of us do not. Some of us prefer loyalty to and security from an organization and its reputation, resources, policies, culture, and brand, while others of us do not. Firm size can matter in your career choice. "Although it is very important to choose a firm that meets your financial and practice needs and provides you with compatible colleagues, it is also important for you to look at the firm structure. If partnership is your goal, take a look at the partner/associate ratio and determine the potential for partnership." BLAKELY, FRIENDS AT THE BAR, at 94.

Takeaway: **Law firms come in all sizes, where size can matter.**

Response: "The most intriguing criterion I am investigating right now is the size of the law firm in which I will practice. Large firms attract me for their influence and resources, but smaller firms attract me for their collegiality and independence. Who knows right now? I may even decide to go solo."

Reflect: Have you worked for a large company? If so, then what was your experience of its policies, politics, and culture? How loyal are you to organizations and their missions? Are you a joiner or a loner? Do you prefer to control your own destiny or to share a collective destiny?

Engage: Rate each of these statements on a scale of 0-strongly disagree, 1-disagree, 2-neutral, 3-agree, or 4-strongly agree: (a) I am more secure as part of a large organization; (b) I navigate corporate culture well; (c) I am diplomatic in my dealings with co-workers; (d) I am patient with office politics; (e) I like sharing my financial success with others; (f) I like others sharing their financial success with me; (g) I commit readily to corporate missions; (h) I like committee work; (i) I am not proprietary with my work; (j) I share credit easily with others; (k) I dress and act to fit in with others easily; (l) I readily sacrifice my time to support less-effective co-workers; (m) I respect and value seniority and hierarchy; (n) I am willing to wait for and earn my due like others; (o) I take direction and supervision well. Add up your score, then divide by 15 to arrive at your average. If you averaged above 3.00, then consider work for a large firm. If you averaged 2.00 to 3.00, then consider working for a mid-size firm. If you averaged below 2.00 but above 1.00, then consider working for smaller firms. If you averaged below 1.00, then consider practicing solo.

Snapshot: She loved the mid-sized firm that she had joined right out of law school. It had a premier reputation for quality law services. The partners were not only skilled lawyers and abundant rainmakers but also of such high integrity as to make the best of mentors. She had all the work she could handle, as did all other lawyers in the firm. The firm was neither too large nor too small but instead just right in every particular. She wouldn't change a thing about it. And yet after two years, she knew that she should leave the firm for solo practice. While the firm was perfect in itself, she realized after she had made some important adjustments to practice that she had no special need for it, nor it for her. Her work at the firm was sort of like a marriage of convenience, and both the firm and she had too much integrity for that. With the full blessing and support of every member of the firm, she started her own practice, in which she quickly thrived, finding her own clients but also taking referrals from her former firm and other firms. Now she had both the perfect firm size and the perfect practice.

36 Large Firms

Large firms vary significantly in their organization, governance, missions, financing, compensation systems, supervision, and practice areas. Give any large-firm opportunity a chance until you have discerned the variables that are most important to you. Yet large firms also tend toward certain attributes. They uniformly require effective management. More management tends to mean more policy through which managers approve and disapprove of certain behaviors, more procedures that you must do things like conflict check, and more supervision to ensure that you comply with policies and procedures. Large-firm culture tends then to be more formal and less informal. Culture can influence and regulate not only professional behaviors but personal demeanor and dress. Large firms also tend simply by their size to have more resources. Yet large firms also by their size require more revenue. "If the large law firm setting is what you choose, be prepared for the reality. Life as an associate in the very large or "mega" law firms, referred to today as Big Law, is often described to me as "brutal." Associates report being on call, and they say that working for a partner who does not have family responsibilities is especially difficult." BLAKELY, FRIENDS AT THE BAR, at 94.

Large does not necessarily mean secure. Large can mean greater demand for more productivity, translating into longer hours. Large firms have traditionally organized under financial models that encourage associates to compete on hours, productivity, and rainmaking to prove fitness for partnership. Large firms can be more competitive and less collegial places to work. Every one of these observations can be a positive or a negative for you, depending on your goals, capability, personality, and disposition. Know large-firm dynamics before making large-firm practice your answer to *the question*. "Do you get a rush from all-nighters, or do you prefer to see the sun from time to time? Do you want a firm you're expected to put in face time at the office of a firm that's flexible about working from home? How much do you have going on in your life other than work—significant other, marathon training, culinary school, whatever—that you'll need to fit in with your busy life as a young associate?" HAHN, GUIDE TO LAW FIRMS, at 45-46.

Takeaway: **Large firms can be highly regulated and competitive.**

Response: "I hope to practice in a large firm serving the largest corporate clients having the greatest influence and resources. I want my work to have global impact, and I see that happening best through the multinational work that large firms often do."

Reflect: Think of large-firm lawyers whom you have met or know. How do they regard their work and firm? What do you know of their balance and lifestyle? Are they making tradeoffs to work for a large firm, and if so, then how?

Engage: List three major advantages of working for a large firm. Then list three major disadvantages of working for a large firm. Then put your two lists together, ranking in priority those advantages and disadvantages. Do the advantages or the disadvantages of working for a large firm come out on top for you?

37 Mid-Size Firms

Mid-size firms of from 20 to 50 lawyers can make for some of the most fascinating firms and exciting workplaces. They are small enough that a charismatic founder or manager may lead them, stamping an invigorating imprint on the culture and reputation of the firm. Yet they simultaneously involve a large enough number of lawyers to give the firm good variety in character, skill, and perspective. They are small enough to remain reasonably informal in structure but large enough to gather substantial financial, professional, and reputational resources.

Mid-size firms may serve multinational corporate clients in complex matters on one hand but also mom-and-pop businesses, families, and individual consumers on the other hand. They may be in a growth mode, creating significant opportunity for new partners, new offices, new practice groups, and new clients. They may be able to change, move, reform, adapt, and innovate in ways that larger firms find difficult, particularly in developing new and boutique practice areas and implementing new billing methods and practice systems. Their management may be more willing to hear your input and draw on your own innovation and management skills, and to grant you a partnership.

On the other hand, managers of mid-size firms may lack necessary management, finance, marketing, systems, and political skills. Mid-size firms may not be able to attract premier corporate clients while simultaneously having too many conflicts to represent small-business and individual clients. Depending on the particular firm and your own view, mid-size firms can combine either the best or worst of small-firm and large firm practice, but a mid-size firm could be your answer to *the question*. "Some firms are neither large nor small; in a sense these are transitional organizations. When a firm reaches a size of about ten lawyers, it becomes institutionalized: it hires more regularly; it departmentalizes; it becomes more structured administratively. Such a firm will become more and more like other large firms as it grows, even though it may try (usually unsuccessfully) to retain its small-firm attributes. These medium-sized firms that do not make the transition to large firms often splinter into smaller firms again or find themselves taken over by larger organizations." MUNNEKE, THE LEGAL CAREER GUIDE, at 234.

Takeaway: **Mid-size firms offer advantages of large and small firms.**

Response: "I expect to practice in a mid-size firm where my voice and contribution count but I have the full resources of a good-size firm."

Reflect: Search online for two or three mid-size firms in the geographic area where you are most likely to practice. What brand do they project? What mission do they pursue? What clientele do they serve? Who are their most-prominent corporate clients? What individual client populations do the firms serve? How many offices do they maintain?

Engage: Picture yourself as the managing partner of a firm of 30 lawyers. List in order the priority you would give to each of the following issues for the firm: (a) recruiting and developing talented new lawyers; (b) retaining and compensating talented senior lawyers; (c) ensuring sustainable finances timely paying all bills; (d) returning adequate profits to equity partners; (e) branding and marketing for new clients; (f) service quality for current clients; (g) maintaining lawyer and staff morale; (h) ensuring fair compensation for all lawyers; (i) providing adequate community and professional service; (j) maintaining attractive and accessible physical facilities; and (k) providing responsible employee health, disability, and retirement benefits.

38   Small Firms

While large firms get the media attention, with lawyers in large firms as the stars of television shows and films, small firms are the engine for legal services in America. Small firms do the abundant hard work of advising, guiding, and representing the nation's millions of small businesses, local governments, nonprofits, families, and individuals. The profession offers few opportunities more manageable, meaningful, honorable, and satisfying than small-firm practice. "Small firms don't have the personnel to fill several layers of management, so you have a lot more control over what you do. While some people feel more comfortable in the cocoon-like environment of a larger organization, most people like the idea of having more direct control over what they do. That's a tremendous plus of small firms." WALTON, AMERICA'S GREATEST PLACES TO WORK WITH A LAW DEGREE, at 681.

Lawyers form small firms for various synergies that working with a small number of like-minded lawyers can provide. Lawyers in small firms cover for one another during vacations and illness. They trade clients and matters when their expertise varies. Indeed, they match differing expertise within their small firms to give clients one-stop service. The earnings windfall of one lawyer covers the earnings shortfall of another, a wet season for one covering a dry season for another. The seniority of one lawyer both tempers and draws upon the youthful energy of another. The administrative skill of one lawyer matches the people skill of the other. Small firms enable diversity. Lawyers in small firms are the early adopters and innovators. They represent the little client, underserved client, and unpopular client, using specialization and technology to level the playing field against larger firms and opponents. Consider a small-firm practice as an answer to *the question*. "Smaller firms and firms located in more remote geographic areas might be better for you. You should not shy away from these options. There are many styles of practicing law, and they are all rewarding in their own ways. Just because you might not be designed for the pressures and demands of large law firm practice does not make you any less of an attorney. Some of the most professionally satisfied lawyers I know are practicing in small firms and small communities throughout America." BLAKELY, FRIENDS AT THE BAR, at 109.

Takeaway: **Small firms offer abundant opportunity to help people.**

Response: "I want to practice in a small firm with a few other lawyers who are just as committed and engaged as me."

Reflect: Locate online four small firms in the geographic area in which you most expect to practice. Examine their websites. How do their practice fields differ? Who are their clients, and what are their clients trying to accomplish? How do the firms identify their missions? How are the firms alike, and how do they differ? Which if any of the firms would you like to join, and why? Which would you prefer not to join, and why?

Engage: Rate 1 to 5 from least to most your probable effectiveness at each of the following small-firm activities: (a) renegotiating the office lease and copier/scanner lease when they expire; (b) balancing the checkbook or ensuring that the bookkeeper does so; (c) approving the firm's advertising, subscriptions, and sponsorships; (d) deciding staff compensation, increases, and bonuses; (e) following up with clients who have not paid their bills; (f) deciding when to upgrade the firm's computer and smartphone technology; (g) organizing and conducting seminars for marketing; and (h) attending luncheons and chamber meetings for networking.

Snapshot: Out of law school, he had initially joined two other lawyers who were already practicing together. Within their small firm, they each shared income and expenses with small financial adjustments along the way. Their partnership worked well enough. Their practices mixed well, they got along great, and his work in the three-lawyer firm helped him get his feet on the ground. Yet those small financial adjustments were soon draining if not straining relationships within the small firm. He finally decided that they would all be better off if he went solo, which he did, remaining in the same office suite but no longer as part of the small firm. They still got along great, referred cases back and forth, and helped one another out where they could. Five years later, the arrangement was working as well as ever, although by then he had a second office in a nearby town.

39 Solo Practice

Solo practitioners have it all, literally and figuratively—all the assets and liabilities, risk and reward, liberty and responsibility, accumulation and accountability, blame and credit, and you name it. To practice solo is to take full and lone responsibility for all aspects of the law practice, without sharing that responsibility with other lawyers. With risk and responsibility go reward. Many solo practitioners become and remain solo precisely because they are so successful financially and in other ways without the support of other lawyers in a law firm. Lawyers who all in one are effective rainmakers, time managers, financial managers, administrators, organizers, producers, openers, and closers have little need for a law firm. Some solos feel that law firms are where free-riders go to have other lawyers carry them. "It has never been easier to open a solo law practice. Both the barriers to, and costs of, entry are lower than ever before, thanks to computers and the Internet. In addition, virtually every state bar association can provide you with thousands of dollars' worth of free law office management consulting advice through their law practice management program." HERMANN, FROM LEMONS TO LEMONADE IN THE NEW LEGAL JOB MARKET, at 100.

Solo practitioners often do not exactly practice solo or at least not in the sense of being isolated from other lawyers. Solo practitioners often share office suites, co-counsel cases with other lawyers and firms, share referral arrangements, and work within other fruitful formal and informal networks of lawyers and other professionals. Solo practitioners may have just as much professional interaction as lawyers in firms or more so, especially insofar as they most often get to pick and choose their professional relationships rather than have to put up with lawyers with whom they do not necessarily get along within their own firm. Solo by choice can be an excellent answer to *the question*. Solo because no firm is hiring in your area can be an excellent way to develop quickly and confidently all of the skills necessary to make yourself a well-rounded and effective lawyer. "If you want to fly solo today, you don't need a law library; you won't have to pay a fortune for access to a legal research database; you don't need a secretary; you don't even need an office—initially, anyway, you could work from home. If you do decide to rent office space, you can find a reasonable situation in virtually every small community." HERMANN, PRACTICING LAW IN SMALL-TOWN AMERICA, at 314.

Takeaway: **Solo practice offers the full rewards of law practice.**

Response: "I want to practice as a solo so that I get the full responsibility and reward of my practice."

Reflect: How well do you work when independent of others' support, guidance, and influence? Are you a self-starter? Do you have strong self-management skills? Do you draw energy from starting a day free to make your agenda, or do you waste time and lose direction when you have no particular accountability to others?

Engage: Rate yourself from 0 to 5 from weak to strong on each of these self-management skills: (a) time management; (b) schedule management; (c) relationship management; (d) financial management; (e) technology management; (f) self-marketing and branding; (g) reputation management; (h) self-evaluation and reflection; (i) grooming and self-care; and (j) mental-and-physical-health management. Add your scores, then divide by 10 to get your average score. If you score 3.5 or less, then be cautious about solo practice, and consider finding solid mentor lawyers in a firm.

40 Management

You can see that differences in firm sizes have a lot to do with the management for which individuals lawyers in the firm may be responsible. Lawyers must manage to some degree in all firms but obviously have more responsibility to manage or support the management of the firm, the smaller is the firm size. Solos do it all. Lawyers in two- and three-lawyer firms do most of it. Yet lawyers in all firms do some management, if primarily of their own matters. Management opportunities and obligations within firms begin with managing the work. Clients have needs, and their matters have urgency and deadlines. Management extends to the client's payment, that lawyers must receive sustainable income for their services, and to the client relationship, that the work must satisfy clients often enough that they return for more work or send other clients. These management activities are at the core of any lawyer's work. "The rapid growth of the profession, as well as technological advances, and changes in client expectations, have provided tremendous opportunity to law school graduates who want to work within the profession without practicing law. In some law firms, former practitioners with business skills have created niches for themselves as managers and office administrators." ARRON, WHAT CAN YOU DO WITH A LAW DEGREE? at 105.

A highly suitable answer to *the question* may thus be that you want and expect to produce valued work for clients who are willing and able to pay often enough that you can continue the work. Once you arrive at that answer, you will have accomplished something mature and fundamental in your commitment to the work. Give that answer to any managing partner who interviews you, and they will respect you highly for it. Most legal work you must manage responsibly, or you will be quickly out of work. "Law firms don't run themselves. They require capable business management to oversee the firm's day-to-day operations and long-term strategy." FURI-PERRY, 50 UNIQUE LEGAL PATHS, at 84.

Takeaway: **Appreciate the core value of managing work effectively.**

Response: "I want to practice law so efficiently and productively that clients I always have enough paying clients to continue."

Reflect: To whom have you been accountable so far in your various volunteer activities or careers for producing valued work? How highly did the persons for whom you worked value your service? How highly did you value producing work for them? Do you take satisfaction in managing assignments to completion? Are you merely a starter or also a finisher?

Engage: Complete each of the following statements with the word or phrase that best describes the quality of your work productivity and management: (a) "others usually find me _____ when a work assignment is due"; (b) "if I was one of ten employees from whom my work supervisor had to assemble a production team, my supervisor would pick me _____"; (c) "when I get a challenging new work assignment, my natural reaction is '_____.'"

Snapshot: The thing that surprised her most about the eight-lawyer firm that she joined right out of law school was how poorly the three partners managed it. She did not make the discovery right away. She just noticed little things at first. As she applied herself to the work with her usual diligence, she noticed that one of the other associates was equally diligent, while the others were not. More concerning, one of the partners was supremely responsive to all concerns and requests, while the other two were abjectly not. The diligent partner was plainly an outstanding lawyer, rainmaker, and manager, but the other two partners seemed so much less so, as to threaten the firm's survival. Paychecks were late on a couple of occasions. Then came the rotating furloughs and pay cuts for all of the associates, both the diligent and the not so. She had had enough of poor management and in difficult conversations told the partners so, that she was preparing to leave. The diligent partner took her aside, suggesting that she give the partners two weeks to work it out. In two weeks, two of the not-so-diligent associates were gone, the furloughs had ended, and she had a nice pay raise. Management comes in all forms including from the bottom up.

41 Rainmaking

A law firm's size influences whether the firm requires its lawyers, particularly its new lawyers, to attract paying clients. Lawyers call *rainmaking* this skill of attracting paying clients. Firms of larger size may require little or no rainmaking especially from new associates, who instead provide the labor for work that partners generate. Large firms might actively discourage new lawyers from bringing clients to the firm, for the conflicts of interest that those clients would create. "As one associate from a huge firm ... told me, "Our real estate practice is so huge that you *can't* bring in business, because it's going to be hard for you to find anything that doesn't conflict out" — meaning that the firm can't take the work because of current or former client conflicts." WALTON, AMERICA'S GREATEST PLACES TO WORK WITH A LAW DEGREE, at 19.

Yet lawyers in firms of all sizes must ordinarily do at least some rainmaking at some point in their careers. Solo practitioners must find clients immediately. Lawyers joining small firms often must do so either immediately or as soon as they get their professional network and reputation reasonably established. Rainmaking is also an essential skill within large firms. As associates in large firms approach the partnership evaluation usually after around seven years with the firm, their performance criteria subtly shift from production to rainmaking. A lawyer without a client is like, well, spring without rain, or sunshine without flowers. A responsible answer to *the question* may thus be simply to practice the kind of law that will attract a sufficient number of paying clients. While that answer may sound too overtly profit-minded, consider that clients pay only when they recognize value in your offering. Your goal may be to offer law services, whether corporate, family, consumer, or otherwise, that have such obvious and deep value as to attract an inexhaustible line of clients. "As a rule of thumb, the smaller the firm, the larger rainmaking will loom in your early career. ... If you're outgoing, you like talking to people and think you'd be good at it, a place where those skills can turn to bucks in your pocket is something you should be aware of, and that's likely to occur in a smaller rather than a larger firm." WALTON, AMERICA'S GREATEST PLACES TO WORK WITH A LAW DEGREE, at 19.

Takeaway: **Choose a practice area where enough paying clients seek your service for you to be able to continue to practice.**

Response: "I want to practice law so effectively that I always have a line of paying clients waiting for me."

Reflect: Think back to the last time that you sold something, whether as part of a job, volunteer activity, or household endeavor. How like or unlike that experience is your sense of offering your law services to paying clients? Should your clients know your price in advance? Should they have price options? How will you be accountable to your price and the quality of your service?

Engage: List in order the client populations you think would be most likely to retain you given your character, interests, skills, personality, and affinities, clients who: (a) speak a specific foreign language that you also speak; (b) have a recreational interest that you also have; (c) went to an undergraduate institution that you also attended; (d) were members of the same fraternity/sorority of which you were a member; (e) are of your same ethnicity or cultural heritage; (f) are members of your same faith community; (g) belong to your same social community or club; (h) eat and shop where you do so; (i) live or work near your law office; (j) visit the same websites you visit; (k) are in your social-media circles; (l) do the same volunteer work you do; (m) have children attending the same school as your children; (n) use the same accountant as you use; (o) see or hear your advertisements; (p) visit your website; (q) read your blogs; (r) drive by your office; (s) see you speak in public; (t) respect your leadership on community boards; (u) value your friendship; (v) trust your former clients who recommend you. How, then, might you strengthen and build upon the highest three connections you just listed, to develop a practice field?

42 Firm Finances

Firm size also influences the degree to which lawyers in the firm must concern themselves with the financial management of the law firm. Lawyers in firms of all sizes have financial responsibilities, but the degree of responsibility varies considerably. In some firms, some lawyers just work, while other lawyers or managers concern themselves with the firm's finances. In other firms, each lawyer has substantial responsibility for firm finances. That responsibility may include not only billing but following up on bills, discounting bills, analyzing accounts receivables, monitoring cash flow, managing payroll, managing lines of credit, and so on. "Today's lawyer must have a basic knowledge of law firm economics to understand the factors that will influence her career. In a nutshell, your job security hinges on the economics at work in a firm. Any leverage that you may be able to exert in terms of negotiating salary, bonuses, or alternative work arrangements will come from your being aware of the bottom line. Long-term planning for your career and properly evaluating your partnership potential depends on your ability to comprehend the business of the law firm and now it operates." CAREY, FULL DISCLOSURE, at 119.

Solo practitioners and lawyers in small firms must be knowledgeable about finances, aware of the financial condition of the firm, and responsible to firm finances because no one else will be. Lawyers in larger firms may not be involved to any degree in the firm's finances, which managing partners may instead manage, or those lawyers may have limited financial responsibility around certain clients, billing practices, or practice areas. Regardless of firm size, some practice areas require substantial financial management, while other areas require little or at least less so. Some of us are effective with financial matters, while others of us are not. Some of us live and breathe finances as an integral part of everything we do, while others of us prefer not to think at all about money, leaving that thought to financial managers. Some of us are skilled at finances, while others of us are not. Your answer to *the question* about a field of practice may depend on your interest in and skill with law-practice finances.

Takeaway: **Choose a practice area that matches your interest in and skill with financial matters.**

Response: "I want to practice in an area like plaintiff's personal injury where I control the risk, reward, and responsibility of my financial future."

Reflect: Are you skilled with budgeting, estimating, analyzing, and otherwise dealing with finances? Do you have financial, accounting, or business education? Are you naturally interested in financial matters? Do you prefer to control your own finances or leave that control to others? Do you trust others making financial decisions that affect you?

Engage: Rank from highest to lowest the following law practices in terms of your financial preferences: (a) unpredictable high financial management, risk, reward, and responsibility plaintiff's contingency-fee personal-injury practice; (b) predictable low financial management, risk, reward, and responsibility insurance-defense practice; (c) demographic-trend and economy-dependent medium management, risk, reward, and responsibility consumer-law practice; (d) cumulative-effect low financial management, risk, and responsibility estate-planning practice; (e) cyclical high financial management, risk, reward, and responsibility real-estate-development practice; (f) most predictable low financial management, risk, reward, and responsibility legal-services practice; (g) judicial staff attorney having no financial responsibility.

43 Practice Fields

When family and friends ask you *the question* about what you plan to do with your law degree, they expect you to answer with a practice area like estate planning, taxation, criminal defense, or personal injury. For the non-lawyer public, practice field is the obvious distinction among lawyers. By professional dress alone, they can tell a trial lawyer in a $1,000 tailored dark-blue suit and red silk scarf (women) or tie (men) from a transactional lawyer in business-casual attire with open collar. To the public, practice field is about all that matters in distinguishing among lawyers. And to some degree, the public is right. As the saying goes, jack of all trades, master of none. Lawyers tend to specialize because of the complexity of law and its practice. Yet you have seen from the discussion so far that you have many other answers to *the question* that do not refer to the practice area. The practice area may not be the most important consideration for you. "How do you make choices about substantive practice areas without pinning yourself down? How do you establish priorities about practice areas when you have no earthly idea what lawyers actually do in those areas? Part of the answer to these questions is that you must simply explore different possibilities. Although you may not make a decision to specialize until you have practiced for several years, or you may decide not to specialize at all, you can begin to educate yourself early in law school about various substantive options." MUNNEKE, THE LEGAL CAREER GUIDE, at 271.

You could and perhaps should be thinking about other answers outside of the obvious answer of a certain practice field. If you get the other criteria right, then the practice area may not matter. Practice areas often enough take care of themselves. For many lawyers, practice area does not matter, while the other conditions of practice matter a lot. Be sure that you think productively about the other conditions we have so far considered. Your elective-course selection, clinical experience, and, yes, family and friends will all encourage you to think about practice field. Get the other practice conditions right before you choose a practice field. "[T]he day-to-day life of a brain surgeon is very different from that of a pediatrician, which is very different from the life of a geriatric cancer specialist—even though all three would qualify as a 'doctor.' Similarly, your day-to-day life as a 'lawyer'—how flexible your hours are, the types of people with whom you interact, what sorts of cases you work on, maybe even the city in which you live—will depend largely on what practice area you enter." HAHN, GUIDE TO LAW FIRMS, at 85.

Takeaway: **Practice field is not the only consideration or even necessarily the primary consideration in what to do with a law degree.**

Response: "I plan to choose a practice field after choosing other practice conditions like location, firm size, and financial sustainability, which I am narrowing down right now."

Reflect: How much does the practice field matter to you? Could you be just as engaged and effective in one field as another, or for you is it all about the practice field? Do you want others to identify you as a lawyer who practices in a specific field?

Engage: Rank from highest to lowest your priority for each of these practice conditions: (a) practice field; (b) firm size; (c) practice location; (d) prospect for increasing income; (e) control of financial risk and reward; (f) avoiding financial matters and responsibility; (g) affinity for clients; (h) commitment to clients' cause;   (i) law firm mission;   (j) practicing on the right side;   (k) practicing in a conducive forum;   (l) leaving a legacy of practice; and (m) ensuring work-life balance.

Snapshot: As a lawyer, he was actually quite hard to describe. No handy label applied to him. If he had consulted with a marketing consultant, the consultant probably would have told him that he had a problem with his brand. Yet what might look to some like an identity problem was in fact his greatest professional asset. No one could pigeonhole him. No one could predict where he would appear next. No one could find his weak point. He was a sort of Renaissance lawyer, good — no, not just good, but *great* at everything that he touched. Whether civil or criminal cases, trials or appeals, ethics matters or transactional work, writing or oral advocacy, negotiation or strategic win-at-all-costs litigation, he did it all so well that he had virtually no parallel. And the most amazing thing was that he did it quietly, with no fanfare, almost stealthily, so that he sort of snuck up on unsuspecting opposing counsel, not sandbagging but just being humble about things. And then it was over. He had won and won big again. Any lawyer who dealt with him knew that he was the best, even if few advertised it.

44 Practice Mix

The question of practice field looks to a lot of attorneys more like a question of practice mix. Many lawyers practice in more than one field. The relationship of one field of practice to another field of practice can be critical to the success of a lawyer and law practice. Some fields go together like milk and honey or peaches and cream. Examples include worker's compensation and Social Security disability, intellectual property and contract licensing, employment rights and civil rights, estate planning and guardianship practice, or business advising and tax practice. If you practice in one of these fields, then you should or could practice in the other. Your clients tend to have needs in both fields. "Most law firms do not practice in just one field and most lawyers do not limit their practice to just one area. Even lawyers who practice in a discrete specialty often are called upon to deal with other areas of law that intersect their specialty." MUNNEKE, THE LEGAL CAREER GUIDE, at 270.

Some fields, although requiring different skills, can make surprisingly good combinations, like criminal defense and bankruptcy. (Yes, getting charged with crime can adversely affect one's job and finances.) Other fields, like administrative practice or constitutional law, can arise within and therefore go with just about any other field (to extend the food analogy, think bacon). Lawyers welcome practice mixes. Diversifying revenue sources reduces revenue risks. When one field is down, another is often up. Practice mixes also create variety in a day, when (as the saying goes) variety is the spice of life. Practice mix may matter to you as much or more than practice field. The following descriptions of practice fields thus include brief mention of related fields that might make for a good practice mix.

Takeaway: **Think of law practice as likely to involve a mix of practice fields rather than restricted to one field.**

Response: "I would like to have a mix of two synergistic practice areas (1) real-estate development and (2) construction law."

Reflect: Read the professional biographies of several leading practitioners on law firm websites. What mix of practice areas do you see any one practitioner pursuing? What fields seem to go together most frequently? What fields seem not to mix? Can you infer why certain fields seem to go well together?

Engage: Pair each practice area in the A list with a good match from the B list. Then choose your top three pairs that you think would make good mixes for your practice. A: intellectual property; aviation law; military law; contract law; alternative dispute resolution; civil litigation; nonprofit law; family law; malpractice; labor law; Social Security disability; real-estate transactions; insurance law; computer law; media law; pension law. B: criminal defense; employment law; personal injury law; administrative law; estate planning; business start-up; taxation; municipal law; civil rights; bankruptcy; guardianship; juvenile law; environmental law; entertainment law; banking law; poverty law.

Snapshot: The combination seemed a bit odd at first, but he realized pretty quickly that he had hit on a solid practice mix in bankruptcy and criminal-defense work. What made the combination odd was that one field was transactional while the other litigation, one field civil while the other criminal, one field mainly administrative while the other more adversarial, advocacy, and negotiation. He had entered practice with an interest in both fields but never figured that they would actually work together. Yet work together, they did, and when he thought about it, the combination made nearly perfect sense. What happens when most wage-earners get charged with crime like drunk driving and lose their driver's license and for a few days or months their freedom? They lose their job, which means they lose their ability to pay their ongoing obligations. Even beyond those clients whom he thought of as facing the "double whammy" of criminal charge and bankruptcy, he found that doing a lot of criminal-defense work for working people made a reputation for him to represent wage-earner bankrupts and vice versa. In the old way of looking at it, he had a working-class clientele, hardworking and hard living, plus occasionally too hard drinking. Bankruptcy and criminal defense made for him the perfect practice mix.

45 General Practice

While practice fields and practice mixes are possibilities, so too is general practice. A general practice is one in which the lawyer does not restrict services to one or a small number of specialized fields. One tends to find general practices in rural and small-town locales where the smaller number of lawyers requires that they serve all needs. Specialization is not an option because no single specialty offers enough work. If the few available lawyers specialized, then clients would not find lawyers for their other work. One less often finds general practitioners in metropolitan areas where the larger numbers of lawyers make specialization both practically possible and prudentially important. "The term 'general practitioner' brings to mind a lawyer in the mold of Abraham Lincoln—a pillar of the community who represented shopkeepers, farmers, businesses, and accused criminal defendants while also finding time to be involved in politics and local government. Today's small firm and solo practitioners, whether in rural or metropolitan areas, handle a myriad of legal problems, may serve as part-time prosecutors or government employees, and are active in bar associations and other community activities." ABRAMS, THE OFFICIAL GUIDE TO LEGAL SPECIALTIES, at 389.

Yet one also finds general practitioners (or at least generalists) filling some of the most challenging and respected of lawyer roles at the highest levels, like general counsel, corporate counsel, attorney general, solicitor general, and appellate judge. General practice is at once more possible today because of the available technology and technical resources but also more challenging because of law's increasing complexity and specialization. General practices can thus be constantly stimulating, involving ongoing learning and ever-growing expertise. You have few things as satisfying as saying that yes, you can help (no matter what is the client's matter). General practices can also be hazardous, relying on uncertain knowledge and under-developed skills. Some of us like to embrace every challenge thrown our way, while others of us prefer to take on only those few things in which we feel ourselves most expert. Know your preference, and let it guide your answer to *the question*. "As a lawyer, you tend to be goal-oriented, and intent on achieving results and closure. With that single-mindedness, it's possible you may suppress or ignore your own preferences, and end up competing with those whose own preferences naturally lead them to that type of work. The result is often failure, either because you can't muster the enthusiasm that impresses employers, or you lack the commitment that motivates you to hammer away at potential leads. With greater self-awareness, you'll be able to create a vision based on your strengths and preferences, and be motivated enough to bring that vision to life." ARRON, WHAT CAN YOU DO WITH A LAW DEGREE?, at 52.

Takeaway: **Consider general practice in which you constantly learn and adapt to fill many service needs.**

Response: "I want to have a general practice that will allow me to serve all the needs of any particular client."

Reflect: Do you see yourself as a generalist or specialist? Where have you served when that service drew most broadly on a range of experiences and skills? Would you prefer to serve a trusted client even if it meant learning new law and skills, or would you prefer to send a trusted client to a lawyer already skilled in that field? Is there a position to which you aspire at some distant point in the future that requires the skills of a generalist?

Engage: How many, from 1 to 20, of the following consumer law services do you think you could competently provide? How many, from 1 to 20, would you want to provide? Estate planning; business planning; personal injury; drunk-driving defense; minor-in-possession defense; driver's license restoration; real-estate transactions; insurance claims; worker's compensation; Social Security disability; taxation; vocational licensing hearings; unemployment claims; discrimination claims; boundary disputes; municipal-ordinance enforcement actions; nonprofit startups; condemnation actions; divorces; juvenile delinquency.

Snapshot: She thought of herself as having the classic general practice. Her two-lawyer office was in an old storefront down a quaint side street just a couple of short blocks from the county courthouse next to the big park in the center of the small town. She did everything that her individual, family, and small business clients brought to her—everything. She felt that she was reasonably good at it all but excellent at none of it. She had no illusion that her clients were getting from her any big-firm, big-fee, bells-and-whistles products. Rather, her clients were getting the simple law products and services that they could afford. Nor did she feel at any particular risk of committing malpractice by practicing in so many fields. Her clients simply did not have big, complex matters. If anyone in the small town did have such a matter, which was pretty rare given the nature of the small town, then they knew well enough to go to one of the fancy big-city law firms and lawyers in the nearest metropolitan area. She was perfectly comfortable with her general practice even when she traveled to big-city forums for bankruptcy, worker's compensation, or administrative-law work. The judges and magistrates in those forums knew how to treat the small-town general practitioner.

She was competent, her services affordable, and her practice general, and her clients loved her for it.

46 Specializing

You may decide that you prefer specialization over an all-comers general practice. Many lawyers do specialize. Sound reasons to specialize include that your skill and efficiency increase as you repeat and improve work you have done before. You get better at it, and you get quicker at it. Clients value your being good at something. They also value when you can do it more quickly, at least when you then offer it more affordably. The first time you do anything, it simply takes you longer. When you systematize and commoditize work, you make it more reliable and consistent, and less expensive. Specialization enables these improvements. You may also make more money. You cannot master all fields, so why not master one? "Another trend that is having a wide-ranging impact on the legal profession is specialization. Increasingly, lawyers are utilizing their legal skills in combination with the skills they have acquired in other disciplines. Specialization includes not only formal recognition as a specialist under a jurisdiction's rules of professional conduct, but also *de facto* specialization in the form of practice concentration or limitation." MUNNEKE, THE LEGAL CAREER GUIDE, at 33.

Specialization, or (more precisely) service differentiation, is also an important marketing tool. When clients see you as a specialist within the law field where they need service, they should prefer you over the services of a general practitioner who might not be so affordable or skilled. Specialization can also reduce malpractice risk. Law practice specialties are too numerous to list other than by example. Some of the more common specialties offered to individual consumer clients include criminal defense, bankruptcy, estate planning, business planning, real-estate services, civil litigation, worker's compensation, and Social Security disability. Consider whether you want to specialize including whether the geographic area where you plan to practice will support it. "Choosing the right specialty is key, and it should start in law school. ... The business world in general has become very specialized, and the field of law is no exception." BLAKELY, FRIENDS AT THE BAR, at 31.

Takeaway: **Consider choosing a specialty practice area to master.**

Response: "I definitely want to develop a practice niche and am thinking about family law, real-estate work, and consumer law. My spouse and I know a lot of couples who use or need legal services, whom I would like to help."

Reflect: Do you see yourself as more of a specialist than a generalist? Why or why not? Do you like to master things beyond basic competence? What specialty would you choose as your favorite? What specialty would you absolutely refuse to practice if offered to you?

Engage: Sort the following specialty practices into these five groups, (a) definitely willing to practice, (b) willing to try, (c) not sure about practicing, (d) likely unwilling to practice, or (e) definitely unwilling to practice: employment law; personal-injury law; administrative law; environmental law; school law; aviation law; business planning; insurance law; estate planning; civil litigation; alternative dispute resolution; military law; family law; intellectual property; taxation; criminal defense; bankruptcy; municipal law; civil rights; consumer law; real estate; immigration law; tribal law; agricultural law.

47 Boutique Practice

Specialization, though, is not the only question when it comes to choosing a practice field. Some lawyers restrict very tightly their practice field to the point that they develop unusual expertise within a sort of sub-field of a specialty practice area. Lawyers who are particularly effective not only at serving clients solely within one field but at distinguishing their work from the work of other practitioners have a *boutique* practice, implying not merely specialized but elite practice. "The rise of small so-called "boutique" firms containing clusters of focused, experienced attorneys of high quality is a phenomenon in many practice fields...." MORRIS, ASK THE CAREER COUNSELORS, at 24.

One does not necessarily have a boutique bankruptcy or criminal-defense practice because both bankruptcy and criminal defense are large specialty fields having many lawyers providing the same service. Yet one might develop a boutique practice in defending prominent healthcare professionals against Medicare- and Medicaid-fraud charges or other similar federal crimes. Similarly, one might develop a boutique practice in bankruptcy reorganization of manufacturing suppliers in an economic downturn. While boutique practices are at the opposite end of the spectrum from general practice, boutique practices have their own allure. The boutique practitioner may not be able to do much of anything else, but the one thing that they can provide, they provide with such natural alacrity, skill, effectiveness, and aplomb that one can only marvel. "True boutique firms afford associates many advantages. Senior lawyers and partners at these firms have a high level of expertise in their field. Generally attorneys achieve some level of success or recognition on the local, state or federal level before deciding to join or form a boutique." CAREY, FULL DISCLOSURE, at 264.

Takeaway: **Consider not only choosing a specialty field but developing a boutique practice within the specialty field.**

Response: "I want to be so good at just one thing, like protecting First Amendment rights, that clients will seek me out from across the country."

Reflect: Do you have the natural focus and drive to be the best in a narrow field? Could you create a new field, that is, see as a boutique practice what others saw only as another case or collection of cases? Do you already have something in your network, education, or experience that would give you the special resources and insight to build and sustain a boutique practice?

Engage: For each of the following pairs of a specialty practice area with a boutique practice within that specialty practice area, choose which one you would prefer: (a) specialty personal-injury practice or boutique practice only in vehicle-defect-crash cases; (b) specialty intellectual-property practice or boutique practice only in information-technology patents; (c) specialty real-estate practice or boutique practice only in inverse-condemnation cases; (d) specialty employment-law practice or boutique practice only in employee welfare-benefits plans; (e) specialty criminal-defense practice or boutique practice only in defending finance executives against charges of federal crime; (f) specialty family law practice or boutique practice in representing victims of domestic violence; (g) specialty business-planning practice or boutique practice helping family businesses transfer ownership and control; (h) specialty estate-planning practice or boutique practice helping parents provide in trust for the care of severely disabled children.

Snapshot: He knew that he had one of the rarest of boutique law practices, but hey, he thought, someone had to do it. Every year brings the smallest handful of commercial airliner crashes, not often in the U.S., but occasionally in the U.S., and always somewhere around the world. His first case representing the estate of an air-crash victim involved a domestic airliner crash. He thought that his involvement in the field would end with that one case, given the paucity of U.S. crashes. Yet he soon realized from the calls and referrals he began getting that most any airliner crash anywhere in the world stands a good chance of having a U.S.-resident victim. Then it simply became a question of personal jurisdiction in U.S. courts over the airliner, and the applicable law. He was a lawyer. He could figure out those questions of law. Before too long, airliner-crash cases in U.S. federal courts all over the country made up the bulk of his practice, around which he focused his office location, staffing, marketing materials, everything. He knew that his unusual boutique practice was due to a combination of his natural warmth with and compassion for grieving people, willingness and ability to take on case costs and risks, and skill with judges and jurors, and then maybe also a good measure of dumb luck. Yet he also knew that he was the best.

48 Transactions or Litigation

One of the choices that lawyers make when choosing a practice field is to decide whether that field should involve transactional work or litigation. Transactional practice identifies, negotiates, structures and documents client agreements, interests, and relationships. Litigation practice involves invoking the authority of courts or other tribunals to decide disputed rights and claims among contesting parties. "[T]hink of the labels 'litigation' and 'transactional' not as distinct practice areas but rather as categories that transcend all the substantive practice areas. For instance, in the realm of entertainment law, some transactional lawyers represent talent and corporations in negotiating contracts, and then there are entertainment litigators who are called in when a contract goes awry." HAHN, GUIDE TO LAW FIRMS, at 94.

The difference between transactional practice and litigation practice is one of the clearest divides in all of law practice. Many transactional lawyers refuse to participate in any litigation practice, instead referring to other lawyers any litigation matters that arise out of their transactional work. For a transactional lawyer to take sides in litigation could create conflicts of interest and disrupt longstanding relationships. "[M]any law students are convinced they know what career path to pursue even though they've had zero exposure to it. Those who just 'know' they would be good litigators, or just 'know' they would do well at transactional work, most likely base those statements on *overconfidence*, not work experience." SCHNEIDER, SHOULD YOU REALLY BE A LAWYER? at 151.

Conversely, many trial lawyers have little or no interest in undertaking transactional work involving the negotiation, drafting, and execution of elaborate agreements documenting important rights. Trial lawyers tend to exercise a different skill set involving procedure, investigation, and written and oral advocacy. Trial lawyers may not even be competent for highly technical transactional work, lacking the knowledge, training, experience, and resources for it. Fewer lawyers combine the knowledge, skills, and character to be effective at both litigation and transactional work. Appreciate the choice that you may face between litigation and transactional work. "Your first summer or post-graduate job won't be your only job—just one in a series of stepping stones in a long career. If you're like a lot of lawyers, you'll change practice areas and settings, maybe even leave law altogether. People who have enjoyed satisfying law careers simply chose each of their jobs based on what sounded like the most fun." SCHNEIDER, SHOULD YOU REALLY BE A LAWYER? at 149.

Takeaway: **Discover whether you are more fit for and comfortable with transactional work or litigation.**

Response: "While I go about discerning my preferred practice area, I want first to be sure that I make the right overall choice between litigation and transactional work. It may be that I could practice in any niche as long as I was first comfortable as either a litigator or transactional lawyer."

Reflect: Make a point of meeting and talking with both litigators and lawyers involved in transactional work. How do they regard their work? How do they seem alike in how they approach their work, and how do they seem different? Can you identify lawyers who are both effective litigators and effective at transactional work? What characteristics seem most associated with which kind of work?

Engage: Classify each of the following services as either litigation or transactional work: (a) drafting wills for two 65-

year-old spouses; (b) helping an 18-year-old client decide whether to fight a minor-in-possession ticket; (c) preparing a bankruptcy petition for a low-income wage-earner who just lost his job; (d) helping a property owner evict a deadbeat tenant; (e) drafting documents to form a limited-liability company for two friends; (f) challenging the state's denial of a foster-care-license renewal for an elderly couple; (g) making a claim for no-fault-insurance benefits for an injured motorist; (h) drafting a consumer contract for a new small business; (i) reviewing a proposed lease for a new retail tenant; (j) handling the closing on the sale of a small strip small; (k) making the city pay for a sewer backup in a resident's basement; (l) helping a neighborhood form an association for snow-plowing services; (m) defending a homemaker charged with drunk driving. What are the criteria you were using to make the distinction? How did you distinguish litigation from transactional work? Did you find yourself having an affinity for one kind of work over the other?

49 Transactional Practice

Transactional practice simply has a different character to it than litigation. The difference is so distinct that transactional lawyers carry a different outlook on their practice. Some lawyers say that the work of a good transactional lawyer is to ensure that the parties will have no litigation. Transactional work in that sense looks forward from the present, trying to anticipate events and equip the parties to deal collaboratively in advance with those events for the surest, swiftest, and best outcomes. Transactional practice at once assumes both the best of intentions by all interested parties that they will respect one another's rights and interests, and yet also assumes the worst of actions by at least some of those parties from whom others will need to protect and provide for their rights in advance. Transactional practice is diligent, prudential, protective, and predictive, crossing i's and dotting t's until everything looks in the best order possible given that scoundrels populate a hazardous world. Due diligence is a key transactional-practice skill. "Virtually all 'transactions' (in the broadest sense of the term) start with due diligence. Due diligence can be described as a detailed review of information related to a company or of the legal structure of an entity for purposes of ascertaining whether a conflict exists or a problem needs to be addressed before a[] transaction takes place." CAREY, FULL DISCLOSURE, at 134.

Transactional practice is creative, innovative, and productive, organizing and ordering rights and interests so as to build things up before others try to tear them down. Transactional practice can be like offering a bulwark of order and prosperity in a sea of chaos and need. Consider the deep value of transactional practice. "Some of the most successful stories that I hear come from women who chose nonlitigation specialties like intellectual property, health care, financial and investment services, real estate, bank regulation, elderly law, estates and trusts, tax, ERISA, and adoption and family law. Most of these women are still practicing, and they have been able to manage their law firm and public-sector practices in addition to having satisfactory personal lives." BLAKELY, FRIENDS AT THE BAR, at 94.

Takeaway: **Transactional practice organizes, orders, and documents rights and interests for best outcomes.**

Response: "I look forward to a transactional practice in which my skill at negotiating, organizing, and documenting rights and interests creates substantial value for my clients."

Reflect: Recall an instance when your proactive measures made for a better outcome when later events occurred. Is that your character to see and prepare for things before they happen? Are you a planner and organizer? Would people who know you call you prudential? Do you like assembling teams? Have you ever done so? Are you a creator and administrator? Are you good at discerning, describing, and ordering relationships?

Engage: For each pair of words, choose the word that first attracts you: (a) prudent or venturing; (b) predict or react; (c) collect or distribute; (d) organize or share; (e) document or investigate; (f) proactive or reactive; (g) collaborate or compete; (h) negotiate or advocate; (i) detailed or general; (j) rely or invent; (k) see or discover. Then, count the number of times that you chose the first word in each pair. If your count exceeds six, then consider transactional practice. If your count is less than four, then consider not doing transactional work.

Snapshot: He was a transactional lawyer. That was it. No litigation. He had estate-planning, real-estate, and business-planning clients, no litigation. He would have been up to litigation. He had the courage of his convictions. He knew a rat when he saw it. He could confront wrongs, advocate for justice for his clients. He did that kind of advocacy all the time in his estate planning, real-estate work, and business planning. Families and deals had their scoundrels, just like in litigation. Rather, he just did not see himself as a litigator. It felt like something genetic more than having anything to do with his skills or preferences. He was a transactional lawyer, and a darn good one at that. He did not want to be an average or poor litigator, which he suspected he would be. Whenever his transactional matters led to litigation, he simply referred the matter to the civil litigators in the local bar. They often referred their transactional matters back to him. He didn't have to be everything to all people. In law practice, he found that he could be true to both his clients and to himself.

50 Litigation

Litigation, which again involves invoking a tribunal's authority to decide disputes, has its own character entirely distinct from transactional work. The public caricatures litigators. Loud, contentious, and flamboyant trial lawyers make for news and entertainment. Like any mockery, the caricatures have just a grain of truth. Some of us like to make people do what they do not want to do. Some of us like to disagree. Some of us like healthy confrontation of perceived wrongs. Some of us like to compete. Those of us who favor these things can make good trial lawyers. Trial lawyers need to stand up for people and things. They need to tell it like it is, even when certain authority suggests that it is not. These actions can be powerful, when trial lawyers understand, always respect, and sometimes even enjoy power. "In litigation, trial practice skills are applied to many specialties, or subject areas, within the large body of law. There is employment litigation, personal injury litigation, contract litigation, estates and trusts litigation, civil rights litigation, and myriad other types of trial practice." BLAKELY, FRIENDS AT THE BAR, at 88.

Yet a litigator need not necessarily be contentious and certainly not flamboyant. Litigators in fact tend to be highly reasonable professionals, knowing that the limbs out which they climb had better be sturdy enough to support their weight. Litigators can nonetheless question what others assume to be true. They can hold issues open when others see them as closed. Above all, litigators have the passion and skill for advocacy. They know that they are not always right. No one can be. While every trial lawyer will tell you that they hate to lose, trial lawyers actually understand and accept more

Dear J.D.

readily than most that advocacy means wins and losses. They have, in other words, the courage of their convictions, often valuing most simply to be in that arena where truth and justice should prevail.

Takeaway: **Litigators confront and address wrongs, adjusting important rights.**

Response: "I so look forward to getting into litigation practice to help clients address some of the really concerning things that I see going on in the community. I want just want to advocate in ways that improve opportunity and order in our community."

Reflect: When you hear the words *trial lawyer*, what do you instantly think? Are your associations positive or negative? Do you respect or disrespect litigators? Can you identify with a model litigator, whether historical or present, famous or unknown? Do you like to confront others when you see something wrong? Are you effective at confrontation? What skills and character do you think effective confrontation takes? Do you like advocating for different outcomes? What skills and character do you think advocacy takes? Are you effective at advocacy?

Engage: Rate each of the following phrases with 1—strongly agree, 2—agree some, 3—neutral, 4—disagree some, or 5—strongly disagree: (a) I stand in the gap when others don't; (b) I stand alongside others who need it; (c) I am a champion of justice; (d) I won't let others push people around; (e) I hate when others take advantage of people; (f) I love being in the contest, win or lose; (g) I hate standing on the sidelines waiting for outcomes; (h) I would prefer to go down fighting; (i) evil prevails when people remain silent to injustice; (j) I'd rather risk losing than miss a chance at winning. Then total your score, and divide by 10 for your average. If your average is 2.0 or less, then consider litigation practice. If your average is 4.0 or above, then consider not practicing litigation.

Snapshot: She knew that she thrived on litigation. She drew such energy from it, needed and wanted to be litigating so badly, that it was almost scary. She had learned to temporize her enthusiasm for it simply for the good of all involved including herself. She even tried taking breaks from it but only found herself picking up extreme sports and even gambling, which she hated but somehow seemed to salve her need for stimulation. Better to litigate, she thought, than to skydive, deep-sea dive, and gamble. The more that she litigated, the more she felt made for litigation. Litigating was like wearing a perfectly fitted glove or a perfectly tailored suit. Without it, in the rare lulls between pretrial hearings and jury and bench trials, she felt lost, as if she had no identity. She would mope about the office, trying to look busy but feeling depressed, until the next deposition, oral argument, or jury draw approached, when she would feel her mood rise again to the occasion. Thank God for litigation, she often thought, for a forum in which we can speak important truths with an authority that actually matters.

51 Dispute Resolution

Litigation practices have changed with the advent and refinement of the field of alternative dispute resolution, also known as ADR. While litigation involves getting an authority like a judge or magistrate to decide disputes that the parties have not decided, alternative dispute resolution presumes that the parties may yet be able to agree. If litigation is the traditional avenue to resolve disputes by imposed mandate, then ADR alternatives involve special procedures like mediation and case evaluation that hope to reveal to the parties that they may yet control their own destiny by compromising and agreeing. In that sense, ADR is an adjunct to litigation, like a side door or back door out of the courthouse. "Lawyer-Peacemakers strive to bring order out of chaos. They work hard to create an atmosphere in which enemies lay down their swords and sign meaningful treaties. To do so, they help their clients concentrate on common interests rather than emphasizing differences." ARRON, RUNNING FROM THE LAW, at 55-56.

Lawyers who specialize in ADR as mediators and case evaluators thus tend to have litigation experience, to know how to evaluate disputed claims and generate options for resolution, while appreciating the litigation stances and strategies of the parties agreeing to attempt alternative dispute resolution. Litigation and ADR go hand in hand, even if ADR involves a somewhat different skill set. Lawyers engaged in ADR need not necessarily have the litigator's investigation, confrontation, and advocacy skills. Mediation, for instance, can involve the opposite willingness to forgo confrontation and advocacy in favor of finding points of agreement pursuing a restorative form of justice. Lawyers involved in ADR should have strong interpersonal, negotiation, and strategic skills, influential, articulate, and engaged in their own right. "Getting certified as an Alternative Dispute Resolution (ADR) professional can be done easily, quickly and relatively cheaply. Most ADR certification programs take only about one week. Getting certified as a mediator is the first step toward gaining experience doing actual mediations." HERMANN, FROM LEMONS TO LEMONADE IN THE NEW LEGAL JOB MARKET, at 97.

Takeaway: **Consider alternative dispute resolution if you prefer resolving disputed matters over advocacy.**

Response: "I so value healing broken situations and relationships that I hope to pursue practice in alternative dispute resolution, particularly through restorative justice."

Related Fields: civil litigation, appellate practice, personal injury, worker's compensation, malpractice, family law, civil rights.

Reflect: When you speak and interact, do you tend to bring groups, sides, and people together around common commitments? Or do you tend naturally to see and raise differences that divide? Do you like agreement and unanimity, or do you prefer competition and contention? Do you naturally see the world as involving competition over limited resources or as constantly creating new opportunities through new methods and resources? Are you effective at generating new options when people get stuck in disagreement? Do you like making a pie or dividing the pie?

Engage: For each of the following disputes, try to envision a proposal that as a mediator you would make to attempt to bring the parties closer together toward resolution by agreement, while concluding as to each dispute whether agreement is possible: (a) formerly abusive father demands resumed parenting time with fearful children in mother's custody; (b) separated non-resident spouse demands renewed access to workshop behind marital home in which resident spouse has a new boyfriend; (c) business partners in dissolution contest rights to business's unique and valuable trade name; (d) neighbor demands that adjacent resident remove deck that resident inadvertently built across the property line; (e) employee demands reinstatement after allegedly discriminatory firing that employer alleges was for theft. If you were able to envision proposals for three or more of these five situations and concluded that resolution was possible in four or more, then consider alternative dispute resolution as a career option.

52 Criminal or Civil

After transactional practice versus litigation, another broad divide in practice fields involves the criminal justice system versus the civil justice system. Both the prosecution and defense of criminal charges on one hand, and the pursuit or defense of civil liability on the other hand, involve litigation. The skills of litigators in either criminal or civil justice systems are similar skills to the extent that they involve written and oral advocacy, and court procedures. Some lawyers do practice in both civil and criminal cases. Melvin Belli, Johnnie Cochran, and Gerry Spence are famous trial lawyers to have represented both criminal defendants and civil plaintiffs. The laws, systems, procedures, and conventions, though, are quite different for civil and criminal cases, meaning that lawyers tend more often to practice primarily or solely in either civil or criminal cases rather than both. "A good approach for a new attorney is to start building a practice around a few key areas of interest. If possible, limit yourself to no more than three or four fields of law that interest you. This will allow enough diversity in your practice to maintain sufficient cash flow in the early days of your practice, but will also provide an escape from the impossible task of being an expert on everything." PFEIFER, HOW TO START A SUCCESSFUL LAW PRACTICE, at 9.

Indeed, the difference between criminal and civil practice is more profound than many assume. Governments charge and prosecute crimes on behalf of the public, while civil litigation typically involves private enforcement of private rights and interests. That one difference having to do with government involvement in criminal cases has far-reaching implications for practitioners around important theoretical considerations like duties to the public and equally important practical

Dear J.D.

considerations like attorney fees. One good answer to *the question* would be to choose between criminal and civil justice systems.

Takeaway: **If interested in litigation, then consider choosing between criminal and civil justice systems.**

Response: "While I am pretty sure that I want to litigate matters, I am still exploring whether I prefer handling criminal or civil matters. I could do both, but the civil and criminal justice systems are pretty different."

Reflect: If you see yourself practicing some form of litigation, then do you see yourself handling matters involving criminal charges on one hand or civil liability on the other hand? Who are the litigators whom you most admire, and which (civil or criminal) do they practice? Do you think that you might want to pursue practice in both civil and criminal cases?

Engage: For each of the following situations, choose whether you would prefer to handle the resulting criminal charges or claim for civil liability: (a) drunk driver causes fatal vehicle crash; (b) aviation engineer conceals fatal design defect; (c) pharmaceutical maker conceals fatal drug defect; (d) financial advisor conceals fraudulent Ponzi scheme; (e) sweepstakes company defrauds contestants in mail scheme; (f) homemaker writes fraudulent check for home repairs; (g) hospital administrator accepts kickbacks from device supplier; (h) employer conceals medical-exam results on worker chemical exposures; (i) nuclear-plant operator falsifies records to conceal radiation release; and (j) lobbyist bribes legislator on behalf of utility company. If you chose civil in eight, nine, or ten of the ten examples, or criminal in eight, nine, or ten, then consider pursuing that field rather than the other.

Dear J.D.

Snapshot: "I love representing drug dealers," the lawyer found himself saying one day, "because they always pay up front and never lie to you." The other lawyers laughed at their professional colleague's insider joke. "Don't get me wrong," he continued, "I hate crime, hate drug dealing, hate the harm that dealers do to themselves and others. But as clients go, telling you the truth and paying up front, well, those parts you can get to like." Still, the lawyer admitted, he was already planning to move into business and other civil work, indeed had already gained his first commercial-litigation clients. "I couldn't do it the rest of my life," he said of defending those charged with drug crimes, "it's nasty business, and while everyone needs representation, you have to keep that ugly part of it at arm's length. You're always hoping that they find another line of work, and they all do, sooner or later, either in prison or out of it, dead or alive."

Part 3

Practice

53 Criminal Justice

The criminal justice system is at once both fascinating and yet in some respects mundane, hugely important while also often neglected, and enormously controversial while also often regarded as sacrosanct. It certainly holds room for advocates of different kinds, beginning with the great divide between prosecution and defense. While many practice areas involve sides, few practice areas involve such stark differences in sides as do prosecution and defense. While criminal justice routinely involves serious issues, it also often involves significant limitations on resources, meaning that lawyers often find themselves working with what little they have available while knowing that better is probably out there. "The true life of the criminal lawyer differs dramatically from the romanticized versions often portrayed in film and on television. Both public defenders and prosecutors must process numerous cases on limited budgets through an over-burdened and under-funded criminal justice system." ABRAMS, THE OFFICIAL GUIDE TO LEGAL SPECIALTIES, at 109.

Yet vigorous opposition is just one thing that distinguishes criminal practice from other practice areas. The opposition of state to citizen, with the attendant imbalance in power, is another distinguishing aspect. So too does the area's moral content, that crimes involve wrongs, often serious or even abhorrent wrongs that demand condemnation. The vulnerability of the victims of those wrongs is another distinguishing characteristic for which the involved lawyers must account, as is the vulnerability of the wrongly accused. Criminal practice attracts lawyers who want to do sobering, serious, and weighty work, confronting our worst intentions and actions. Criminal practice is also an area of surprising ministry, where lawyers on both sides hold broken lives and uncertain futures in their hands with the real prospect for shaping them for the better. If you wish to have an impact on your community, to wield real power on the one hand, or to ensure that those who do hold power use it judiciously, then consider criminal practice. "Jobs in criminal justice are plentiful, and they can cover a wide array of career options[including] parole and probation careers, criminal defense organizations, state and local police[and] other law enforcement careers, jobs in homeland security, careers with government entities such as the FBI, Department of Justice, and Bureau of Prisons, [and] careers in corrections and the prison system." FURI-PERRY, 50 UNIQUE LEGAL PATHS, at 60-61.

Takeaway: **Consider criminal practice if you wish to do serious and impactful work around most-difficult situations.**

Response: "I definitely plan to practice in the criminal-justice system where I feel that I can do the most good, although I have not yet decided on prosecution or defense."

Related Fields: prosecution, criminal defense, drunk-driving defense, federal defense, white-collar defense, public defender, license defense.

Reflect: What is your professional experience so far with the criminal-justice system? What was your interest in the criminal-justice system when you started law school? How has your interest changed? Do you see your future in criminal justice long term? Do you see short-term opportunities in criminal justice? What skills would you build if you practiced in the criminal-justice system at least to start your career? How could doing so advance or retard your long-term career goals?

Engage: Count the number of the following events where you could see yourself providing that professional service: (a) interviewing a child victim of physical abuse to identify the perpetrator; (b) attending an autopsy to confirm homicide as cause of death; (c) helping next of kin identify a decomposed body; (d) investigating a rape victim's sexual history; (e) notifying a mother of charges against her for shaking her baby to death; (f) evaluating a sentencing report on the impact on five children of their father's death by vehicular homicide; (g) obtaining forfeiture of a single mother's home for on-site manufacture of illegal drugs; (h) counseling a convicted defendant on the terms of a life sentence; (i) interviewing an admitted murderer for acts in mitigation of sentence; and (j) reviewing photos of a decapitation homicide with a crime-scene expert. If you counted three or less, then consider choosing a different field. If you counted six or more, then consider choosing the criminal-justice field.

54 Criminal Defense

When a lawyer switches sides from prosecution to defense work (or less commonly vice versa), former colleagues will joke about the lawyer having "gone over to the dark side." Despite the good-natured joking among lawyers about switching sides, to move from prosecution work to criminal defense is not to join the bad guys. While the lay public may question how lawyers can defend those whom the government accuses of crime, lawyers know how important criminal-defense work is. Not only do the innocent find themselves wrongly accused, but even the guilty need and deserve fairness in procedure and proportion in penalty. Indeed, criminal-defense lawyers find deep meaning in the work in the opportunity that defending clients charged with crime gives them to guide and influence the most-obviously broken and vulnerable among us. We are not simply attorneys but also counselors. Few clients are more willing to listen to our counsel than those, charged with crime, who face losing everything. "Defense attorneys are often faced with factual situations that are extremely unfavorable to their clients. They work closely with their clients when preparing for trial and generally attempt to resolve the case before trial by seeking dismissal of the case or negotiating a plea agreement with the prosecutors." ABRAMS, THE OFFICIAL GUIDE TO LEGAL SPECIALTIES, at 111.

If you have ever had a calling to help the poor and oppressed, then consider criminal-defense work where the clients are often financially, socially, and spiritually poor, and whose own wrongs (when properly accused) or government (when improperly accused) severely oppress them. Public-defender offices and indigent-appointment systems make the work financially sustainable, as do substantial fees for the higher-profile clients and defenders. Yet criminal defense more than most fields involves a social rather than financial call. Family and friends may have had good reason to abandon these accused clients, but every needs an advocate, and these clients far more than most.

Takeaway: **Criminal-defense work has great social value in addressing the rights, character, needs, and responsibilities of the accused.**

Response: "I am eager to stand alongside the criminally accused not just to defend the innocent but to influence, guide, and protect the guilty who need lawyers more than most."

Related Fields: prosecution, drunk-driving defense, federal defense, white-collar defense, public defender, license defense.

Reflect: Have you been guilty, if not of a serious crime than of something? How much do you feel that the accused need counsel? Could you see yourself helping an innocent client fight a serious accusation? Could you see yourself advising a guilty client to admit a wrong as a first step toward recovering a life? Would you find value in helping guilty clients advocate for fair and rehabilitative sentences? Do you believe that people have the capacity to change for the better? Do you think that your counsel could help some do so?

Engage: Rate each of the following as a +1 (can see myself doing), 0 (neutral), or -1 (cannot see myself doing): (a) advising a guilty client to admit to a homicide charge to avoid life sentence without parole; (b) advising an innocent client on advantages to accepting a guilty plea to a lesser charge; (c) representing a client whose guilt seems obvious to you but who maintains innocence; (d) continuing to represent a client who at first maintained innocence but now admits guilt to you; (e) representing clients whose actions you rightly condemn and abhor;   (f) requiring full payment of your fee before representing a client who claims innocence; (g) continuing to represent your client after the matter has exhausted your retainer fee with the client unable to pay more;   (h) representing indigent clients for appointment fees that are often inadequate for the required work; (i) learning that non-lawyer friends question your integrity for representing the guilty;   (j) doing work that non-lawyers often do not understand or even respect. If your total plusses against your minuses are five or more, then consider criminal-defense work. If your total plusses against minuses are zero or less, then consider other work, or re-examine your responses.

Snapshot: "Oh, sure," the lawyer replied in answer to the other lawyer's question about her practice area, "I represent mostly university students charged as minors-in-possession, or with open intoxicants, or for disorderly conduct, and occasionally drunk driving. You'll find me at one of the area's three district courts for arraignments most Monday mornings." The other lawyer marveled at how specific her practice was. "Yes," she replied, "It's sad, of course, but with them away from mom and dad for the first time, I'm kind of like a stern big sister to them, although I don't have to be *too* stern because the judges take care of that part. Most of them get it straight quickly. I don't have many repeat clients, and with the diversion programs, I feel like I am saving some of them from much worse, at least those who listen to me." The other lawyer asked if she had any other practice plans. "Not really," she replied, "I've been doing this work for a few years now, and although it never really changes, every client is unique, so it always seems fresh. I haven't come close to tiring of it." The lawyer paused for a moment before turning back to conclude with a huge smile, "And I always wanted to be a big sister."

55 Drunk-Driving Defense

Criminal-defense work can involve several subspecialties one of which is drunk-driving defense. Odd though it may seem, drunk-driving charges are so common as to make for a relatively substantial practice niche. Some lawyers do little other work outside of drunk-driving defense. These lawyers know the sad patterns that these crimes involve. Lawyers handling drunk-driving-defense and minor-in-possession charges meet Monday mornings at the courthouse nearest a university campus or entertainment district, where their clients face arraignment after late-Friday-night and late-Saturday-night arrests. Certainly, many such cases involve ensuring reliable cause in the stop, science in the blood- or breath-testing, and procedure following arrest. Many more such cases involve fair treatment in the charge, plea, and sentence. "[M]any criminal defendants hire private criminal defense attorneys to represent them at arraignments, pretrial hearings, settlement conferences, trials, and sentence hearings. Private criminal lawyers are obligated to provide their clients with legal counsel that is in their best interest. ... All final decisions on any matter, however, are made by the defendants." ECHAORE-MCDAVID, CAREER OPPORTUNITIES IN LAW, at 26.

Sound representation can mean the difference between the client's saving or losing an education, vocational or professional license, job, or even marriage. Your ability to counsel and arrange for drug- and alcohol-treatment plans and other rehabilitative steps can be key to effective practice. Consider defending those charged with driving under the influence of alcohol or drugs, if you want to do work that the community needs. "What are your career priorities? By priorities, we mean what is truly important to you when it comes to a job? ... Many people don't realize the importance of having a job that's in line with their priorities until they're in one that isn't." SCHNEIDER, SHOULD YOU REALLY BE A LAWYER? at 158, 160.

Takeaway: Consider drunk-driving defense if you want to help save and rehabilitate broken lives.

Response: "I have a passion to help alcoholics and others with life-controlling addictions, which oddly enough makes drunk-driving defense a good area for me to practice."

Related Fields: prosecution, criminal defense, federal defense, white-collar defense, public defender, license defense.

Reflect: Do you have personal or family experience with addictions and their treatment? Research the impact of alcoholism and other addictions on individuals, families, employers, communities, and the economy. Do you see an opportunity in drunk-driving defense and related law practice to help those whose addictions are most threatening themselves and others?

Engage: Rate each of the following with +1 (interested), 0 (neutral), or -1 (not interested): (a) breathalyzer and blood-alcohol science; (b) Alcoholics Anonymous and other addiction-treatment programs; (c) keeping client college students in school; (d) saving a working client's job under difficult circumstances; (e) negotiating frequently with prosecutors; (f) cross-examining police officers; (g) helping clients deal with short-term and medium-term incarceration; (h) helping clients recognize that they have substance-abuse issues; (i) earning regular fixed fees for predictable work; (j) requiring that clients pay fees up front. If your total plusses against your minuses are four or more, then consider criminal-defense work. If your total plusses against minuses are zero or less, then consider other work, or re-examine your responses.

Snapshot: "Yep," the drunk-driving-defense lawyer replied, "That defense has been all the rage up here for the past few months. As soon as they get arrested, they call their girlfriend or whomever to meet them at the hospital with a bottle of hard liquor to drink before the hospital can get the blood drawn." The other lawyer asked whether this odd defense of drinking *more* liquor after arrest on a drunk-driving charge worked. "Not usually," the defense lawyer replied, continuing, "These knuckleheads don't know anything about absorption rates. It only works if the hospital bumbles around for a while before the blood draw, and even then the prosecutors don't buy it, which doesn't surprise me." The two lawyers remained silent for a few moments while an assistant prosecutor walked past. The defense lawyer then resumed, "I'd never counsel it, but I suppose they'll keep doing it until the next great idea comes along." The two lawyers laughed.

56 Federal Defense

There are crimes, and then there are federal crimes. Practice in the federal courts is in many jurisdictions pretty starkly different than practice in the state courts. While the generalization is not always true, lawyers still often find that federal criminal prosecutions involve more prosecutorial resources, finer and more technical points of law, more court procedure and formality, and higher expectations of counsel on the part of the court. If you are looking for a professional challenge, then try discrediting an FBI investigation while disputing the conclusions of the IRS, EPA, Labor Department, Justice Department, or other federal agency. If you are looking for a challenging forum, then consider that federal judges have lifetime appointments and are beholden to no one, unlike state-court trial judges whom local voters typically elect. Federal judges do not suffer fools gladly. What passes as competent counsel in state court may not meet a federal judge's higher standard. Federal criminal defense work is not for the faint of heart, in part because of the exacting demands of federal judges and in part because of the serious and often-complex nature of the federal charges, particularly with enterprise crimes. "The federal government has made the war against drugs a priority with stiff penalties for those defendants proved guilty of importing, selling, and distributing drugs. ... Drug cases include those brought against neighborhood dealers as well as those brought against organizations involved in large-scale drug trafficking and money laundering (the transfer and concealment of large amounts of cash generated through sales of drugs through various bank accounts)." ABRAMS, THE OFFICIAL GUIDE TO LEGAL SPECIALTIES, at 112-113.

Clients charged with federal crimes need strong and expert representation. Lawyers who defend clients on federal charges are often members of a small and elite local bar whose members have earned their way onto the federal appointments list. Those lawyers may also travel statewide, regionally, or even nationally for federal criminal-defense representation. New lawyers are less often members of that elite bar but may certainly aspire to it and soon attain it. You know that you have accomplished something significant when you do so.

Takeaway: **Consider federal criminal-defense work if you like to undertake high-level, challenging, and technical advocacy work in the most-formal forum.**

Response: "My aim is to become so skilled at the representation of those who are charged with crime that I can handle the most-serious federal charges in that premier federal-court forum."

Related Fields: prosecution, criminal defense, drunk-driving defense, white-collar defense, public defender, license defense.

Reflect: Do you like taking on high-stakes matters? Do you respond well to high expectations? Do you have a firm sense of your own skills and professional worth? Are you willing to challenge the most-resourceful and most-respected authority, to put it to its proofs? Can you stand for an indigent individual against the power, prestige, and mechanisms of the federal government?

Engage: Count how many if any of the following commitments match your professional goals or stir your professional passion enough to pursue criminal-defense work: (a) limit the reach of the federal government into state and local matters so as to maintain constitutional government; (b) preserve and restore a reasonable sphere of individual liberty and privacy against federal scrutiny and control; (c) humanize and hold accountable technical bureaucratic systems to economic realities and social norms; (d) resist and reduce regulatory oppression to sustain and enable responsible and innovative economic and proprietary activity; (e) challenge and reform regulatory regimes and enforcement mechanisms having disparate impact on disadvantaged populations; (f) ensure fair and equitable exercise of charging and sentencing discretion; and (g) restrict prosecutorial and judicial powers to the proper limits of their delegation.

Snapshot: She had come to law school thinking that criminal-defense work would be the last practice area in which she would ever engage. She gradually realized, though, that the work would put her alongside the most vulnerable of all persons, indeed the most in need. Her outstanding academics and strong writing skills had won her an appellate-court research attorney's job immediately after law school, but she had stayed only a few months. She wanted to work with and for people, especially people who need the most help. She began taking state-court assignments to represent indigent defendants, quickly growing skilled at and respected for her trial work. Her volunteer work teaching prison inmates to research and write honed her interpersonal skills and won her more respect. She taught as an adjunct at the local law school and university, organized law conferences and programs, and involved volunteer students in her trial and research work, giving her even greater standing and confidence. Within a few years after graduating from law school, her reputation for thoughtful, skilled, and earnest criminal-defense work had earned her way onto the local federal court's assignment list, from which she frequently tries challenging federal criminal-defense cases. This practitioner had found and embraced her life work.

57 White-Collar Defense

Federal criminal matters can involve securities fraud, mail-and-wire fraud, contractor kickback, and other charges against brokers, bankers, business persons, and other professionals. These so-called *white-collar* criminal cases can also involve state court proceedings. White-collar criminal defense is another sub-specialty of a broader criminal-defense practice. "Many large law firms have a white-collar criminal defense division. White-collar defense attorneys also work at small firms and as solo practitioners. ... Unlike crimes such as burglary, murder or rape, white-collar crime rarely includes a physical component. Embezzlement, fraud, price-fixing, racketeering and bribery are all considered white-collar crime." VISWANATHAN, VAULT GUIDE TO LITIGATION LAW CAREERS, at 22.

Not all lawyers who practice in criminal cases will handle white-collar charges. White-collar clients tend to have more financial resources than other criminal-case clients. They can often afford to hire premier counsel for substantial fees. The lawyers who graduate to white-collar work tend to be the buttoned-down lawyers with whose firms non-lawyer professionals might already have dealt in other matters and would also most value and respect for criminal defense. White-collar defense is often a small and elite bar within the larger criminal-defense bar. "[W]hite collar practitioners ... all know each other and, for the most part, behave with a higher degree of civility than general litigators. ... These attorneys have to like battling the government. They see themselves as 'The Fixer,' called in at the last minute to clean up a bad situation." MUNNEKE, THE LEGAL CAREER GUIDE, at 376.

White-collar defense also differs from other criminal defense in the nature of the charges, usually having to do with finances and fraud rather than drunkenness and violence. The evidence therefore often involves communications and accounts rather than scenes and acts. The expert witnesses are more often accountants and analysts than medical examiners and toxicologists. The law itself, in the precise definition of peculiar white-collar crimes, can be more technical and obscure. The look, feel, and conduct of white-collar cases is simply different in so many respects that some lawyers find it so fitting as a subspecialty not to do much of anything else or at least not any other criminal-case work. "As technology advances and a larger percentage of the country's jobs are classified as white-collar, the incidence of white-collar crime will probably increase. It follows that this area of practice will grow as well in the coming decades." MUNNEKE, CAREERS IN LAW, at 78.

Takeaway: **Consider white-collar criminal defense if criminal law attracts you but you favor financial and technical issues over the behavioral and anatomical.**

Response: "White-collar criminal defense interests me because of the criminal-case work, technical and financial issues, and reputations and interests at stake."

Related Fields: prosecution, criminal defense, drunk-driving defense, federal defense, public defender, license defense.

Reflect: Remember Dostoyevsky's *Crime and Punishment*? The definition and occurrence of crime, and the secretive workings of the criminal mind, fascinate. Would criminal defense interest you if you could avoid working with violent crimes and criminals? Are you interested in how swindles, schemes, and scams work? Or are you curious about swindlers, schemers, and scammers? Have you ever wondered why professionals with so much at stake may risk it all for the excitement of approaching and crossing lines? Can you identify with an innocent professional getting accidentally caught up in a complex scheme?

Engage: Choose one of each pair: (a) few large matters or many small matters; (b) few large fees or many small fees; (c) larger financial interests or smaller financial interests; (d) greater client resources or lesser client resources; (e) larger client reputations or smaller client reputations; (f) technical matters or behavioral matters; (g) financial issues or anatomical issues; (h) numbers or words; (i) working with professional clients or non-professional clients; (j) working on professional matters or non-professional matters. If you chose six or more of the first of each pair, then consider white-collar criminal defense over other criminal defense.

58 License Defense

License defense relates to the subspecialty of white-collar criminal-defense work. When professionals commit crimes or engage in other serious misconduct, they can face license proceedings in which they badly need and will pay handsomely for your legal representation. Doctors, nurses, therapists, counselors, and others in the healthcare field, social workers, daycare operators, foster-care aides, and others in the social-services field, and lawyers, accountants, securities brokers, and others in administrative and financial fields, hold licenses. These professionals have substantial financial and reputational interests in their careers. Misconduct related to their field, such as an allegation that a nurse has physically abused a patient, threatens loss of their licenses and hence loss of their careers. Even misconduct unrelated to their careers, such as a drunk-driving conviction, can lead to a license proceeding. License proceedings have the complexity of other legal proceedings including administrative rules, evidence rules, researchable precedent, written advocacy, direct and cross-examination and oral advocacy at hearing, and appeals. "Approximately one-fourth of one's life will be spent in the workplace. This venue can be a virtual dungeon or paradise. The strategic objectives of work are: money, fun, intellectual satisfaction, community service, and, once again, fun. It is rare that a job will offer all of these elements. However, a guiding principle could be 'Get a life,' which means finding a rewarding balance between work and leisure." BEAN, CAREERS IN NATIONAL SECURITY LAW, at v.

Only a foolhardy professional would face a license proceeding unrepresented. The adage is that even when lawyers (who have the advocacy skills) self-represent, they have a fool for a client. While akin to traditional litigation, administrative license proceedings are just different enough from criminal-defense work or civil litigation in trial courts that only some lawyers entertain that practice area. The administrative law judges, rules, authority, and conventions are all different, making license proceedings a niche specialty. Consider license proceedings as your answer to *the question*.

Takeaway: **Consider license-proceeding work if you would like working with other professionals to save or restore their career.**

Response: "I most look forward to representing professionals in license proceedings when allegations of their misconduct threaten their careers. Professionals have so much invested in their skills, and their skills are so important to us, that I want to see them do well."

Related Fields: criminal defense, drunk-driving defense, federal defense, white-collar defense, public defender.

Reflect: Would you be more comfortable advocating before administrative judges who specialize in their subject? Would you prefer to be a trusted member of a smaller trial bar practicing in a special forum? Do you think that your personality, experience, and skill could gain the confidence of other professionals in dire need of your services? Do you work well with others who have substantial education, or do you prefer to be the expert working with non-professional clients? Do you have the advocacy skills to place a professional's one-time misconduct within the context of the professional's overall career contributions and considerable skill? Could you influence a professional to accept rehabilitative actions that others recommend but the professional rejects?

Engage: Which of the following professionals would you either be willing to represent or (more so) interested in representing in license proceedings? (a) A gynecologist alleged to have viewed pornography. (b) An anesthesiologist alleged to have abused anesthetics. (c) A surgeon alleged to have botched multiple surgeries. (d) An orthopedist alleged to have harassed nurses. (e) A general practitioner alleged to have advertised as a cardiologist. (f) An accountant alleged to have prepared fraudulent audits. (g) A securities broker alleged to have churned a customer account. (h) A lawyer convicted of drunk driving. (i) A foster-care worker alleged to have berated elderly residents. (j) A daycare worker alleged to have inappropriately touched children. If you chose six or more of these ten professionals, then consider licensing work as your field.

59 Civil Litigation

You may from the above criminal-case and license-proceeding practice-area descriptions already see how closely related and yet different is civil litigation. Civil litigation, like criminal-case work, involves advocacy. Your clients and you take one side arrayed in adversarial stance against the other side, each seeking opposing objectives. Yet the advocacy of civil litigation differs from criminal-case work in that it involves disputes between private parties contesting private rights and responsibilities. "[T]he path to a solid career in litigation is not one of bullying and theatrics, but one of perseverance and flexibility. A litigator focuses on details, on being organized and on satisfying her client's wishes. For a successful litigator, winning isn't everything. Indeed, for most litigators, a successful case never makes it to court, but settles quickly—to the satisfaction of the client, who didn't have to undergo the ordeal and pay for the expense of a trial." VISWANATHAN, VAULT GUIDE TO LITIGATION LAW CAREERS, at 93.

While litigation can involve a declaration of rights and accompanying injunctions, private parties in civil litigation typically contest over an exchange of money compelled by the threat or fact of a civil money judgment, rather than fighting fines, penalties, or incarceration as in criminal cases, or disputing the privilege of continuing professional work as in license proceedings. Civil litigation thus has its own financial look and feel, distinct from those other practice areas. "In addition to the thrills, however, litigation can be a very demanding practice, and it also can be less compatible than others with the desire for an enriched home and family experience. ... 'Just a little litigation' is like 'just a little pregnant.' There is no such thing." BLAKELY, FRIENDS AT THE BAR, at 89, 92.

Often, civil litigation is all about money, meaning who owes how much to whom. Various events can spawn civil litigation, including everything from deliberate or negligent acts causing personal injury or property damage to business disputes, commercial litigation over contract sales and remedies, and intellectual-property disputes. Lawyers find a common denominator in their filing private complaints and other pleadings in the civil courts, and pursuing pretrial discovery and procedures, all while preparing for civil jury or bench trials that are relatively unlikely to occur given the high prospect for resolution by pretrial motion or settlement. Civil litigators constantly prepare for trial while seldom going to trial, using their keen evaluation and strategic skills to measure and negotiate the right settlements. "[Litigation] is the quintessential adversarial practice. The interactions between the parties can be rancorous. This means ou can spend a lot of time drafting arguments that you may never need to use. The reward is victory. You must get satisfaction from winning." MUNNEKE, THE LEGAL CAREER GUIDE, at 373.

Takeaway: **Consider civil litigation if you like strategic advocacy between private parties over monetary adjustments reflecting private rights and interests.**

Response: "Civil litigation's strategic and procedural nature just seem to fit my administrative skills and discipline, especially in that I enjoy advocating for financial and property rights and private responsibilities, all of which I value highly."

Related Fields: federal litigation, class actions, appellate advocacy, personal injury, insurance defense, worker's compensation, malpractice, family law, employment law, civil rights.

Reflect: Are you a strategic thinker? Do you have keen administrative skills, liking investigating, organizing, and preparing? Does private negotiation over monetary compensation interest you? Are you effective at monetizing losses and valuing monetary demands and interests? Do you readily recognize and value rights while advocating for financial responsibility and interests? Are you willing to confront others with monetary demands or, conversely, to contest frivolous and exaggerated monetary demands even when made by those suffering loss or injury?

Engage: Which of the following ten clients would you be willing to represent and (more so) interested in representing in civil litigation? (a) A vehicle passenger who suffered leg and arm fractures, in a personal-injury lawsuit against the vehicle owner/driver. (b) A business partner in a lawsuit against the other partner over the business's dissolution. (c) A retail customer in a lawsuit against the retailer for premises slip and fall. (d) A copier lessee in a lawsuit against the copier lessor for warranty breach. (e) An automotive manufacturer in a lawsuit against a supplier for contract breach. (f) A musician/artist in a lawsuit against a record label for unpaid royalties. (g) A dairy farmer against a grain mill for poisonous feed. (h) A landowner in a lawsuit against a township to increase the township's condemnation offer. (i) A medical-device inventor against the device's manufacturer for license payments. (j) An employee in a discrimination-and-harassment suit against her employer. If you chose six or more of these ten fields, then consider civil litigation as a practice field.

Snapshot: "Hey, you again?" the debtor's lawyer greeted the collections lawyer in the courthouse hallway, adding, "You really get around!" They both laughed. They had met once before on a different collections matter in an adjacent county. "Be right with you," the collections lawyer said politely as he finished talking with a couple of unrepresented debtors and then turned back, saying, "I think we've got something we can do here. I'm fine with what you proposed so long as we get the equipment back." The debtor's lawyer breathed a silent sigh of relief, replying, "Want it on the record?" "Nah, I trust you," the collections lawyer said good-naturedly with a big smile, adding with a quick wave of his hand, "I'll shoot you the paperwork," before turning to usher the two unrepresented debtors back into the courtroom to be sworn for debtor's exams in an office down the hallway. "See ya," the debtor's lawyer waved back, but the collections lawyer had already disappeared back into the courtroom.

60 Commercial Litigation

Businesses have disputes with one another, requiring dispute resolution. Because their disputes are relationship based rather than one-offs like much tort litigation, businesses tend to engage in substantial alternative dispute resolution before litigating. Yet when they cannot resolve their issues voluntarily, they do so through litigation that can seem to them and their lawyers like much more than simply business. The saying is that nothing is harder and more emotional for the parties than a divorce case—other than litigation between business partners. Conflicts of interest are one reason why business-planning lawyers often eschew commercial litigation, referring it when it arises to the trial lawyers and litigation practice-groups in their firm or other firms. "Litigation attorneys, or litigators, deal with the judicial process, with civil disputes or criminal cases that are headed to court. ... Those attorneys who handle conflicts between individuals, whether over personal injuries, domestic disputes or other matters, are civil trial lawyers. Commercial litigators are trial attorneys whose clients include corporations and businesses." KOURI, VAULT GUIDE TO CORPORATE LAW CAREERS, at 5.

Commercial litigation actually can take many forms, only one of which is an internal dispute among the owners of one business. Different businesses sue one another over disputed goods-and-services contracts, equipment and real-property leases, licenses of intellectual property, unfair competition, and a host of other issues. Another reason that commercial litigation can be more difficult to resolve than other litigation is that insurance is usually not available for compensation. What one party demands, the other must be able to pay, making commercial litigators wary of the bankrupt defendant.

Commercial litigation can be highly strategic, with multiple possible outcomes, some win-win creative and others lose-lose destructive. "Note that being a litigator doesn't automatically put you in a courtroom. Public defenders may indeed be in court every week. But litigators who work on corporate or commercial matters might never go to court. They serve their clients by filing motions and briefs and settling conflicts without actually going to trial." KOURI, VAULT GUIDE TO CORPORATE LAW CAREERS, at 5.

Takeaway: **Consider commercial litigation if you have strong advocacy skills and business and strategic sense, but can also be a creative problem solver.**

Response: "I would enjoy the challenge, excitement, creativity, and strategy of commercial litigation, especially for sustainable enterprises trying to act and get others to act responsibly."

Related Fields: business planning, civil litigation, federal litigation, alternative dispute resolution.

Reflect: Are you interested in litigating? Do you have strong advocacy skills? Do you have a strong professional identity and substantial confidence in your positions? Do you like resolving disputes where resolution does not seem possible? Can you generate options and see opportunities where others cannot and do not? Do you like working with business owners and managers on business issues?

Engage: Which of the following clients would you like to represent in commercial litigation? (a) The lessee of a poorly designed, non-working $200,000 piece of custom machinery against the machinery's lessor manufacturer. (b) The reinsurer of a $40 million building-collapse loss against the contractor that installed equipment incorrectly causing the collapse. (c) A feed distributor against the bulk commodity supplier that shipped livestock feed laced with poisonous heavy metals. (d) The seller of a property-management business against the buyers who failed to pay for the purchase while raiding the business of cash deposits held in trust. (e) The installer of a commercial paper cutter sued by the cutter-owner printing company when the cutter worked poorly. (f) One co-owner of a computer-installation and repair service sued by the other co-owner over the equity of compensation and distributions. If you count three or more, then consider commercial litigation as a practice area.

61 Federal Litigation

As is true with criminal cases, civil cases filed in federal court or removed to federal court offer a different and often stiffer challenge than civil cases contested in state court. The diversity jurisdiction that gets many cases into federal court requires damages of at least $75,000, meaning that the average diversity case involves more money than the average state-court case. The federal-question jurisdiction that gets other civil cases into federal court means that the cases often involve important constitutional or federal statutory rights. The procedural rules can be different, and federal judges often require a significantly greater degree of formality and precision in following those rules, adding to the complexity and expense of federal civil litigation. "'What kind of lawyer are you?' In order to turn introductions into new clients, you must be able to answer this question with confidence. Yet an amazing number of attorneys get the 'deer in the headlights' look when asked to describe what they do." PFEIFER, HOW TO START A SUCCESSFUL LAW PRACTICE, at 5.

Federal courts draw jury pools from wider districts than state county courts, meaning that local counsel may be less attuned to juror profiles, biases, and expectations. Federal judges can have different views of the rights and responsibilities of litigants than locally elected state-court judges have. Most if not all of the advantages that local counsel may have in a state county court—familiarity with the rules, procedures, relaxed norms, judges, jurors, and court staff— disappear in federal court, which is much of the point of federal jurisdiction. Some skilled trial lawyers refuse to practice in federal court, while others disdain or prefer not to do so, while other skilled trial lawyers seek out the federal forum for the same reasons. The federal bar is simply a different bar than the state-court bar, as new trial lawyers soon find out.

Takeaway: **Consider federal civil litigation as a practice area if you prefer to deal with national over local entities and interests.**

Response: "I look forward to establishing a federal-civil-litigation practice involving national entities and interests. I have the confidence in my skills to develop and maintain a state-wide practice and even national practice."

Related Fields: civil litigation, class actions, appellate advocacy, personal injury, insurance defense, malpractice, employment law, civil rights.

Reflect: As a trial lawyer, would you prefer a local state-law practice primarily within your own county before your local judges, or would you prefer a federal district-wide or state-wide practice involving federal law and national interests? Would you prefer to sue national and multinational companies defended by high-powered lawyers or sue local individuals and companies defended by local lawyers? Would you prefer to have the same lawyer on the other side of multiple cases, making you familiar with that lawyer's character and practices, or would you prefer to have different lawyers from outside the area on each new case?

Engage: Count the number of the following ten parties that you would like to represent in these federal-court cases: (a) a test-instrument designer suing a school for copyright infringement; (b) a citizens-action-committee chair suing the city for First Amendment violations; (c) a public employee suing his state-government employer for unreasonable search and seizure relating to a drug test; (d) a city bus driver suing her city employer for due-process violations in terminating her employment; (e) a minority prospective tenant suing an apartment complex for housing discrimination; (f) a foreign-corporation importer suing a local distributor for breach of contract; (g) a medical-device manufacturer suing a federal agency over product approval; (h) a hospital defending a federal antitrust action to stop a merger; (i) a securities dealer defending a customer's action alleging inappropriately risky investments; (j) an airplane-engine manufacturer defending a products-liability claim brought by the estate of an air-crash victim. If your count reaches five or higher, then consider pursuing federal civil litigation.

Snapshot: The seasoned litigator gripped the podium to steady himself, his knees literally shaking. With wide eyes, he stammered back answers to the federal judge's demanding questions shot at him in rapid fire one after another, "Y-y-y-yes, Your Honor…. N-n-no sir…. Y-y-yes sir." When the brief hearing was over, a lawyer friend met the seasoned litigator in the hallway outside, asking in an amused voice, "Hey, what are you doing here? I didn't know you practiced in federal court." "Nah," the seasoned lawyer growled as he regained his composure, "I hate coming up here where they treat you like…." At this point his friend smiled broadly, clapped the seasoned lawyer on the back, and gestured toward the courthouse exit while interrupting, "Ah, my friend, we each have our job to do and place to do it, and it is good to know one's place. But we should be careful because courthouses have ears."

62   Class Actions

Civil litigation, whether state or federal, is only a broad practice area rather than a true specialty. Most civil litigators focus their practices in specific areas within that broad category. While their skills and familiarity with the civil procedural rules may make them candidates to handle just about any civil litigation, they tend nonetheless to handle only certain types of cases with which they have the greatest familiarity. Class-action practice is a prime example. A class action is a peculiar animal, as any student of civil procedure knows, so peculiar that lawyers make a specialty area out of class actions. Class-action rules are distinct, with class certification an exercise unto itself, not to mention the distinct issues and concerns surrounding class representatives, class counsel, notice to the class, settlements, and fees. Setting aside the unique legal issues, the time and financial resources necessary to pursue class actions are alone obstacles to entering class-action practice. "Whether out of interest or merely to make polite conversation, most people will ask what kind of law you practice, and they will assume you can answer this question relatively easily. You never hear doctors stammering around trying to describe their specialty field of medicine...." PFEIFER, HOW TO START A SUCCESSFUL LAW PRACTICE, at 5.

For these and other reasons, few civil litigators actually file or defend class actions. Civil litigators can go a whole career without being involved in so much as one class action. On the other hand, those litigators who do handle one or more class actions are more likely to handle several or many. Once one handles one class action, other class actions seem more manageable. A lawyer's reputation, confidence, client contacts, and resources all tend to grow with experience, particularly in niches. Those attributes need to grow for class-action practice, particularly insofar as much of it occurs in federal court because of favorable removal laws. Some skilled lawyers develop a practice niche emphasizing class actions, finding the work all at once challenging, meaningful for ending or establishing the lawfulness of broad practices, and financially rewarding if high-stakes and risky.

Takeaway: **Consider class-action practice if you like challenging law, high financial stakes, and work having broad impact.**

Response: "I would love to get to the point that I am able to handle class-action litigation for its high stakes and broad impact."

Related Fields: civil litigation, federal litigation, appellate advocacy, personal injury, insurance defense, employment law, civil rights.

Reflect: Would winning cases for individual clients satisfy you, or do you think that you would soon want your work to have broader impact on the rights, remedies, and practices of others? How skilled could you become at the representation, discovery, and other administration of dozens or even hundreds or thousands of claims? Do you have the patience for assembling large databases, developing elaborate notices, using merge files, and otherwise managing the technology and communications peculiar to class actions? What percentage of your own time and money are you willing to risk on a single matter?

Engage: Choose one or the other within each of these ten pairs, the first being typical of class actions and the second being typical of other civil litigation: (a) large numbers of plaintiff clients in one case or many cases each with one or two plaintiff clients; (b) a few large cases or many smaller cases; (c) federal court or state court; (d) extra pretrial motions and procedures or less pretrial procedure; (e) large time investment in single cases or small time investments in many cases; (f) large amounts of money advanced in one case or small amounts advanced in multiple cases; (g) longer time between large investment and large return, or shorter time between smaller investments and smaller returns; (h) class-member databases, spreadsheets, and merge files, or individual client records; (i) class-member notices or individual client relationships; (j) settlement hearings or private agreements. If you counted five or more of the first choice within each pair, then consider class-action practice.

63 Appellate Advocacy

Like class-action practice, appellate practice is a sub-specialty within civil litigation, one that applies to criminal cases, too. Only some lawyers handle appeals. Parties appeal litigation losses. You might reasonably assume that parties would hire their trial counsel to appeal a trial loss, but many trial lawyers have no interest in appellate work, and some parties have little interest in hiring the lawyer who lost their trial to lose their appeal. Parties often turn to appellate specialists for appeal work.

Only certain lawyers within large and small firms, and in solo practices, have the skills and interest to review lengthy trial transcripts, do extensive legal research, write lengthy appellate briefs, and conduct oral argument in front of panels of inquisitive appellate judges. "The day-to-day work involves only legal research and writing. There is no fact development work such as discovery, depositions, etc. It is not as adversarial or time-sensitive as trial litigation; it's great for introverts who want a predictable schedule." MUNNEKE, THE LEGAL CAREER GUIDE, at 372.

Brief writing alone discourages or intimidates some practitioners who limit their writing to standard pleadings, routine discovery papers, and short motions. The intellectual challenge of appellate arguments can be deeper, more theoretical, and more policy-oriented, and less practical and strategic, than trial work. Appeal work can take prodigious mental energy and significant discipline, even compulsion, in citation format, editing, revising, and proofreading skills. Oral arguments condense those intellectual challenges into 15-minute, 20-minute, or 30-minute pressure cookers, exciting to the appellate lawyer but frightening to others. "With low success rates—only a fraction of decisions are overturned—this practice is not for the faint of heart. So why do appellate lawyers like their job so much? The pure intellectual thrill of crafting arguments that could alter the direction of the law make this practice worth the uphill battle." HAHN, GUIDE TO LAW FIRMS, at 105.

Client contact, witness contact, opposing-party contact? Often none. Appellate lawyers tend to deal with the trial lawyers, insurance claim representatives, or corporate counsel, and of course opposing counsel. To the disinterested, appellate practice can look isolating, pressure-filled, high stakes, and arcane, while the appellate practitioner rightly sees it as lawyers' law, policy-shaping, and the pinnacle of litigation practice. "Attorneys specializing in appellate work are generally employed by law firms or by state or federal government organizations. Large and mid-size law firms with trial practices often have departments dedicated to appellate work. Small firms that handle trial work, such as plaintiffs' personal injury law firms or criminal defense firms, may have attorneys who work on appeals, or they may turn for assistance to an outside practitioner who specializes in appeals." ABRAMS, THE OFFICIAL GUIDE TO LEGAL SPECIALTIES, at 33.

Takeaway: **Consider appellate practice if you have excellent research and writing skills, and abundant mental energy, and like working with other lawyers on policy-based advocacy.**

Response: "My strong research and writing skills should give me good opportunities for appellate practice, where I look forward to shaping the law while advocating for clients."

Related Fields: civil litigation, federal litigation, class actions, personal injury, insurance defense, worker's compensation, malpractice, family law, employment law, civil rights.

Reflect: Does researching and writing a 20-page brief sound daunting or attractive? How about a 50-page brief? Does reviewing and summarizing a 500-page transcript sound daunting or attractive? How about a 1,000-page transcript? Do you enjoy editing, rewriting, and revising to satisfy other professionals' critiques, or do you prefer that your written work be your written work as you see it best? Would you prefer to work with other lawyers on appellate cases than with clients and witnesses on trials? Do you prefer books or people? Are you an introvert or an extrovert?

Engage: How many of the following five issues could you see yourself spending 30 to 40 hours researching and then writing about as an appellate advocate, while finding the work reasonably satisfying? (a) Whether cause-in-fact in a legal malpractice case is an issue for the judge or jury. (b) What is the appropriate definition and test for who is an employee for worker's compensation purposes? (c) Whether a trial court may reform a disputed development agreement to meet the parties' intent at the time of its execution. (d) Whether a consent judgment of divorce terminating life-insurance interests bars an ex-spouse from re-designating the other ex-spouse as beneficiary shortly before death. (e) Whether a federal law mandating health insurance grants a no-fault insurer a setoff under a state statutory provision. If your count is three or more, then consider appellate practice.

Snapshot: He slipped into the back of the appellate courtroom just as the first oral argument began. He liked to arrive early to watch the full docket unfold and get a sense of the judges' moods and interaction, even when his argument was not for a couple of hours. He was going to re-read things anyway, so why not sit in the courtroom? Looking around the half-empty courtroom, he recognized several of the lawyers. You could usually tell the one-timers and first-timers from the experienced appellate advocates. The experienced lawyers were completely at ease, while the new lawyers fidgeted. The nervous tics of the new lawyer sitting closest to him reminded him of his first oral argument when his heart beat so hard that the papers in his hand shook with each beat. Thankfully, he had not been too breathless in that argument, not like some of the new lawyers he had seen over the years. On the way home later that afternoon, thinking again of the nervous lawyer seated next to him, he had a twinge of regret that he could not get as nervous about oral argument as he once had. Then he laughed out loud alone in the car. Not really. He loved being at ease in an appellate courtroom.

64 Personal Injury

As specialties within civil litigation, federal cases, class actions, and appeals all involve forums and procedures rather than substantive law. Civil litigators, though, often specialize around substantive-law areas. Personal injury is one of the more-common substantive-law practice niches within civil litigation, indeed a potentially lucrative one in which the better lawyers can make substantial incomes from contingency fees without having to count hours to bill for hourly services. A personal-injury lawyer is one who represents individuals who have suffered physical injury due to the negligence of others. Motor-vehicle accidents are by far the most-common source of personal-injury claims, comprising as much as 60% of civil torts cases, but personal-injury lawyers may also represent clients injured in slips or trips and falls or by product defects, highway defects, medical care, workplace accidents, construction accidents, and other causes. "In the civil litigation arena, the term 'trial lawyer' typically causes us to think of the plaintiffs' and defense personal injury bar. Personal injury lawyers provide access to the civil court system for those without financial means by handling cases on a contingency fee basis, which means that the attorney is only paid a percentage (usually one-third) of any recovery." ABRAMS, THE OFFICIAL GUIDE TO LEGAL SPECIALTIES, at 445.

Perhaps surprisingly, personal-injury lawyers tend not to represent the victims of intentional torts, whether assault and battery or worse, because of the absence of liability insurance and usually uncollectible defendants. Personal-injury lawyers can have a public reputation as troublemaking ambulance chasers who stir up claims by irresponsible malingerers, but the work instead often seeks critically needed compensation for responsible clients badly injured by irresponsible actors whose insurers pay for everything (both indemnity and defense). Personal-injury lawyers often help people who are in very bad physical and financial circumstances by no fault of their own and instead the obvious fault of others. Medical knowledge can help in personal-injury practice, as can strong professional identity, good negotiating skills, solid trial skills, and good bedside manner for the most-seriously injured clients. Personal-injury lawyers also handle wrongful-death cases, extending the practice area into the profound.

Takeaway: **Consider personal-injury practice if you like helping people in most-difficult situations while advocating for their compensation out of which you earn contingency fees.**

Response: "I want to help the seriously injured make liability-insurance recoveries so that they can get back on their feet as quickly as possible. Injuries are a huge drain on the economy and significant disruptor of careers and families."

Related Fields: civil litigation, worker's compensation, Social Security disability, federal litigation, appellate advocacy, insurance defense, malpractice.

Reflect: Does reconstructing events interest you? Would you enjoy working with accident-reconstruction experts and engineers? Are you comfortable with anatomy issues? Would you appreciate reviewing medical and autopsy records? Would you like working closely with non-lawyer clients who have no knowledge of law and procedure? Are you a financial risk-taker for bigger reward? Could you consistently step into the middle of clients' personal disasters to give them the sense that things will soon be better, in other words to gain and hold their trust and confidence?

Dear J.D.

Engage: Count the number of the following cases in which you would be willing to advance $10,000 or more of your own money and work dozens or even hundreds of hours on the reasonable probability of recovering compensation for your plaintiff client out of which you would receive a contingency fee: (a) T-bone vehicle collision at an intersection fracturing your vehicle-passenger client's hip; (b) steering-linkage failure causing truck to hit your pedestrian client at her mailbox; (c) retail products display collapse knocking over your elderly client fracturing her shoulder; (d) slip and fall on ice outside shop door due to gutter problems, fracturing your client supplier's forearm and wrist; (e) chainsaw centrifugal clutch flies apart fracturing your chainsaw-repair client's eye orbit; (f) abrasive grinding wheel flies apart severing tendons in your client worker's knee; (g) carbon-fiber arrow splinters on release of compound bowstring, severing multiple tendons in your client's hand; (h) conveyor belt drags your client worker into mechanism amputating his arm; (i) high-speed head-on wrong-way freeway collision kills your estate client's decedent; (j) your child client mistakenly shuts winter coat-string in van door causing van-driver to drag child fracturing child's arms, legs, and ribs. If your count was six or more, then consider personal-injury practice. If your count was three or less, then re-examine your answers or consider a different practice area.

Snapshot: "You recognize him?" one of the local lawyers asked one of the out-of-state lawyers while pointing at a well-groomed, handsome, silver-haired man sitting in the back of the courtroom. The man did not wear a suit and tie but had a big silk scarf puffing out the open collar of his custom-tailored, cuff-linked shirt under his expensive navy-blue blazer. The out-of-state lawyer hesitated a moment before answering, "The guy on the billboard on the way in from the airport?" "You got it," the local lawyer smiled back, adding, "He's got several of these bus-crash cases like our one case." The local lawyer explained that the well-groomed man on the billboard and in the back of the courtroom, though licensed to practice law, never really did so, only referring cases to skilled trial lawyers throughout the state as, in effect, a broker. "Nice work if you can get it," the local lawyer concluded with a chuckle. "Nah," the out-of-state lawyer replied, "I'd rather be a trial lawyer than another pretty face." They both laughed at that one.

65 Insurance Defense

Personal-injury practice divides itself into sides much like prosecution and defenders in criminal cases. Lawyers who represent injured persons find it difficult at the same time to represent defendants whose negligence has injured. Insurers retain defense counsel in personal-injury cases. Insurers do not like retaining lawyers to defend their insureds when those same lawyers are suing their insureds in other cases. Some lawyers manage to stay in the good graces of one or more liability insurers in order to receive defense assignments from those insurers while simultaneously representing personal-injury plaintiffs whose claims involve other insurers, but doing so risks losing the confidence of the insurer, when that confidence may mean hundreds of thousands of dollars in fees to the firm. "Insurance defense attorneys may be part of small, mid-size, or large firms that specialize in insurance defense work, or they may work in-house for corporations or insurance companies. Sometimes, they work in the insurance defense litigation departments of large general practice firms." ABRAMS, THE OFFICIAL GUIDE TO LEGAL SPECIALTIES, at 448.

If you do not have the compassionate character, strong identity, and risk-taking nature to represent personal-injury plaintiffs but still like civil litigation, hourly or fixed-fee work for financially responsible insurers, and the constantly fascinating carelessness with which we act and the violent mechanisms of serious injury, then consider insurance-defense practice. Many civil litigators first learn their craft doing insurance-defense work, some sticking to it throughout a career while others move over to plaintiff's work or more complex litigation.

Takeaway: **Consider insurance-defense practice if you prefer low-risk hourly or fixed-fee civil litigation working primarily with other professionals.**

Response: "I like civil litigation, and my preference would be to do defense work ensuring that my assigning insurers pay only reasonable compensation for reliable claims."

Related Fields: civil litigation, personal injury, worker's compensation, federal litigation, appellate advocacy, malpractice.

Reflect: Do you like litigation more than working with the parties for whom you litigate? In other words, do you like strategic work interacting primarily with other professionals more so than substantial interaction with individual clients? Would you be comfortable preparing litigation budgets, writing litigation reports, and keeping claims representatives informed? Do you enjoy cross-examining claimants to discover contradictions and exaggerations? Could you comfortably recommend refusing settlement to an opposing claimant who suffered serious injury, where the claimant cannot prove your defendant client's fault? Could you work for insurers who routinely offer less in compensation that you think the claims are worth?

Engage: Count the number of the following claimants to whom you could advocate firmly that your defendant client's insurer pay significantly less than demanded, notwithstanding your client's fault in causing their injury: (a) an infant suffering permanent brain injury at birth due to delivery delay and trauma; (b) a young child suffering permanent shoulder injury on a defective playground swing; (c) a high-school track star whose running career a motor-vehicle accident ended; (d) a young mother disabled by a mistaken medication switch from caring for her children; (e) a young man whose face and throat a vicious dog bit and permanently scarred; (f) a pony-tailed woman accidentally scalped by a defective machine; (g) a mid-career tradesman permanently disabled by a defective tool; (h) an experienced tool-and-die worker whose finger a defective machine amputated; (i) an elderly wheelchair-rider permanently restricted to bed after a handicap-bus accident; and (j) the estate of a woman who died from asphyxiation due to a defective heater. If your count was six or more, then consider insurance defense as a practice field. If your count was under three, then consider a different field, or re-examine your answers.

66 Worker's Compensation

Worker's compensation is a practice area that relates closely to personal-injury practice because so many injuries happen in the course of work. Worker's compensation is a no-fault system that compensates the injured worker while barring the worker's suit against the employer and co-workers. In that no-fault respect, worker's compensation claims are different from personal-injury claims. Fault is not the issue. Worker's compensation issues, though, can be similar to personal-injury-case issues, particularly around whether the accident caused the injury and disability, and to what extent the claimant has an actual disability. Because some of the issues and skills for both worker's compensation and personal-injury cases are the same, lawyers who handle personal-injury cases sometimes also handle worker's compensation cases. "Lawyers who admit to having chosen their job largely based on the salary tell us they wish they had asked a lot more questions—about the projects they would be given, the clients they would represent, how work was assigned to associates, the opportunities for training and mentoring, the people they would work for and with, the office culture, the billable-hour demands, and the overall workload. Besides salary, these are the other big issues you need to focus on before accepting a job." SCHNEIDER, SHOULD YOU REALLY BE A LAWYER? at 148.

Yet worker's compensation cases have different laws and rules, and administrative forums and procedures. Many personal-injury lawyers refuse to handle worker's compensation cases, instead referring them to worker's compensation lawyers who may not handle any personal-injury cases. Worker's compensation is usually a higher-volume, lower-fee practice, with comp lawyers simultaneously handling not just dozens but a hundred or many more cases, nearly all of which are likely to result in recovery of at least modest comp-insurance benefits out of which the lawyer will receive a statutory contingency fee. Despite safety improvements, workplaces continue to hurt millions of workers, some of them severely and permanently. Worker's compensation is an important and substantial practice specialty, in which lawyers take sides in either representing claimants or working for employers and their comp insurers.

Takeaway: **Consider choosing worker's compensation as a practice area, if you like presenting important compensation claims in an administrative forum where no one's fault is at issue.**

Response: "My greatest interest right now is in helping injured workers recover worker's compensation medical-expense and work-loss benefits until they are able to return to work to support themselves and their families."

Related Fields: civil litigation, personal injury, Social Security disability, insurance defense, employment law.

Reflect: Would you be more comfortable practicing in an administrative forum where no party must prove or defend accusations of fault, and recoveries are of medical-expense and work-loss benefits? Do you like meeting and serving working people? Conversely, would you prefer to work for employers and insurers disputing and resolving the benefits they will pay to working people? Would you like the fast pace of a volume practice with as many as hundreds of small files? Could you work well with orthopedists, physical therapists, and occupational rehabilitation and vocational experts?

Engage: Count the number of the following activities that would interest you in doing in a worker's compensation practice: (a) meeting injured workers in hospital or convalescing at home after serious workplace injury; (b) meeting with injured workers' treating physicians to obtain opinions and reports; (c) reviewing and analyzing medical records of workplace injury; (d) retaining and working with vocational rehabilitation experts; (e) negotiating with defense counsel and insurance-claim representatives over medical services, bills, and benefits; (f) mediating multiple comp claims in one half day of private caucuses at the comp bureau; (g) preparing briefs and analyses for the administrative law judge; (h) preparing and summarizing medical-record and rehabilitation-report exhibits; (i) presenting or challenging the testimony of claimants and experts at administrative hearings; (j) advising and counseling claimants and claim representatives about claim values and settlements. If your count exceeds six, then consider worker's compensation as a practice area. If your count is less than three, then consider a different field, or re-examine your answers.

Snapshot: The personal-injury lawyer loved referring worker's compensation cases to his friend whose practice was nearly all comp, especially when she came to his office for the first client introduction, counseling, and interview. She was a masterful lawyer from whom he had learned much about client relationships, file management, office systems, and the other things that make a practice efficient. With so many clients on usually smaller matters, comp lawyers have to be organized and efficient, he had learned, and so the systems and practices of a good comp lawyer were a revelation to the personal-injury lawyer. On this occasion, she deftly guided the client through the hour-long initial consultation while the personal-injury lawyer just sat back and marveled. When it was done, she had already dictated a memorandum to the file that her legal assistant would copy back to the client who had listened to the dictation, correcting small things as they went along. The best part, though, was watching how encouraging she was to each client. While still telling everything straight with no promises or exaggeration, she managed to make each client feel heard, respected, and valued. He had no particular interest in comp work, but from her he learned great respect for it.

67 Social Security Disability

Social Security disability is another field closely related to both personal-injury and worker's compensation practice. When someone suffers a serious enough injury (whether or not in the workplace) to be disabled permanently or long term, they may qualify for Social Security-disability benefits whether or not their disability resulted from work or negligence. While some lawyers who practice worker's compensation or personal injury may occasionally help a permanently disabled client make a Social Security-disability claim, other lawyers practice solely or primarily in Social Security-disability claims. Social Security claims are administrative claims usually made first without counsel. When the Social Security Administration denies a claim, though, the appeal, marshalling and analysis of medical evidence and the administrative hearing require skills like those of a trial lawyer. "Every career decision requires a strategy. Developing the right conceptual framework can enhance a law student's or lawyer's thinking about a profession.... The challenge is balancing immediate needs (money, health benefits, and social security) with broader needs (a fulfilling career, intellectual challenges, and exciting opportunities)." BEAN, CAREERS IN NATIONAL SECURITY LAW, at 1.

The Social Security Administration permits trained non-lawyer agents to assist claimants many of whom opt instead to retain a lawyer on contingency fee. Lawyers who make a practice solely out of these appeals may have well over 100 and possibly even 200 or 300 pending claims at a time. They provide critical services to some of the nation's most-needy residents who must have worked long enough to make qualifying contributions to the system. Medical knowledge or aptitude, skill in analyzing vocational reports, and people skills are as important as, or more important than, trial skills in this field.

Takeaway: **Consider a Social Security-disability practice if you wish to use medical and vocational knowledge and people skills to advocate in federal administrative forum for some of the nation's most-deserving and neediest residents.**

Response: "I would find most satisfying and meaningful helping permanently disabled workers qualify for critically needed Social Security disability benefits. This work would serve some of the most-needy and deserving clients."

Related Fields: civil litigation, worker's compensation, personal injury.

Reflect: What aptitude do you have or are you willing to develop for medical and vocational knowledge? Do you enjoy reviewing, summarizing, and analyzing records, reports, and information? Do you have compassion for those who are permanently and prematurely disabled from their careers? Would you like to advocate in an administrative forum that relaxes rules of evidence and other trial formalities and conventions? Could you manage and sustain a practice involving hundreds of matters each involving a modest contingency fee?

Engage: Count the number of these skills you have or would be interested in developing relating to Social Security-disability practice: (a) using client-relationship-management (CRM) software to track your many clients' profiles; (b) using financial-management systems to track your anticipated cash flow from many matters generating modest fees; (c) maintaining sound working relationships with specific vocational experts retained to examine your disabled clients;

(d) relying heavily on legal assistants and other staff to obtain and process records and information; (e) appearing frequently before the same administrative law judges knowing their practices and preferences; (f) each week reviewing hundreds of pages of medical and vocational records on dozens of clients; (g) typing or dictating many summaries and analyses in the strict form preferred by certain judges; (h) having no party opposing your client as you evaluate and advocate for your client's benefits; (i) disputing matters directly with opposing lawyers only if and when you agree to appeal a hearing loss; and (j) practicing at your office, experts' offices, the administrative-hearing location, and locations convenient to your clients.

Snapshot: He had not gone to law school thinking that he would join a small firm handling primarily Social Security disability claims, but in retrospect the work fit him perfectly. Before law school, he had led programs in foreign countries for homeless youth and urban substance abusers. The work had been immensely challenging and rewarding in every way but financially. Now, he had family members for whom to care. When he realized that Social Security disability work meant helping some of the most physically, financially, and emotionally broken working people, he jumped at the chance. He was quickly so good at the interpersonal interaction, the medical and vocational evaluations, the office systems, and the administrative advocacy that the practice burgeoned. He made partner in just over three years. A lawyers skills were powerful tools, when matched with the right practice area, experience, and commitment.

68 Malpractice

Many lawyers who have personal-injury practices do not handle medical-malpractice cases and cases against other professionals because of the specialized knowledge that malpractice cases require. On the other hand, some lawyers specialize in medical-malpractice cases, or dental, legal, or accounting malpractice, to the exclusion of all or nearly all other types of personal-injury cases. One of the peculiarities of medical malpractice is that the cases require proof of the medical standard of care, meaning that medical experts must testify to that standard. Lawyers taking medical-malpractice cases must thus develop and maintain relationships with physicians who are willing (and whom the lawyers pay) to review cases and testify as experts. Medical-mal lawyers must thus have the professional skill and confident personality to gain and hold the trust of medical experts and strong intellectual interest in medical practice. "Claims against professionals such as doctors, lawyers, and accountants are known as malpractice cases. These cases arise when a plaintiff claims that a doctor, lawyer, accountant, or other professional failed to exercise the ordinary skill and capacity that a prudent and reputable member of that profession would exercise under the circumstances. ... Professional malpractice cases are often incredibly complex and are often handled by defense attorneys who specialize in the area." ABRAMS, THE OFFICIAL GUIDE TO LEGAL SPECIALTIES, at 447.

Plaintiff's med-mal lawyers must also have strong trial skills because physicians and other medical practitioners do not admit malpractice easily. A plaintiff's medical-malpractice firm must also have and deploy substantial monetary resources to retain experts and otherwise finance this complex and highly uncertain litigation. Because of the cost of preparing and pursuing any one case, each case must have relatively substantial value, and the stronger medical-malpractice firms tend to take only major wrongful-death or permanent-injury cases. Consider medical malpractice as your answer to *the question* if you feel you can develop premier skills supported by supreme confidence and backed by substantial resources.

Takeaway: **Consider medical malpractice as a practice area if hard-fought, high-stakes litigation around medical procedures causing death or serious injury attracts you.**

Response: "I hope to develop the skill, acquire the resources, have the medical aptitude, and gain the confidence to handle major medical-malpractice cases. Medical injuries both scare and fascinate me, and I want to see safer medical practices."

Related Fields: civil litigation, appellate advocacy, personal injury, insurance defense, license defense.

Reflect: Could you think and speak like a physician, at least after intense study of one specific limited topic at a time? Could you, with intense study of medical procedure, effectively contradict and impeach a medical expert in the expert's own field? Could you read and understand an excerpt of a medical-procedures text by research, without having had extensive medical education? Would you have enough confidence in your abilities to do these sorts of activities effectively enough that you would bet tens of thousands of dollars and hundreds of hours of your time on each medical-malpractice case in which your fee depends on winning?

Engage: Rate each of the following medical procedures with +1 (could stomach, understand, and litigate), 0 (unsure of any conclusion), or -1 (could not stomach, understand, or litigate): (a) laparoscopic cholecystectomy mistakenly severing the urethra; (b) cervical fusion mistakenly performed at the wrong level; (c) laminectomy of the thoracic spine mistakenly leaving a cottonoid embedded inside the surgical site; (d) late-term multiparous vaginal delivery of macrosomic infant causing permanent brachial-plexus injury; (e) high-forceps delayed vaginal delivery of cord-restricted 0-APGAR brain-injured infant following extended labor; (f) embolism death of 28-year-old woman following mistaken reverse hookup of transfusion equipment; (g) through-and-through open femur-fracture failure to unite due to mistaken order for manipulation causing severe leg shortening of 14 year old. If your total plusses and minuses are greater than three, then consider medical malpractice as a field. If less zero or less, than consider not pursuing medical malpractice as a field, or re-examine your answers.

Snapshot: The achievement had taken him years, but he knew that he now had the premier plaintiff's medical-malpractice practice in the region. His small firm reviewed 1,000 potential cases every year to take just 10. Each of those 10 cases involved the patient's death or serious permanent injury by a compelling breach of the standard of care. Each year his small firm had some of the largest malpractice verdicts and settlements in the state. Success built on success. Yet it had never been about the money. In some ways, the 990 potential cases he turned down were just as important as the 10 cases he took. He and his skilled staff, which included a physician and former nurse, were educating these patients and family members of deceased patients in ways that their medical-care providers had not. Some local physicians and hospital administrators decried the firm's services because of their potential malpractice liability. Yet in by far most of the cases that the firm reviewed, the firm's staff was educating the potential clients to the other causes of the injury or death, explaining in a credible way that malpractice was either not present or had not caused the loss. The firm filed suit only in the most egregious instances of malpractice causing the greatest loss. Now that, he concluded, was a practice that had been worth building.

69 Civil Rights

Another practice niche for the skilled civil litigator involves civil-rights cases. Federal law authorizes private damages actions against government entities the agents of which violate individual constitutional rights. The individual plaintiffs whom lawyers represent in these cases may be citizens whom police officers arrest and search without cause while using excessive force in violation of Fourth Amendments search-and-seizure rights. They may be prisoners whom prison officials deny critical care for known serious medical conditions in violation of rights against cruel-and-unusual punishment. They may be citizens whom public officials deny First Amendment rights of free speech, free association, and freedom of religion. "I'm in private, solo practice. I can tell people 'no.' It doesn't hurt me. So I only work with clients who are trying to create something or protect something they've created. If somebody comes along and tries to stomp on my clients' creativity, they're going to get the lion out of me. As lawyers, we have the power and the responsibility to enforce barriers—barriers that protect people, property, and principles. We can support those barriers from a place of power instead of force. That power comes from our passion." HOUCHIN: FUEL THE SPARK—5 GUIDING VALUES FOR SUCCESS IN LAW & LIFE, at 33.

Federal and state laws also prohibit discrimination against many protected classes in education, employment, public services, and public accommodation, giving civil-rights lawyers the opportunity to represent individuals in private suits against private persons and entities. Civil-rights lawyers, who typically represent these plaintiffs on contingency fees (with prevailing-party fees also available), may have political, ideological, policy, social, moral, and humanitarian commitments that attract them to civil-rights litigation. Some lawyers handle little other than civil-rights cases, while other personal-injury lawyers, employment lawyers, and civil litigators simply add a few compelling civil-rights cases to their practice mix. No matter their commitments or niches, civil-rights lawyers must first have strong litigation skills.

Takeaway: **Consider civil-rights cases as a practice niche having compelling social value, if you expect to have strong litigation skills.**

Response: "I have always wanted to do civil-rights work and so expect to take civil-rights cases as soon as I have the litigation skills and confidence."

Related Fields: civil litigation, appellate advocacy, personal injury, employment law.

Reflect: What do you know of the history and significance of the civil-rights movement in the United States? Do you have a connection of any kind, whether family history, volunteer service, leadership positions, or otherwise, with civil-rights initiatives? Do you have affinity with one or more protected classes? Would you like your legacy to include civil-rights advocacy?

Engage: Which of the following civil-rights plaintiffs would you like to represent? (a) A 17 year old delivering drugs for his dealer mother whom a police officer shot in the back as he lay face-down trying to give himself up. (b) An elderly drunken bicyclist whom a police officer intentionally struck in the throat and knocked to the ground for no apparent purpose as the bicyclist pedaled past. (c) A middle-aged prisoner with a burst appendix denied medical care for several days until convulsing and near death. (d) An elderly prisoner denied his insulin until he required a lower-leg amputation due to uncontrolled diabetes. (e) A minority sandwich-shop patron denied service and called a racial slur. (f) Sheriff's officers demoted for announcing support for the losing sheriff's candidate. (g) A public-school bus driver denied a hearing over her termination for objecting to an unsafe driving practice. (h) A medical student dismissed from a public university without a hearing and prior notice of the grounds for dismissal. If you chose at least three of these matters, then consider civil rights as a practice niche.

70 Family Law

A civil litigator's skills extend beyond personal-injury, civil-rights, and public-interest cases to other civil cases involving personal rights and interests. Family law is an example of another substantial practice area involving skill in civil litigation. The core of many family law practices involves representing divorcing spouses. Although self-represented divorces are possible, indeed fairly common, most marriages involve sufficiently substantial personal, social, financial, and property interests to warrant competent legal representation. Divorce cases include custody and parenting-time disputes, child-support and spousal-support enforcement, and property divisions. "Family lawyers help divorcing spouses work through issues concerning their own financial needs and those of their children. This involves an analysis of the income of the payer and the needs of the payee. These issues can be complicated." ABRAMS, THE OFFICIAL GUIDE TO LEGAL SPECIALTIES, at 166.

Fewer than half of all American households involve married couples. Beyond divorce work, family law practice can also mean drafting prenuptial and cohabitation agreements, resolving paternity disputes, and negotiating separation agreements. Family law can involve not only skill in civil litigation, negotiation, mediation, dispute resolution, and drafting, but also knowledge of real property law, tax law, and business valuation. "The court's first priority is providing a safe environment for children, but its second concern is keeping families together. When these priorities clash, the situation can become emotionally charged and troubling. A litigator entering this field should be prepared for such logistical and emotional challenges." VISWANATHAN, VAULT GUIDE TO LITIGATION LAW CAREERS, at 17.

Although family law practice becomes and remains simply routine legal service for many practitioners, family law can also be a ministry to the broken and hurting individuals involved and also a policy mission. Family demographics, structures, and relationships have changed significantly in the past two generations in trends that appear to be accelerating, after already having had substantial social and economic effects. "Family law attorneys agree that the *ability to empathize* with the problems of others is critical to success in the field. ... Another important skill is the *ability to remain objective* about highly sensitive matters, even when the client is facing a life crisis." ABRAMS, THE OFFICIAL GUIDE TO LEGAL SPECIALTIES, at 174.

Takeaway: **Consider family law practice if you have the counseling, negotiation, dispute-resolution, and litigation skills to help families of divorce.**

Response: "I want more than anything to get involved in family law where I can help individuals and families recover from broken trust and relationships."

Related Fields: civil litigation, appellate advocacy, bankruptcy, taxation, real property, estate planning, probate practice, juvenile law, school law.

Reflect: What personal experience do you have of healthy or unhealthy family relationships that would help you value a family law practice? Do you have the patience, character, interaction skills, and relational insights necessary to counsel a divorcing party? Do you have a passion for protecting children? Would you see family law as simply an appropriate service offering in your practice mix, or do you think that it might be a calling, ministry, and mission? Could you practice family law and nothing else? What policy interests do you have in family trends and dynamics?

Engage: Rate each of the following common family law practice conditions with +1 (like), 0 (neutral), or -1 (dislike): (a) high-emotion clients; (b) strained party relationships; (c) immediate service needs; (d) mixed relational-financial issues; (e) personal interests predominating; (f) court-access office-based practice; (g) significant pretrial procedures; (h) frequent negotiation and mediation; (i) frequent short hearings but few trials; and (j) income and asset valuations. If your total plusses and minuses are greater than four, then consider family law as a field. If less zero or less, than consider not pursuing family law as a field, or re-examine your answers.

71 Juvenile Law

Children face issues that in one way or another involve law, legal proceedings, and lawyers. Some lawyers specialize in child and juvenile issues. In many cases, the parents create those issues, as in the family law matters mentioned above involving paternity, child custody, parenting time, and child support. Sometimes, the parents in those cases do not adequately represent the children's interests. When, for instance, those matters involve allegations of parental abuse or neglect, the court may appoint a guardian ad litem who may be a lawyer or may retain a lawyer to advocate for the child. Unfortunately, states frequently must terminate parental rights for abuse and neglect, in which cases the courts must ensure that both the parents and the child have lawyers representing them. "What subjects genuinely interest you? By this we mean, what subjects interest you intellectually and would you enjoy thinking about on the job every day? ... It's easy to see why it's so important to consider what subjects you enjoy thinking about when you're deciding which jobs to pursue. Because if you're bored by what you have to think about at work, the profession itself will probably come up short." SCHNEIDER, SHOULD YOU REALLY BE A LAWYER? at 155.

Children may also often require short-term representation, as when law enforcement briefly arrests and jails the parents, leaving uncertain custody and guardianship, or when an older child attempts suicide or otherwise requires temporary mental-health commitment. Of course, children also get into their own trouble, resulting in juvenile-delinquency proceedings in which they must have representation. Disabled children and their parents also have federal educational rights about which they often need representation. Lawyers who wish to represent children in a niche practice have plenty to do and can also advocate for effective law reform around issues affecting children.

Takeaway: **Consider juvenile law as a practice field if you have a passion for helping children.**

Response: "I want to help children and so am focusing on juvenile law including advocacy for policy changes."

Related Fields: family law, civil litigation, school law, probate practice.

Reflect: Do you have a commitment to helping children? If so, then what motivates your commitment, and how could you draw from that experience in law practice? How strong are your advocacy skills? Are you a problem solver in social situations?

Engage: How many of the following children would you care to represent in a juvenile-law practice? (a) A child sexually abused by a single parent. (b) A neglected child whose parents police arrested after discovering illegal guns and drugs in the home. (c) A child whom an older sibling had seriously injured multiple times. (d) A child brain injured and mentally incompetent after huffing butane and suffering cardiac arrest. (e) A child whose parents refused her cancer treatment on religious grounds. (f) A delinquent child whom law enforcement caught vandalizing commercial property. (g) A 13-year-old child driving the get-away vehicle as an accomplice to murder. (h) A child whose parents both died in a vehicle crash. (i) An anorexic child hospitalized for malnutrition. (j) A morbidly obese child physically unable to leave the home. (k) A child film star whose parents filed suit against one another over the child's earnings. (l) A child who was one of eight children fathered by a pro-basketball star by different mothers across the nation. If you counted eight or more, then consider juvenile law as a practice area.

Snapshot: After nearly 30 years, he had developed widespread reputation as the go-to lawyer on child-advocacy issues. He was so reliable, trustworthy, and effective that both the state and federal courts frequently appointed him to represent children in the most-difficult cases. He found himself at the center of every pilot program or reform initiative in any way involving the rights and interests of children. Early in his career when he was practicing business law at a large law firm, no one would have expected him to have anything to do with children and the law, no less to become the region's leading child-law expert. His expertise with juvenile law might have had something to do with his having raised his own three children as a single parent. He never could quite explain it, but he was not going to complain. He could think of no better work with which to cap a long and engaging career than to be the region's premier advocate for families with children.

72 School Law

While juvenile law addresses the interests of children generally, school law is a subspecialty practice area addressing the specific concerns of students and schools. Both state and federal law heavily regulate schools, school funding, student rights, teacher rights and obligations, and other issues having to do with schooling. Lawyers thus specialize in school law, while law firms develop and advertise school-law practice groups. Some lawyers frequently represent children in school disputes both having to do with suspensions and dismissal, and with disability rights, educational rights, privacy rights, anti-harassment and anti-discrimination rights, and rights to educational-program access. "'All my life I thought I wanted to work for a big firm, have a cushy office and have my name on the letterhead. By the time I made it, I was miserable. It took someone I respected to tell me it was okay to take a pay cut and allow myself to be happy instead of rich.' — Elizabeth, attorney at a small firm." SCHNEIDER, SHOULD YOU REALLY BE A LAWYER? at 170.

Other lawyers frequently represent the schools in disputes with parents of children and with regulators, bond issuers and other financiers, teachers, unions, media, suppliers, and others. Schools are just unique enough in their missions, structures, governance, norms, and practices that tort law, contract law, labor law, constitutional law, and other general fields of law take a slightly different shape and require a different perspective.

Takeaway: **Consider school law if academics, education, access, and learning interest you, and you have broad law knowledge and skills to apply confidently in this unique environment.**

Dear J.D.

Response: "I would like to represent schoolchildren and their parents for a while but eventually move into representing schools in all of their concerns. My parents were both educators, and so I highly value and want to promote sound academic environments."

Related Fields: family law, juvenile law, municipal law.

Reflect: While every professional has spent a lot of time in school, do you have any substantial employment, consulting, board leadership, volunteer, or other qualifying experience with schools? Have you had or helped students with special needs, in dealing with their schools? Do you have a degree in education or public administration?

Engage: Count the number of the following clients you would like to represent: (a) a physically disabled child whose school officials refused to accommodate in gym class; (b) a mentally disabled child whose school counselors refused special-education assistance; (c) a gifted child whose school teachers refused entry into an advanced program for older students; (d) a Christian child whom school officials suspended for bringing his Bible to read on free time; (e) a truant child whom school officials suspended for excessive absences; (f) a high-school student who attempted suicide after a school bullying incident; (g) a grade-school student kept working by her parents for eight-to-ten-hour days in a home upholstery business throughout the school year, interfering with studies; (h) a school board negotiating a new contract with its teacher's union; (i) a school board negotiating better terms for its construction bond; (j) a teacher in a tenure hearing involving allegations of physical abuse of students; (k) a school custodian suspended for a positive drug test; (l) a school librarian refusing to remove certain books from the school library on the demand of parents. If your count is six or more, then consider school law as a practice area. If your count is three or less, then consider other practice areas.

Snapshot: She had raised a severely mentally disabled daughter, fighting with the school at every step for the services she felt federal law mandated to provide her daughter with a free and appropriate public education. She had won enough of her battles that she decided to go to law school to help other parents gain education services for their disabled children. Now, advocating for parents with disabled schoolchildren comprised most of her part-time solo practice. She still provided the daily physical care for her disabled daughter who was now out of high school and still at home. Yet the lawyer found plenty of time and technological means to research, write, communicate, and advocate for her parent and student clients from home. She also got out frequently to attend meetings at the schools and was also able to conduct litigation. In fact, even though the juggling of work from home was at times tiring, she realized from comments others made one day at the court-ordered evaluation of one of her cases that she had made quite a name for herself. In a way, her daughter had given her a career gift that she could not have imagined and accomplished for herself. Sometimes challenges are what we need to discover what lies deepest within us.

73 Employment Law

Some practice areas include both transactional and litigation practice. Those practice areas may involve substantial transactional, contract, policy, and procedure work but also occasionally or frequently give rise to litigated claims. Employment law is one of those bridge fields. "Employment law offers a mix of litigation and counseling. In large firms, the litigation work tends to dominate and it is unusual for a large firm to maintain a purely counseling position. The proportion of each type of work varies from firm to firm." MUNNEKE, THE LEGAL CAREER GUIDE, at 357.

Employment law is a large, complex, and constantly changing field in which many lawyers practice. The field is so large that lawyers often specialize in only certain subspecialties within employment law such as in Americans with Disabilities Act (ADA) claims, Family and Medical Leave Act (FMLA) rights, pension and welfare benefits, unemployment taxes and claims, and Occupational Safety and Health Administration (OSHA) compliance. Like other fields, employment law tends to divide itself between lawyers who represent employers and lawyers who represent employees. Conflicts of interest and client loyalties discourage lawyers from frequently representing both sides. "If you have passion for civil rights and like to root for the underdog, you might find working on the plaintiffs' side of the employment bar a good fit. While plaintiffs aren't always the underdog, many plaintiffs' lawyers report that they at least feel like the underdog most of the time." GRUBB, VAULT GUIDE TO LABOR AND EMPLOYMENT LAW, at 36.

Litigation is common around claims for discrimination in hiring, promotion, pay, and firing, for retaliation and harassment, and also over FMLA and ADA rights, whistleblowing, wrongful discharge, unemployment benefits, labor-law violations, and other rights and interests. Because employers have substantial economic interests in productive employees, they will commonly pay hourly or fixed fees for competent representation. Because employees have substantial financial interests in employment wages and benefits, lawyers are often able to represent them in employment disputes on contingency fees. "Because there are so many different kinds of laws governing employment and workplace issues, attorneys usually specialize in a particular area of law— whether ERISA, workers' compensation or employment discrimination." VISWANATHAN, VAULT GUIDE TO LITIGATION LAW CAREERS, at 17.

Takeaway: **Consider employment law as a vast, important, and dynamic practice field.**

Response: "At first, I want to represent employees to ensure that they continue to work to care for themselves and their families, but soon I hope to develop a practice helping employers maintain consistent non-discriminatory policies and practices."

Related Fields: civil litigation, worker's compensation, labor law, civil rights.

Reflect: Do you have human-resources education or experience? How hard a time do you think employers have keeping up with all of the employment laws these days? Would you like to help them do so? Have you ever been involved in or witnessed an employment dispute in which an employer mistreated or discriminated against an employee? Would you prefer to represent employees against employers, or represent employers against employees? Or would you prefer a mediation service bringing the two sides together?

Engage: Choose your preferred client, employer or employee, in each of the following disputes, or indicate that you prefer not to be involved in the matter: (a) a minority candidate for employment suing an employer for the disparate impact of using criminal histories to rule out candidates; (b) an executive employee negotiating with an employer over terms of hire; (c) an employee disputing as unlawfully retaliatory an evaluation system the employer adopted; (d) an employee contesting the employer's zero-tolerance absence policy as violating the Family and Medical Leave Act; (e) an employee whom the employer fired shortly after the employee began advocating that other employees join him in organizing a union; (f) an employee with a machine-amputation injury suing the employer for an intentional tort of knowing to a certainty that the machine would injure someone; (g) an employee whom the employer suspended after calling in OSHA inspectors over unsafe chemicals; (h) an employee seeking a hearing over the employer's denial of unemployment benefits after termination for alleged misconduct. If you chose the same side at least four times, then consider employment-law practice on that side.

74 Labor Law

The field of labor law is a practice niche within the larger field of employment law. Labor law involves unions organizing workers to bargain for employment terms in a collective bargaining agreement otherwise known as a labor agreement or union contract. Labor law is union law, primarily federal law under the National Labor Relations Act. The Act authorizes the National Labor Relations Board to establish offices to take enforcement action determining employer violations of the Act. Employers have substantial management and financial interests in the terms on which they employ and compensate workers. Many employers would prefer not to have a union, but federal officials ensure that employers respect workers' rights to organize and bargain. Employers frequently hire lawyers to advise them about those federal rights to ensure compliance. "Traditional labor practice deals with the relations between workers and their employers. Attorneys play an important role in labor relations matters, providing assistance to both labor and management. These lawyers counsel their clients concerning plant closings, unfair labor practice charges under the National Labor Relations Act, and collective bargaining negotiations." ABRAMS, THE OFFICIAL GUIDE TO LEGAL SPECIALTIES, at 291-292.

Lawyers also represent employers in labor negotiations over union contracts and in labor disputes over the alleged violation of those contract terms. Unions also hire legal counsel for the same purposes, making this field another one in which lawyers and firms tend to represent only one side or the other (employers or unions). "According to many union-side lawyers, working on the side of labor requires an incredible amount of flexibility because attorneys must juggle such a variety of issues—from standard litigation to dealing with arrests of union officers engaged in a civil disobedience protest." GRUBB, VAULT GUIDE TO LABOR AND EMPLOYMENT LAW CAREERS, at 29.

Federal labor law has unique provisions, procedures, and practices, and its own elaborate history and precedent. Lawyers thus tend to either handle a lot of labor law or none of it because of the investment it takes to learn and stay updated on it. Like so many other specialties, labor law is ordinarily not for dabbling.

Takeaway: **Consider labor law if you wish to learn and apply a complex body of federal law regulating organizing and bargaining rights of workers, where both sides (employers and unions) have the resources and need for counsel.**

Response: "The history and law of labor unions fascinates me. Worker wages and rights, and working conditions, are so important that I plan to represent unions and workers."

Related Fields: employment law, civil litigation.

Reflect: Do you know anything of the history of the labor movement worldwide or in the United States? Have you followed the major national news about labor law lately? Have you or any of your family been union members? Have you or your family owned or operated union-shop businesses? Do you have strong labor or management views? Could you represent labor-law clients who hold strong views?

Engage: Rate each of the following labor-law matters as +1 (would like to be involved), 0 (neutral), or -1 (would not like to be involved): (a) regional grocer wants counsel on how lawfully to resist union organizing of its bakers and butchers; (b) multinational office-furniture maker wants representation negotiating new labor agreement for its truck drivers; (c) automotive supplier wants representation to arbitrate a dispute whether the worker's get paid for donning and doffing painting gear; (d) union wants to hire counsel to advocate stronger enforcement of domestic-worker organizing rights; (e) union wants representation in contract negotiation with fish-processing plant; (f) union wants representation in arbitration over leave-time dispute with textile mill; (g) steelworker wants to sue union for violating duty of fair representation when refusing to process grievance over seniority-bump rights; (h) local NLRB office wants to hire counsel full time to direct investigations. If your total plusses and minuses are at least plus four, then consider labor law as a practice field.

75 Bankruptcy

Bankruptcy practice is a large, important, and cyclical field to which many lawyers devote their full practices. Fewer practitioners today make bankruptcies part of a general practice because of bankruptcy practice's increasingly complex and burdensome technological and certification requirements. "At the heart of all of the bankruptcy lawyer's functions lies one central role: rescue worker. Companies are in bankruptcy for a reason—they've hit the perfect storm, and somebody's gotta come in and haul that boat into port, or least make sure there are enough lifeboats to go around. That someone is the bankruptcy lawyer—out to salvage the equipment, the crew, or, with luck, the whole boat." STUHL, VAULT GUIDE TO BANKRUPTCY LAW CAREERS, at 1.

Bankruptcy practice can be either a consumer or corporate service. Some lawyers devote their full practices to preparing and filing bankruptcy petitions, and obtaining bankruptcy discharges, for individual consumers. Other bankruptcy lawyers devote their practices to representing corporate debtors (both private and public) in bankruptcy liquidations or reorganizations, and to representing creditors in those corporate proceedings. Bankruptcy practice can thus have either a highly human side to it, helping struggling income earners recover from financial collapses, or a purely business side to it, helping companies shed or collect debts between one another in the most efficient, orderly, and secure manner. "[Bankruptcy] practice combines the representing and counseling of clients who are considering or going through bankruptcy, or the representation of creditors of such companies. The basic premise is that there is a limited pool of assets and all the creditors are fighting to get the greatest amount possible. This practice is a hybrid litigation/ counseling/ contract practice." MUNNEKE, THE LEGAL CAREER GUIDE, at 344.

The public may assume that bankrupt debtors brought their collapses on themselves through irresponsible financial management, which in some cases is true. Yet individual bankruptcies are often due to sudden medical emergencies, disability, layoffs, property damage, and other uncontrollable and even uninsurable loss and expense. Bankruptcy practice can thus be a professional ministry to broken individuals and struggling families. It can also be an economic savior of struggling businesses and employers on the survival of which communities depend. "Looking for an exciting, recession-proof legal practice that allows you to engage in a hybrid of litigation and transactional work? If so, bankruptcy law might be the right fit for you." HAHN, GUIDE TO LAW FIRMS, at 108.

Bankruptcy is federal litigation and can involve contested hearings, meaning that litigation and advocacy skills are necessary. Yet bankruptcy is often more of an administrative than trial practice, leaving plenty of room in the field for practitioners who do not identify themselves as charismatic trial lawyers. "The bankruptcy attorneys we talked to described a wide range of daily activities. 'There's no typical day, thank goodness!' says Paul Gaynor. 'Every day unfolds differently. I'm on the phone a lot, and I attend a lot of meetings. The tasks vary with whether I'm representing a debtor or a creditor corporation.' Paul notes that a good bankruptcy lawyer has to be familiar with numerous areas of the law. 'You really have to be a general practitioner to be an effective bankruptcy lawyer,' Paul says." ABRAMS, THE OFFICIAL GUIDE TO LEGAL SPECIALTIES, at 62.

Takeaway: **Consider bankruptcy practice if you have strong administrative and financial skills.**

Response: "I plan a consumer bankruptcy practice so that I can help individuals and families struggling with finances because of unexpected medical emergencies and sudden job, business, and property losses."

Related Fields: collections, civil litigation, federal litigation, business planning, family law, criminal defense.

Reflect: What skills do you have with personal or business finances? Are you a sound money manager? Do you have strong administrative skills? Could you train and supervise non-lawyer staff to prepare elaborate schedules accurately? Are you willing to go to court at least for routine hearings?

Engage: How many of the following bankrupt debtors would you be interested in representing? (a) An unemployed 27 year old who ran up tens of thousands of dollars of credit-card debt for consumer items while living in his parents' basement and is now charged with drug crimes. (b) A 30-year-old single mother of two children whose employer laid her off making her unable to pay furniture, car, and home loans. (c) A 35-year-old married tradesman who incurred over $150,000 in uninsured medical bills due to cancer treatment. (d) A 40-year-old couple who bought a half-million dollar home at the top of the market and are now a quarter-million dollars underwater and in foreclosure. (e) A 45-year-old woman whose staging business a flood destroyed leaving her deeply in debt for real and business property she no longer holds. (f) A 50-year-old divorced woman whose former husband left to pay substantial consumer, vehicle, and mortgage debt when he ran to Acapulco with his girlfriend. (g) A 55-year-old physician now disabled by vascular dementia while owing a seven-figure uninsured malpractice judgment. (h) A 60-year-old couple who had put all of their assets into a small bookstore business that then collapsed following a fire. (i) A 65-year-old couple who had depended on the husband's coal-miner pension and medical coverage until the mine went bankrupt and who now have substantial medical-expense and consumer debt. If you chose five or more, then consider bankruptcy practice.

76 Collections

A collections practice, while related to bankruptcy, is a distinct niche to which some lawyers and firms devote their full practices. Collections lawyers handle volume unpaid accounts for businesses, hospitals, professionals, credit-card companies, and other providers or financers of consumer goods and services. Collections firms file hundreds of simple breach-of-contract complaints usually for small amounts of a few hundred or few thousand dollars. Collection agencies have usually already tried unsuccessfully to collect on those debts by means other than litigation. Default judgments and post-judgment debtors' exams, garnishments, and execution on assets are common. "Good things happen to people all the time, but only to people who **Show Up**. I'm continually amazed at the number of people who never show up and complain about not getting what they want. ... You'll be amazed at the number of lawyers who don't show up for community or networking events and whine that they don't have enough business. You'll be amazed at the number of lawyers who do not blog, have lame Web sites, never contribute articles to publications, or never give free lectures to gatherings of their potential clients and wonder why other firms get all the business." HOUCHIN: FUEL THE SPARK—5 GUIDING VALUES FOR SUCCESS IN LAW & LIFE, at 22.

Collections firms typically work on contingency fees, so that their lawyers must be sensible and systems and practices efficient. While collections work against debtors who have suffered serious financial misfortune due to no fault of their own may seem hard or heartless, collections lawyers can be in a unique position to offer debtors responsible workouts. Collections laws like the federal Fair Debt Collections Practices

Act and corollary state acts also provide a strong regulatory framework ensuring fairness by threatening statutory penalties for unscrupulous debt collectors. Together, debtors' rights and creditors' rights require collections lawyers to know and follow elaborate administrative and legal procedures. Collections work is thus at once both precise work and volume work, while also both financial and personal. Good lawyers make good work of it for all concerned, both debtors and creditors.

Takeaway: **Consider collections practice if you like volume work and frequent travel to routine court hearings, and have strong financial and administrative skills.**

Response: *"I would love to develop a collections practice that helps the state's many small businesses and service providers recover small amounts owed to them. I would enjoy frequent local travel for routine court hearings and have the strong administrative and procedural skills to do it."*

Related Fields: bankruptcy, civil litigation, business planning, family law.

Reflect: Do you like to get out and about, or do you prefer to stay behind the desk at the keyboard? Would you like the energy of busy courtrooms handling smaller and more-routine matters? Do you like keeping a full schedule? Do you have the administrative skills to handle volume files? Are you financially minded? Can you tell when someone is telling the truth about money?

Engage: Count the number of the following common collections-practice conditions that you like: (a) many cases; (b) smaller amounts involved; (c) business clients; (d) consumer opposing parties; (e) seldom any opposing counsel; (f) frequent vehicular travel; (g) frequent court appearances; (h) more routine hearings than disputed hearings; (i) contingency fees; (j) elaborate procedures; (k) close statutory regulation; (l) financial field; (m) frequent negotiation; and (n) supervise staff work. If you counted nine or more conditions as favorable, then consider collections practice.

Snapshot: She had done well academically in law school, immediately joining a large statewide firm after graduation and the bar. Although delighted with her job and the firm, she was at first a little disappointed when the firm assigned her to its collections practice group. She didn't like the thought of grinding people down for money and was sure that she lacked the temperament to bully people, if that is what collections took. Yet as soon as she started the work, she realized that she could instead be the voice of reason between her corporate and small-business clients, and their debtor customers, patients, and clients. Her sense of collections practice as a humane ministry only grew as she continued. Her clients appreciated her work, which was plenty productive financially, but she also sensed that the debtors whom she sued and with whom she negotiated so often also came to appreciate her work. Debt is a burden to both creditor and debtor, and she was helping both.

77 Estate Planning

Clients have substantial interests in the orderly transfer of wealth from one generation to the next, which is the goal of estate-planning practice. Estate planning is among the most common of transactional practices, found everywhere from small towns to major metropolitan areas. Americans are wealthy, and an aging baby-boom generation makes the transfer of that wealth a ripe and growing area for needed law services. For clients to entertain estate planning, they must have an estate, which means that estate planners work exclusively for clients who are able to afford their law products and services. "The goal is to efficiently transfer wealth between generations and within families. Similar to tax practice, this is a complex, statutory practice. The law evolves very quickly and there is a wide variety of authority, including case law, revenue rulings, statutes, etc." MUNNEKE, THE LEGAL CAREER GUIDE, at 381.

Uncollectible accounts receivable is not, or should not be, a problem for estate planners, who charge both fixed fees and hourly fees, often without requiring up-front payment from their well-heeled clients who expect respectful billing. Estate-planning practice can have a satisfying commodity-like aspect to it, in that lawyers prepare standard wills, trusts, powers of attorney, and other documents. The estate planner who re-invents the wheel does her client an unnecessary and potentially hazardous service. You should instead be proud of your finely crafted products in estate planning. Yet estate planning is also highly personal for the client who must consider a lifelong legacy while recognizing intimate family relationships. Effective estate planners thus combine commodity skills with custom-fitting practice. Estate planners are also most fully in control of their schedule and work, without court, opposing parties, or opposing counsel, making estate planning a congenial practice. "No matter how big your investment portfolio, how notable your modern art collection, or how rare your collection of antique silver, when the time comes for you to leave this world, you can't take your assets with you. The estate lawyer's role is to help a client arrange his or her financial affairs so that, upon the client's death, the client's assets are distributed exactly as he or she wishes and the tax consequences of distributing that property are minimized." ABRAMS, THE OFFICIAL GUIDE TO LEGAL SPECIALTIES, at 461.

Takeaway: **Consider estate-planning if you look forward to transactional practice for individuals and families of means.**

Response: "I plan to open an estate-planning practice serving first-generation small-business owners and professionals, drawing on my family network and contacts in my home community."

Related Fields: business planning, family law, probate practice.

Reflect: Is family important to you? Do you value legacy? Do you respect individuals whose responsibility, industry, and stewardship enabled them to acquire wealth? Are you skilled at drafting precise, error-free documents? Do you network effectively within communities made up of individuals of means?

Engage: How many of the following estate-planning clients would you be interested in representing? (a) A 28-year-old couple traveling together to the Middle East leaving behind their two infant children. (b) A 38-year-old childless professional couple both earning substantial incomes and together amassing significant wealth. (c) A 48-year-old couple owning a small business they hope to grow large enough to pass on to their college-age children. (d) A 58-year-old unmarried best-selling author who has two children born out of wedlock to different mothers with whom the author has no relationship. (e) A 68-year-old twice-married highly compensated executive and father of three, who has just married his third wife, a 28-year-old performer. (f) A 78-year-old widow recently diagnosed with early Alzheimer's who wishes to cut her four children out of her will for urging her to move into a nursing home. (g) An 88-year-old patriarch who nearing death wishes to convey half of his estate to the winsome young couple next door who have just begun to care for him. (h) A 98-year-old spry woman who, having outlived all relatives, wishes to convey her entire seven-figure estate into trust for the care of her beloved cats.

78 Probate Practice

The other half of making estate plans is probating them. Some estate-planning lawyers seldom if ever approach a courthouse, even to probate decedents' estates (the estates of clients who died). Many other lawyers who draft estate plans also represent estates in probate proceedings. You have some choice, in other words, of whether to take an estate-planning practice beyond the office and into the courthouse. Probating decedents' estates is usually primarily an administrative rather than adversarial activity. You must know court rules and probate procedures but may not need any particular pretrial or trial skills beyond those basics. Yet you never know. Surviving family members can dispute estate plans over fraud and undue influence, and creditors can raise claims against the estate that require hearing. "What do you want in a work environment? By work environment, we mean the type of work setting you would most enjoy—the type of coworkers, the physical surroundings, the office culture, the hours, the dress code, the level of formality, the bureaucracy, the commute, etc. In short, the overall environment in which you'd feel most comfortable." SCHNEIDER, SHOULD YOU REALLY BE A LAWYER? at 157.

Estate planners who lack pretrial and trial skills or otherwise prefer not to litigate may yet probate estates but encourage the personal representative to hire a trial lawyer as co-counsel to represent the estate in contested hearings. Probate practice goes well beyond probating decedents' estates to include important related activities like establishing conservatorships and guardianships for the mentally incompetent and resolving disputes over advance medical directives and other forms of powers of attorney. Beginning of life and end of life each bring unique legal issues over which probate courts hold special authority, invoked through probate practice.

Takeaway: **Consider probate practice if you wish to use administrative and procedural skills to help families with end-of-life issues.**

Response: "My experience in serving the elderly gives me a heart for probate practice, where I can advocate to protect their interests.

Related Fields: estate planning, family law, civil litigation, alternative dispute resolution.

Reflect: Do you have an affinity for the incompetent and elderly and their health, social, family, financial, and legal issues? Do you have administrative skills? Do you have strong skills in procedure? Are you a problem solver, especially in family situations and relationships? Do you have some of the skills of a family counselor, recognizing family dynamics?

Engage: How many of the following probate-practice matters would you be interested in handling? (a) Probating the estate of an elderly, childless decedent who by proper will left all property to a charity. (b) Probating the estate of an elderly decedent whose three adult children are cooperating in dividing the intestate estate. (c) Probating the will of a decedent whose two adult children contest the will as the product of the decedent's new young wife's undue influence. (d) Probating the will of a decedent who died having neglected to amend that estate plan to reflect the decedent's remarriage late in life. (e) Representing the interests of a severely depressed teenager committed to a mental-health facility after attempting suicide. (f) Representing the interests in continuing medical treatment of a 40-year-old husband and father made comatose and severely brain injured from a serious motor-vehicle-accident. (g) Acting as guardian ad litem for a 72-year-old widow whose dementia now makes her incompetent to decide on her own care and medical treatment. (h) Acting as successor trustee over a deceased father's trust for the benefit of two minor children, when the mother trustee died in a plane crash. If you answered five or more, then consider probate practice.

79 Business Planning

The core practice area for transactional lawyers is business planning. For solo practitioners and very small firms, the core business-planning services can be forming and advising new small start-up businesses for individuals, families, and nascent business partners. For mature and sophisticated small and mid-size firms, the core business-planning services can be forming new businesses for existing small businesses and assisting existing businesses with second-stage growth, merger, acquisition, and sale. "I love teaching about creative business—always have. Combine that passion for creative business with my legal degree and you have a snapshot of my practice. But take it a step further. At its essence, what I'm doing is helping people reach their creative potential. That's powerful stuff. I believe one of the things we're all here on the plant to do is to help each other reach our individual and collective potential." HOUCHIN: FUEL THE SPARK—5 GUIDING VALUES FOR SUCCESS IN LAW & LIFE, at 59.

Other lawyers, particularly in larger law firms, form, advise, and represent mid-size and large businesses, often started by other businesses or experienced executives with substantial investment capital. Business planning only begins with choosing and organizing the proper form of entity, whether sole proprietorship, partnership, limited-liability company, corporation, or other form, and assisting with mergers, acquisitions, and sales to achieve the client's business goals. For businesses of all sizes, regulatory compliance is a constant and growing issue, ensuring the need for and value of law services. "Because of the proliferation of government regulatory activity at all levels—federal, state, and local—hardly a business or industry remains untouched by the need to assure compliance with the various rules and regulations. Often the economic well-being of the company is at stake." MUNNEKE, NONLEGAL CAREERS, at 81.

In addition to research, investigation, due diligence, and drafting skills, business planners often have keen strategic sense and negotiation skills. They less often litigate but may work closely from time to time with civil litigators pursuing and defending business claims. Together with family law, business litigation comprises most of the nation's civil dockets.

Takeaway: **Consider business-planning practice if you have strong due diligence, drafting, negotiation, and compliance skills, and an interest in creating and sustaining valuable enterprise.**

Response: "I look forward to a business-planning practice particularly serving individuals and families starting and expanding small businesses. I have an affinity for productive people."

Related Fields: securities law, intellectual property, commercial litigation, alternative dispute resolution, taxation, bankruptcy, estate planning.

Reflect: Do you appreciate how important productive enterprises are to our individual and collective health, comfort, security, and standard of living? Have you a clear sense of the governance, management, and regulatory challenges that productive enterprises face? Do you like business people? Do you have or are you interested in developing skills that businesses would value?

Engage: Count the number of the following common business-planning-practice conditions that you would appreciate: (a) frequent interaction with productive people; (b) office-based rather than court-based practice; (c) due diligence a high value; (d) forms and templates support drafting skills; (e) strategic and problem-solving skills helpful; (f) primarily property and financial rather than social issues; (g) clients able to pay but demand service value; (h) collaboration and negotiation skills helpful; (i) non-adversarial; (j) long-term client relationships possible. If you count six or more, then consider business planning as a practice area.

Snapshot: He seemed to have been born a business lawyer. His business-planning skills just seemed to burgeon once he was in practice with a large firm. He quickly soaked up everything that he could learn from the other lawyers in the firm. Soon, he was beginning to see new solutions to old business problems. Before too much longer, he had the confidence to put those innovative solutions into place. He also wrote constantly for his firm's website and blog on business matters. Clients and other business leaders took note. His service eventually led to his leading the premier statewide business organization. Looking back on his career, he realized that plenty of business lawyers had the knowledge, insight, and skills he possessed. He figured that what distinguished him from other lawyers was that he fairly bristled with positive energy. Indeed, he sort of had the figurative look and feel of a bottle brush. Not a bad image for a business-planner's career, he thought. "Business clients frequently look to their lawyers for advice directly related to the operation of the business but only tangentially related to the law, such as how to deal with special interest groups, how to respond to concerns about product safety, whether to fire an executive, how to plan for the possibility of adverse media coverage, how to create a business plan, how to cope with a serious ethical lapse, whether to close a factory and what kind of compensation plans should be offered to employees." KOURI, VAULT GUIDE TO CORPORATE LAW CAREERS, at 9.

80 Securities Law

Businesses seeking to raise capital by offering stock shares to the public require the help of a securities lawyer. Lawyers who practice business planning have the basic skills to form and advise a closely held corporation, one whose shares a small number of individuals hold and one that has not offered those shares to the public. Federal and state governments closely regulate public offerings of stock shares. "Corporations must follow certain protocols regarding disclosure of information to shareholders and investors depending on the size of the corporation and the type of investor. ... To ensure the companies remain in accordance with these laws, corporate attorneys prepare reports for initial public offerings, yearly and quarterly disclosures, and special disclosures whenever something happens that might affect the price of the stock...." KOURI, VAULT GUIDE TO CORPORATE LAW CAREERS, at 9.

Lawyers who wish to represent companies in public offers must have the additional knowledge and skill of securities lawyers. Criminal and civil penalties for misleading and non-compliant public offerings make this practice area one in which lawyers must have precise regulatory knowledge and strong drafting and due-diligence skills. Securities practice is ordinarily an office-based, transactional practice in which lawyers can largely schedule and control their own work on their own terms meeting client needs and expectations. "Day-to-day work involves due diligence, drafting documents, interfacing with the SEC, negotiating the offerings and/ or financing documents, writing memos, etc. ... [A]ttorneys can also handle stock plans, option plans, employment matters, and the entire gamut of corporate issues." MUNNEKE, THE LEGAL CAREER GUIDE, at 355.

Yet the area occasionally involves communication, negotiation, and even litigation with regulators and affected officers, directors, shareholders, and investors. Securities lawyers often refer litigation and alternative dispute resolution to other lawyers who have those skills and whose advocacy will not create conflicts. Securities lawyers often work within practice groups at larger firms on behalf of corporate clients ready, willing, and able to pay for premier law services. "Both state and federal laws regulate the sale of securities. ... Securities lawyers help their clients through this maze of federal regulations and the equally complex state regulations, which are sometimes referred to as 'blue sky' laws." ABRAMS, THE OFFICIAL GUIDE TO LEGAL SPECIALTIES, at 377-378.

Takeaway: **Consider securities-law practice if you wish to apply detailed regulatory knowledge to the precise drafting and strategic evaluation of public-offer documents on behalf of growing and larger corporations.**

Response: "I would like to practice securities law to help new technology companies raise capital through new public offerings. I like to see innovators financially empowered and rewarded."

Related Fields: business planning, administrative law, civil litigation.

Reflect: What skill do you have for researching and strategizing about regulations? Are you good at discerning regulators' intent? Do you have the skill and interest to draft precise public documents meeting detailed regulations? Do you like working for growing and innovative companies?

Engage: For which of the following securities-law clients would you like to provide services? (a) A penniless and eccentric but brilliant inventor who, tired of giving away his inventions to greedy companies, wants to form a future publicly traded company to bring his inventions to market. (b) A hugely successful new social-media company owned and run by four immature and feuding techies wanting to take the company public. (c) An insecure and untrusting minority-owner non-family CEO of a large family business preparing to go public. (d) A huge private global direct-sales company wishing to raise substantial new capital through public offering to enter new international markets. (e) A small but publicly traded company whose largest shareholder/chief executive wants to take the company private. (f) A publicly traded company in a proxy fight with an activist investor holding nearly ten percent of outstanding shares. (g) A publicly traded company in acquisition talks with another publicly traded company in which the purchase price may involve shares of the acquirer's stock. If you chose three or more, then consider a securities-law practice.

81 Intellectual Property Law

The value of a business is often in its designs and processes, not just in its people and relationships. Businesses innovate, invent, modify, and adapt things of value including not only designs for physical things but also conceptual formulas, systems, and processes. Other businesses will soon discover and adopt those things of value, destroying the inventor's competitive advantage, in a natural and important disseminating process. Yet intellectual-property law grants inventors patent protection for some period to reap a benefit from their investment in their inventions. Intellectual-property law also offers copyright protection for fixed original expressions and trademark protection for names, logos, symbols, and other identifying marks. Lawyers use copyright and trademark law to help clients in any creative business including not only technology, design, and manufacturing but also sports, entertainment, and publishing. Intellectual-property law creates and preserves order in the marketplace, frustrating and penalizing knockoff artists who without any inventive skill or investment would steal the value of designs and inventions, undermining the market for those designs and inventions. "Copyright, trademark, trade secrets, patents, and other aspects of intellectual property (IP) law are not new areas of practice. Companies are recognizing, however, that protection of their IP rights can be critical to the future of their business." MUNNEKE, NONLEGAL CAREERS, at 91.

Lawyers make a practice niche out of intellectual property. Law firms devote their whole practice or significant practice groups to the field. Any metropolitan area and many firms of any size providing corporate and business services will offer intellectual-property representation. That representation first entails the evaluation and protection of designs and inventions. Lawyers who do more than just copyright and trademark work, and also file with the federal office responsible for issuing patents, must become members of the Patent Bar, requiring additional training and examination. Lawyers with engineering education and background have natural advantages in the patent field, but not all lawyers desiring to pursue intellectual-property practice have that education and background, and so many law schools offer graduate programs in intellectual property. Patent lawyers can also succeed in practice on curiosity, design intuition, and on-the-job learning alone. The practice area also involves the licensing and sale of designs and inventions. Intellectual-property lawyers may also litigate patent, copyright, and trademark disputes or work closely with commercial litigators who do. Intellectual-property practice is a traditional but constantly dynamic law field. "As of 2010, almost 80 percent of aggregate American corporate assets were intellectual property (IP) and intangible assets, up from 32 percent only 25 years ago. This stunning rise in IP assets and their increasing critical importance to the U.S. economy has prompted a corresponding rise in the number of IP professionals, and in the array of complex issues with which they must cope." HERMANN, FROM LEMONS TO LEMONADE IN THE NEW LEGAL JOB MARKET, at 150.

Takeaway: Consider intellectual-property practice if you have an interest and talent in understanding how things work, and want to work with creative persons generating new economic activity through innovation.

Response: "My goal is an intellectual-property-law practice where I can help inventors evaluate and patent new things, and help new and growing businesses protect their trade names and trademarks. My engineering background should help."

Dear J.D.

Related Fields: business planning, securities law, administrative law.

Reflect: Do you have engineering education? Do you have strong visual-spatial reasoning? With some explanation, can you see how systems and designs work? Would you like working with designers, engineers, and others who invent things? Would you be willing to study outside of your law school curriculum for the Patent Bar examination? Do you think that you could pass?

Engage: Count the number of the following intellectual-property-law clients you would like to represent and believe you could someday competently represent: (a) a blueberry farmer who has invented a berry-storage rack; (b) a therapist who has invented an adaptation to an assistive device; (c) a computer programmer who has invented a coding logarithm; (d) an automotive supplier wanting to license a car-parts design to an automaker; (e) an internet company wanting to license a patented search engine from a coder; (f) a luxury-goods designer wanting to license a design to a luxury-goods maker; (g) an electronic-device maker wanting to sue another electronic-device maker for screen-design patent infringement; (h) a sporting-goods maker wanting to sue another sporting-goods maker for golf-club-design patent infringement. If you count four or more, then consider intellectual property as a practice area.

Snapshot: "I've seen that before," the 55-year-old lawyer was saying to the client, "and I'd have to research the prior art, but there'd have to be a dozen patents around strap configurations like that." Reading the disappointment in the client's face, he added, "But you might have something here over in this clip. You ever seen one of those before?" He seemed so completely at ease and so knowledgeable noodling around with the design of the transport system with its trucker-inventor that you would have thought he was a degreed engineer and professional designer. He was neither. He had no education or training other than as a lawyer. Yet he had grown up on a farm fixing things and so had always had a simple knack for picturing how things work — and how they might work better. He made no claim to being a designer, but he knew that in his decades of experience in intellectual-property practice at a mid-size firm specializing in that work, his insight must have contributed substantially to the design of dozens of patented inventions. He never tired of the work. He was a fixture at every inventors' and business-development conference in the area, whether in the local universities or in the circles of entrepreneurs, manufacturers, or designers. Every inventor knew him or knew of him for his skill. He might not have been good at anything else in the law profession, but he was good at patent work, and everyone knew it.

82 Taxation

Nothing is as sure as death and taxes, but at least lawyers can give clients a little help with the latter. Tax law is so complex, tax burdens so significant, and lawful tax strategies, exemptions, and other advantages so valuable for clients that many lawyers are able to devote their full time to the practice area. Tax lawyers provide services primarily to those who have income or assets to protect, often substantial income and assets. "Tax lawyers typically fall into four main types: (1) those who come up with and develop transactions, also known as planners; (2) those who advocate a position for a client with a taxing authority like the IRS and sometimes litigate this position in court, known as controversy experts; (3) those who actually complee and file tax returns, known as compliance experts; and (4) certain hybrids who do a little bit of everything.... In addition, tax lawyers are often then further divided by their tax specialty." NASH, VAULT GUIDE TO TAX LAW CAREERS, at 23.

As is true for business planning, estate planning, and some other practice areas involving economically productive or financially advantaged clients, taxation is not an area where lawyers must routinely be particularly strategic about ensuring that their clients are able to pay and do pay fees. Rather, tax lawyers must demonstrate the value of their tax services, which depends on strategic knowledge of tax law and business finance. "[T]he variety of taxes we have—at the federal, state, and municipal levels—and the wide range of activities that are taxed (as well as the wide range of activities that are exempt from taxation) make for a remarkably complex area of law. Tax lawyers help their clients navigate the highly technical statutes which make up our tax laws." ABRAMS, THE OFFICIAL GUIDE TO LEGAL SPECIALTIES, at 411-412.

Tax practice is not for dummies, and yet tax practice requires no particular magic art or personal charisma as some believe that negotiators, mediators, trial lawyers, appellate advocates, and other performance-skill lawyers must possess. Tax practice is also primarily proactive planning work under the common schedule and control of lawyer and client, rather than reactive work done at the whim and demand of claimants, courts, regulators, and others. Tax practice can involve audit response, and clients can also dispute and litigate with the IRS and other tax authorities either with the help of their tax lawyer or other lawyers skilled in advocacy and dispute resolution. Tax work tends strongly though to have a purely financial rather than personal, relational, or social quality to it, making the work less emotional and more rational than some other practice areas seem. "Considering the total activity of a corporate tax department, it is not difficult to understand the perennial debate as to whether tax is a financial or legal function. It is both." MUNNEKE, NONLEGAL CAREERS, at 66-67.

Takeaway: **Consider tax practice if you have financial knowledge and strategic skill that you like to apply proactively for clients to protect and increase their income and assets.**

Response: "I am preparing for tax practice, preferably for businesses of some size but also for small businesses and individuals with substantial income and assets."

Related Fields: business planning, estate planning, administrative law, alternative dispute resolution, civil litigation.

Reflect: Do you have financial knowledge? Do you have education or experience in how businesses use and manage money? Are you decently skilled at using numbers? Do you like helping individuals and companies increase their earnings and assets? Would you be satisfied in a practice that is primarily about money rather than activities, events, and relationships (recognizing that money affects other things)?

Engage: Rate each of the following common conditions of tax practice as +1 (like), 0 (neutral), or -1 (dislike): (a) quantitative concepts more so than qualitative concepts; (b) formulas and numbers more so than text; (c) financial statements more so than descriptive text reports; (d) finance and business more so than personal and relational; (e) clients with income and assets; (f) primarily office based rather than court based; (g) primarily planning rather than responding; (h) primarily individual or corporate rather than collaborative or competitive; (i) affected by economic cycles; (j) frequent law changes; (k) complex code and regulations; (l) regulatory enforcement rather than private enforcement. If your total was greater than seven, then consider tax practice. If your total was three or less, then consider other fields.

83 Real Property

Real-property work is another practice area for lawyers who prefer office-based practices without the advocacy and adversarial aspects of litigation. Property law is complex, having not only to do with real-property title and transfer but also property use, development, and regulation. "Real estate transactions involve hospitals, schools, hotels and resorts, shopping centers, single family homes, multifamily housing developments, farms, churches, parking lots, and even coal mines. Real estate law concerns every aspect of commercial, industrial, and residential transactions and investments." ABRAMS, THE OFFICIAL GUIDE TO LEGAL SPECIALTIES, at 367.

Small-town lawyers in solo and small firm practice, though in relatively sparsely populated areas, may nonetheless find enough real-property work to specialize in residential, agricultural, and small-business commercial transfers and uses of real property. Lawyers in more-highly developed geographic areas specialize not only in those smaller individual transactions but in real-estate finance and development, zoning and land-use regulation including condemnation, and public-bond work for stadiums, arenas, hospitals, schools, bridges and roads, and other public-use structures. "Real estate sales and development constitute one of the two largest groups of employers of lawyers." MUNNEKE, NONLEGAL CAREERS, at 97.

Real-property practice has within it several such niches sufficient to sustain practice groups within mid-size and large law firms. Real-property-law clients can run the gamut from land-poor individuals on family homesteads to multinational corporations managing far-flung real-property assets. Real-property practice can be highly local, even provincial, or regional, national, or global. Real-property practice is classic transactional work involving drafting and due diligence especially around title work but also frequently involves complex negotiation among multiple constituents including landowners, lessees and other users, private and public financiers, local, state, and federal government and regulators, and adjoining property owners and other community representatives. Real-property practice can also involve litigation and alternative dispute resolution, although many transactional lawyers would refer or co-counsel litigation with skilled trial lawyers. Real-property practice is all at once prevalent, impactful, dynamic, and remunerative, a traditional lawyer's core practice area. "[T]he natural gas boom has created thousands of jobs for landmen, the front-line energy company employees who negotiate with landowners and rights holders, document these transactions, and administer the resulting agreements. Many landmen have a law degree." HERMANN, PRACTICING LAW IN SMALL-TOWN AMERICA, at 281.

Takeaway: **Consider real-property practice for impactful and rewarding transactional drafting and due-diligence work on title, transfer, use, and regulation, for individuals, families, businesses of all sizes, financiers, and government.**

Response: "I would love to practice real-property law where my strong drafting and due-diligence skills would do the most good, for corporate and government clients of all kinds and sizes, but also for individuals and families."

Related Fields: municipal law, administrative law, energy law, regulatory work, alternative dispute resolution, civil litigation.

Reflect: Are you a landowner or from a family of landowners? Do you have experience with or affinity for land-use issues? Can you relate well to homeowners, farmers, ranchers, developers, bankers, and local government officials involved in real-property transfers or development, or land-use issues? What specific real-property knowledge, skills, or experience do you have that would help them trust and rely on you?

Engage: How many of the following real-property-practice clients would you be interested in representing? (a) A young couple purchasing their first home from an unrepresented seller without a real-estate agent. (b) A middle-aged couple selling their home by owner without a real-estate agent. (c) A retail-business owner whose building local inspectors have condemned as unsafe. (d) A farmer whose cropland local government has taken to re-sell to an auto manufacturer to build a huge new plant. (e) A club owner whose racy shows local officials have threatened to enjoin under an adult-entertainment ordinance. (f) A church requiring zoning variance to expand its sanctuary and add classrooms. (g) A multinational restaurant chain requiring corporate counsel to direct local acquisition of new locations. (h) A global corporation needing to reduce the size of its real-estate-investment portfolio by sales to local developers. (i) A national bank needing to review and improve its mortgage-brokerage and foreclosure procedures. (j) A community organization challenging the alleged redlining of its neighborhoods by local mortgage brokers.

Snapshot: Real-property transactions just seemed to suit him better than anything else that he encountered in law practice. He had tried litigating once and never tried it again, instead referring away all litigation, even for his best clients. Business planning was fine, and he also liked his good bit of estate work. Yet somehow, real-estate work was just his thing. He took to it like the proverbial duck to water. Part of it had to do with the properties themselves. He had an unquenchable interest in the local community's eclectic mix of land uses and property developments, whether residential, commercial, industrial, or recreational. From his many real-estate contacts, he seemed to know about every deal well before it actually happened. He also liked the fastidious nature of the work. He had always been fastidious himself about his demeanor, dress, papers, and things, so keeping real-property transactions properly documented seemed both natural and quite satisfying to him. He could tell instantly when the smallest detail was out of place. He suspected that he was close to obsessive about things, but compulsion of that kind just made him all the better at documenting each transaction. By the end of his career, he had even developed his own new building holding a suite of offices in which, yes, he had a title company as a tenant. Now, that's perfect.

84 Natural Resources Law

Natural-resource development and management is a ripe and dynamic area for law practice. Energy development, uses, policies, and regulation continue to change rapidly with technological advances, political developments, and environmental concerns. Oil-and-gas law has long been a traditional practice niche in certain regions of the country where the sale or lease of extraction rights comprises an important part of the local economy. Fracking has opened vast new fields while re-opening old fields and at the same time changing significantly the pricing and mix of other energy sources. Coal mining has accordingly declined in some areas as plants convert to gas but resumed in other areas to ship supplies overseas. "What subjects genuinely interest me? Here's a novel thought: some people actually work in careers in which the basic subject matter is of enormous personal interest." SCHNEIDER, SHOULD YOU REALLY BE A LAWYER? at 198.

New rail and pipeline transport of oil and gas from fracking and tar sands raise new safety and environmental concerns. Wind farms, solar fields, their transmission utilities and storage facilities, and other alternative energy sources raise new opportunities and environmental concerns. Water rights, agreements, and uses remain a critical area of industrial, agricultural, and residential concern for tens of millions. Timber, fishery, and wildlife resources all continue to undergo development and need management and regulation, all of which require the services of lawyers. Natural-resource law offers multiple practice niches involving complex transactional and regulatory work, and frequent negotiation and dispute resolution. Practitioners with industry-specific knowledge, education, or experience enjoy distinct advantages serving clients in these niches.

Takeaway: **Consider natural-resources law as a complex and rewarding transactional practice especially if you have experience or interest in specific natural-resource industries.**

Response: "I would love to be involved in the development and regulation of green-energy initiatives around wind, solar, and natural-gas resources but also have interests in water and wildlife law."

Related Fields: administrative law, legislative work, alternative dispute resolution, civil litigation.

Reflect: Do you hunt, fish, hike, camp, participate in water sports, or otherwise enjoy the scenic outdoors? Do you have experience with or interest in energy development and regulation? Are you interested in policy work?

Engage: How many of the following natural-resource law clients would you be interested in representing? (a) A farmer needing to challenge reductions in water rights threatening crops. (b) A woodland owner needing to negotiate new contracts for timber harvesting. (c) An oil-and-gas company needing to negotiate new drilling leases. (d) An industry association needing to respond to proposed new fracking regulations. (e) A fishing company needing to contest proposed shortening of seasons. (f) A local government drafting new ordinances to address wind turbines and solar-energy farms. (g) A citizens group wishing to advocate against wind turbines in a pristine lake. (h) A rail company needing to negotiate with regulators over proposed new oil-transport regulations. (i) A coal company needing to negotiate new supply contracts with foreign governments. (j) A hunting-guide association needing to write new bylaws governing members. If you counted six or more, then consider natural-resources law as a practice area.

85 Insurance Law

Individuals, families, businesses, and governments manage risk through insurance. Life would be a lot harder and more hazardous without the modern miracle of insurance. Insurance shifts the risk from the insured to the insurer, which prices, spreads, and absorbs the cost of loss that is certain in general but uncertain in particular. Insurers insure against death, illness, disability, and workplace injury. They also insure against property loss and damage and business interruption due to fire, flood, and other casualty. They also insure against liability for causing those losses due to negligence, malpractice, products liability, premises liability, commercial operations, errors, omissions, and other wrongful conduct. All of that insuring requires substantial and continuing service from lawyers, many of whom serve insurance companies as clients in private practice and many of whom work in-house or in captive firms within an insurance company. "One major difference between in-house corporate insurance work and working for an insurance company as outside counsel is that, as in-house counsel, you have only one client—the corporation—and the department is viewed as a cost center." MUNNEKE, NONLEGAL CAREERS, at 93.

Insurance law as a practice area extends to litigating claims and defenses involving all of these and other forms of coverage. Yet the claims side of insurance law is only one half of the total insurance-law equation. Insurance law also involves the formation, governance, reporting, regulation, compliance, and underwriting practices of insurers. Insurance-law practitioners tend to work either on the claims side of insurance operations, as advocates skilled in investigation, negotiation, litigation and alternative dispute resolution, or on the underwriting side, as transactional, business-planning, and regulatory or compliance lawyers. Insurance law is a vast and important field offering diverse opportunities. "This practice is very contract driven. The meat of the work is interpretation of the scope of coverage of insurance contracts (auto, home owners, renters, general, employers, directors and officers, etc.)." MUNNEKE, THE LEGAL CAREER GUIDE, at 366.

Takeaway: **Consider practicing in either the claims side of insurance law or the transactional, underwriting, and regulatory side to do important work in a field critical to managing risk in a hazardous world.**

Response: "I plan to practice insurance law primarily on the regulatory side to ensure that insurers continue to manage and reduce risk for individuals and entities in responsible ways."

Related Fields: civil litigation, alternative dispute resolution, personal injury, malpractice, worker's compensation, administrative law.

Reflect: How effectively are you managing personal risk through insurers? What experience do you have or do your family, friends, acquaintances, and community have with catastrophic loss of life, limb, or property? Would you enjoy helping people and companies manage their lives and businesses responsibly as to risks? Would you appreciate helping others recover from catastrophic losses? Do you like or dislike insurers? If so, then think about why, and whether those feelings would help you commit to practice in this area.

Engage: Which of the following insurance-law clients would you like to represent? (a) A motor-vehicle owner trying to get a higher appraisal on a totaled vehicle from a collision insurer. (b) A homeowner the insurer claims deliberately set the insured house on fire. (c) A seafood restaurant suing an insurer for business-interruption coverage when a storm cut power for a week. (d) A disability insurer defending a claim by an allegedly disabled worker whom the insurer video-recorded water-skiing. (e) A life insurer defending a claim by a beneficiary whose spouse the insurer has evidence committed suicide. (f) An insurer that regulators subpoenaed to produce records regarding whether it had adequate reserves to cover present and future claims. (g) An insurer that desires to underwrite new commercial coverage in your state in which the insurer has not yet qualified to operate. (h) An insurer that federal regulators allege must meet new financial regulations and reporting requirements. (i) An insurance-industry association studying proposed new state legislation affecting underwriting practices. (j) Regulators attempting to take over an insurer whose sole shareholder appears to have absconded to a foreign country with company funds. If you counted five or more, then consider insurance law as a practice area.

86 Health Law

Considering that healthcare goods and services comprise approximately one sixth of the U.S. economy under vastly increased federal regulation, you should never have a shortage of work in the health-law field. Traditional health-law concerns include forming, governing, capitalizing, and managing hospitals, physician practices, medical-device makers, and other entities in the healthcare field. State law governed much of the field other than medical devices subject to federal regulation. Newer and emerging concerns include forming and managing health-maintenance organizations, preferred-provider networks, managed-care organizations, insurance exchanges, community-needs assessments, and other innovative entities and initiatives. "[Health law] divides into three pieces: transactional (provider operations, counseling, standard corporate work), regulatory, and litigation. This is a highly regulated environment. The standard hospital practice can include a significant amount of work for non-profit institutions. The day-to-day work centers on disputes regarding medical reimbursement, allegations of fraud, compliance with regulatory issues, etc." MUNNEKE, THE LEGAL CAREER GUIDE, at 365.

The federal Affordable Care Act and accompanying proposed, interim, and final regulations newly compel, govern, or influence these emerging concerns. Coupled with delayed and exempted individual and employer mandates, these new federal laws and regulations will likely continue to drive growth in health-law practices for years to come, particularly as legislators modify state and federal legislation and regulation to account for the unforeseen effects of the federalization of health insurance and medicine. Qualifying for critical public healthcare benefits under complex Medicare and Medicaid regulations add to the extensive healthcare-practice mix. No matter the source or scope of healthcare regulation, healthcare is so significant for the nation's aging baby-boomer population, the resources and political influence of which are so vast, that health law should remain a dynamic field for years to come. "Managed health care, pharmaceutical manufacturing, medical research, nursing, and hospice care are multibillion-dollar industries. These fields are in constant contact with the legal system." MUNNEKE, NONLEGAL CAREERS, at 95.

Takeaway: **Consider health law as a vast and significant transactional practice area especially if you have medical education or interests.**

Response: "I would like to represent healthcare providers both in governance and compliance matters. I have several family members who are professionals in the healthcare field."

Related Fields: business planning, insurance law, administrative law.

Reflect: What healthcare-field education or experience do you have? Do you have family members or friends who are professionals in the healthcare field? Are you interested in helping professional and institutional clients respond to regulatory changes? Do you have strong research, due-diligence, compliance, drafting, and communication skills?

Engage: How many of the following healthcare-field clients would you be interested in representing? (a) A family investigating the sudden death of its 50-year-old wage-earner member during a routine colonoscopy. (b) A hospital review board considering terminating the privileges of an incompetent surgeon. (c) A leading cardiologist planning to form a new cardiac-care practice group. (d) A growing suburban hospital planning to hire a dozen additional staff physicians. (e) A major university hospital seeking a certificate of need from regulators for a new heart-transplant unit. (f) An employer of hundreds of employees attempting to comply with new healthcare and health insurance regulations affecting full-time and part-time employees. (g) A professional school attempting to advise its students and graduates regarding the character-and-fitness effects of refusing to comply with the federal individual mandate. (h) A religious-freedom nonprofit seeking representation for employers objecting to the federal abortion-coverage mandate. (i) A nurse facing a license proceeding over alleged abuse of an elderly patient. (j) A physician attempting to negotiate a sale of her interest in a clinical-practice group in order to take a position in hospital administration. If you counted five or more, then consider practice in the health-law field.

Snapshot: She was finally retiring after 30 years in health law. Her longevity had hardly seemed possible when she left her nursing career in her early 30s to go to law school. She had planned to leave the healthcare field behind but was not surprised when she ended up in a hospital's corporate-counsel office. Her dual professional education and licensure in both nursing and law made her a hot professional commodity. Although she had not enjoyed the clinical side of nursing, she quickly found that she loved the health law work whether it involved clinical, administrative, compliance, liability, or governance issues. She had always taken a keen interest in hospital systems, processes, and operations. Now, as assistant corporate counsel, she found her expertise touching on it all. Her skills grew over the years until she retired as a vice president of risk management and compliance, large and in charge, her associate counsel liked to tease her because of her great warmth and humility.

87 Municipal Law

Local governments face many legal issues requiring that they retain the services of lawyers knowledgeable and skilled in municipal matters. Municipal-law issues can involve such local functions and operations as streets, public transportation, parking, sewers, utilities such as gas, water, electric, and cable, zoning, land use, building inspections, parks, events, and cemeteries. A municipal lawyer's service can include advising city councils, managers, staff, boards, and departments regarding local, state, and federal law, rule, regulation, and constitution. Law services can also include representing the city in civil litigation over tort liability, contract breaches, and constitutional and statutory violations involving zoning, land use, freedom of speech and religion, and privacy and other rights. Law services can further include ordinance enforcement over illegal parking, abandoned vehicles, drug use, excessive noise, and other disturbances. "We naturally tend to think about government as a big-city/capital-city phenomenon. While Washington, D.C., and state capitals almost always employ more government attorneys than any other places, they do not employ the majority of them. … [T]housands of small towns … harbor a significant number of federal and state government lawyers. Moreover, these communities also demand and sustain a considerable legal presence necessary to handle their own governmental affairs." HERMANN, PRACTICING LAW IN SMALL-TOWN AMERICA, at 250.

Municipal lawyers may also represent cities, townships, villages, and other local entities in contract negotiations with cable operators, refuse-collection services, and dozens of other suppliers of goods and services, and labor negotiations with law enforcement, firefighters, public-works employees, and other union workers. Municipal lawyers can have frequent evening events attending meetings of councils, zoning boards of appeal, and other boards and committees. Few practice areas call so regularly on such broad and practical law knowledge and skills as those possessed by municipal lawyers. Effective municipal lawyers can make a greater positive difference in the lives of local citizens than practitioners in just about any other law field. "Local government may present opportunities in fields such as land-use planning, zoning, utilities law, and other substantive areas that correspond to local political issues. Jobs may be funded in departments within city government and in special districts (e.g., water, school, regional planning)." MUNNEKE, THE LEGAL CAREER GUIDE, at 240.

Takeaway: **Consider municipal law if you want to make a daily positive impact on local communities while acquiring and exercising the broadest and most practical law knowledge.**

Response: "I would like most to practice municipal law so that I can daily see the positive evidence of my work on the health, safety, and sustainability of vibrant local communities."

Related Fields: administrative law, civil litigation.

Reflect: Have you been active in any local initiatives? Do you appreciate the operation of local councils, committees, and boards? Do you take an interest in local people, places, and events? Do you frequently notice things that you think local leadership and the local community could do better?

Engage: Count the number of the following municipal-law matters that you would be interested in being involved in and in which you think you could be effective: (a) a township negotiating a new refuse collection contract; (b) a village

Dear J.D.

negotiating a new labor agreement with public-works employees; (c) a city needing to enforce an ordinance not to park vehicles on main streets during snow-removal season; (d) a city council determining whether to approve a request for a permit for a controversial parade; (e) a zoning board deciding whether to grant a variance to enable a landowner to access her property; (f) a village interested in adopting a sign ordinance to improve esthetics to attract more tourism; (g) a township trying to force a rural landowner to clean up a junkyard; (h) a township defending a suit brought by an outdoor-sign company contesting restrictive regulations; (i) a homeowner's association negotiating with the city over an assessment to install curbs and lighting; and (j) a county sheriff sued for a pattern of excessive force deputies have allegedly used against arrested citizens. If you count five or more, then consider municipal law as a practice area.

88 Administrative Law

Despite its common-law heritage and free-market commitments, America is now unquestionably a regulation nation. Local, state, and federal regulations challenge individuals and businesses undertaking all kinds of necessary, productive, and recreational but simultaneously risk-generating activities. Healthcare, insurance, banking, securities, medical devices, motor vehicles, public transportation, gambling, mining, education, pharmaceuticals, insurance, construction, hunting, fishing, and all professions, among many other pursuits, all face substantial regulation. Regulations and rulings, cases, bulletins, and interpretations fill millions of pages of administrative codes, reporters, and registers in dozens of searchable online databases. "Don't expect this regulatory barrage to cease anytime soon. Regulations are not something that regulatory agencies cobble together out of whole cloth on their own initiative. Instead, they are the direct result of the legislative activities that churn out thousands of new laws every year. ... This regulatory barrage, more than anything, accounts for the growth in the local public-sector attorney population, a phenomenon that is found throughout the United States, even in the most economically hard-pressed areas." HERMANN, PRACTICING LAW IN SMALL-TOWN AMERICA, at 170.

When government officials, private patients, clients, or customers, affected members of the public, or interested members of the media suspect private violations of public regulations, government officials initiate elaborate investigations that may lead to administrative fines, license suspension or revocation, cease and desist orders, civil liability, criminal charges, and the collapse and disintegration of enterprises formerly of substantial economic and social value. With so much regulation, and so much at stake over regulatory violations, administrative law is a vast and hugely important practice area in which many lawyers specialize within dozens of significant industry and profession niches. "Given the ubiquitous nature of the 'fourth branch' of government—administrative agencies—you're bound to practice administrative law in some capacity, whether you like it or not. Administrative lawyers practice at the intersection of law, business, and government, helping their clients to navigate the 'alphabet soup' of government regulation." HAHN, GUIDE TO LAW FIRMS, at 101.

Administrative law is a primary reason that you see thriving niche and boutique law practices in gaming law, fish-and-game law, animal law, agriculture law, mining law, art law, aviation law, transportation law, and dozens of other smaller law fields related to specific regulated sectors. Administrative-law practitioners need only have the regulatory research, due-diligence, communication, and strategic skills, and a passion for understanding their clients' industries and professions, to find meaningful opportunities for extensive, impactful, and valuable law service. "The field of administrative law encompasses many subspecialties, from banking regulatory practice to homeland security, from aviation and transportation law to health regulatory practice. Administrative lawyers work with the laws of executive agencies—federal and state—and explore how those agencies regulate the industry in which an attorney works...." FURI-PERRY, 50 UNIQUE LEGAL PATHS, at 24.

Takeaway: **Consider administrative law if your skills are in regulatory research and compliance, and you like working** with professionals and businesses on the integrity of their processes and practices.

Response: "I would like to do administrative work helping businesses in various industries comply with federal and state regulations, given my research and due diligence skills."

Related Fields: health law, insurance law, natural-resources law, immigration law, worker's compensation, Social Security disability.

Reflect: Have you held licenses in other fields or worked with others who do? Have you worked in a heavily regulated industry like insurance, banking and finance, healthcare, education, pharmaceuticals, or securities? Do you have strong research skills? Are you good at due diligence, developing and following protocols? Do you like working with businesses and professionals?

Engage: How many of the following administrative-law clients would you like to assist, be effective in assisting, and be likely to gain their confidence to assist? (a) A physician facing a licensing hearing for alleged misconduct with a patient. (b) A foster-care family facing a license-revocation hearing over alleged neglect. (c) A securities broker facing a license-revocation hearing over alleged reporting non-disclosures. (d) A medical-device maker seeking approval of a design alteration to a heart valve. (e) A pharmaceutical company appealing preliminary denial of a new drug. (f) A bank seeking to remove itself from a regulator's under-capitalized at-risk institution list. (g) A hospital seeking to satisfy antitrust review and approval of a merger with a cross-town rival. (h) A banking association challenging new consumer-credit regulations. If you chose four or more, then consider practicing administrative law.

89 Immigration Law

With advances in transportation, migration is easier and more common today than ever before, and with prevalent civil wars, terrorism, persecution, economic collapse, natural disaster, and starvation, just as necessary as ever. The United States has since its founding been a nation of immigrants and remains the world's leading such nation both as an immigrant destination and in terms of migrant-population makeup. Federal law regulates immigration closely, and states attempt to regulate immigration and control the social and economic impacts of immigration. These circumstances of prevalent immigration and close regulation make immigration law a dynamic practice area even without recent substantial immigration reform, which members of Congress continually discuss in public. "Though some think of immigration law as a field fraught only with administrative practice and paper-pushing, it also involves a lot of human drama. From assisting refugees and immigrants seeking asylum to representing families separated by borders, immigration lawyers help their clients through emotional and life-changing events...." FURI-PERRY, 50 UNIQUE LEGAL PATHS, at 19.

Individuals and families desperately need immigration-law services. Lawful status can make the difference between life and death, medical care and no care, assets and no assets, income and no income, education and no education, marriage and separation, and children and loss of children, among other significant differences. Because of their precarious undocumented status, individuals often find non-lawyers preying upon their insecurity to cheat them out of all kinds of rights and benefits. Immigrants need skilled, committed, and compassionate legal counsel. Businesses also depend on retained or in-house counsel to qualify foreign labor, whether highly skilled or unskilled, to fill roles that U.S. workers are unable or unwilling to fill. U.S. companies even need immigration lawyers' help to qualify U.S. citizens to work for them abroad. "Those attorneys who work in smaller firms may do business immigration work, or they may assist individuals with personal or family immigration issues. Indigent individuals faced with immigration concerns often turn to public interest lawyers who specialize in immigration." ABRAMS, THE OFFICIAL GUIDE TO LEGAL SPECIALTIES, at 230.

As abundant as it is, immigration work simply takes skill in regulatory research, compliance, and advocacy, administrative skill in handling and documenting matters consistently and expeditiously, and the affinities and commitment to address and satisfy these important humanitarian and economic needs. These skills tend to be the skills of litigators more so than transactional lawyers. "Most immigration lawyers spend time in the U.S. Immigration Court and at the Bureau of Citizenship and Immigration Services (BCIS) and, as a result, learn litigation skills very early." VISWANATHAN, VAULT GUIDE TO LITIGATION LAW CAREERS, at 19.

Takeaway: **Consider immigration law as a dynamic practice if you have foreign-language skills or other helpful affinities and like regulatory work helping immigrants obtain lawful status and businesses qualify foreign labor.**

Response: "My foreign-language skills should help me establish an immigration practice helping immigrants qualify for lawful status while also helping U.S. companies qualify foreign workers for domestic employment and global companies qualify U.S. workers for foreign employment."

Reflect: What foreign-language skills or cultural affinities do you or your close family members have that might connect you with immigrant populations? Do you already interact with immigrants? Do you follow immigration matters in the news? Do you think that you would like regulatory work, helping individuals and businesses comply with immigration laws?

Engage: How many of the following immigration-law clients would you like to represent, think that you could represent competently in time, and believe that you could gain the confidence of to represent? (a) An undocumented Mexican laborer arrested for drunk driving and detained for deportation. (b) An undocumented Guatemalan woman who, having been forced to serve as a drug mule, seeks U.S. asylum. (c) An undocumented Iraqi who overstayed a student visa, held for deportation following an incident of alleged domestic violence. (d) An undocumented Nicaraguan who bore a child in the U.S. for whom she wishes to appoint a U.S. citizen guardian while she returns briefly to Nicaragua to bring her undocumented Nicaraguan-born child into the U.S. (e) A major-league sports team needing an exceptional-ability visa for a foreign athlete the team just drafted. (f) A pharmaceutical manufacturer needing an advanced-degree extraordinary-ability visa for a foreign scientist to run a clinical trial in the U.S. If you chose three or more, then consider immigration law as a practice field.

Snapshot: "I guess not so good because I'm so busy doing just about 100% immigration work," the lawyer explained to the other lawyer who had asked how his customs practice was going. The immigration lawyer had extensive experience in international customs, tariffs, and trade before earning his law degree. In fact, he had pursued his law degree with the specific plan in mind to open a customs practice, not just taking the relevant courses but even to the point of developing and (after passing the bar) distributing marketing materials. Yet his first client was in immigration law. And his second. And his third. And most of the rest of them long since then. "I should have known that my Spanish-speaking skills would help, but I had no idea of the need or opportunity," the immigration lawyer explained. "I do always seem to be hustling to be sure I've got enough work," the immigration lawyer replied to the other lawyer's query, before adding, "but I'm not sure why I feel that I need to hustle because the work has been steady since I started. One satisfied client just seems to lead to another." He paused before concluding, "In retrospect, I am so much happier doing this work than the customs work that I had planned. The individual clients mean so much to me. Who wants to work for multinational corporations when they could help immigrants?"

Part 4

Employment

90 Prosecution

Prosecution work is distinct, all to its own, sui generis. Law practice has few roles so clearly defined and constrained. One does not dabble at prosecution work. In most cases, a lawyer who prosecutes crimes does little or nothing else. The role of working for government and representing the people to charge and prosecute crimes involves such singular and peculiar authority that to do so lawyers must ordinarily forgo any other employment and join the prosecutor's office. "The job of Prosecutors is complex and demanding. They carry a heavy caseload and must make sure that the legal process is followed for every case. They might work on a case alone or with other prosecutors." ECHAORE-MCDAVID, CAREER OPPORTUNITIES IN LAW, at 11.

The people elect some prosecutors, usually county prosecutors who then hire assistant prosecutors to share the authority of charging crime. The president appoints federal prosecutors, known as U.S. Attorneys, who do likewise, hiring career Assistant U.S. Attorneys to carry out the work, while also representing the federal government in civil matters. Elected county prosecutors can become powerful, and to some persons even notorious, local public figures given the cumulative effect on certain local constituencies of prosecutorial discretion. U.S. Attorneys wield similar influence. "A great advantage of most government jobs, prosecutor positions, public interest jobs, and small firm associateships is that you get to hit the ground running. You get lots of responsibility, very early on. ... Feeling as though your work has a real impact on someone else from an early point in your career creates an adrenaline rush very little else can match." WALTON, AMERICA'S GREATEST PLACES TO WORK WITH A LAW DEGREE, at 23.

Given their notoriety and public service, prosecutors find a natural path onto the judicial bench, again whether by local election or administrative appointment. Prosecution work with its constant theme of law and order seems more like a lawyer's work than just about any other role. Some lawyers start as prosecutors for the trial work and public service, only to proceed to large- or small-firm private law practice. Many prosecutors, though, stay the full course, making a career of prosecution work. The field is so distinct, that when it comes to prosecution work, it seems that you either have what it takes to confront and charge crime, or you don't. "People just *love, love, love* being prosecutors. The sense of being one of the 'good guys'—they sometimes semi-jokingly refer to 'doing God's work'—the immediate courtroom experience, the lack of billable hour and business generation requirements—no wonder these are such popular jobs!" WALTON, AMERICA'S GREATEST PLACES TO WORK WITH A LAW DEGREE, at 901.

Takeaway: **Consider prosecution work if you have a strong sense of responsibility and the discipline to daily pursue it.**

Response: "I am most interested in prosecution work to protect, preserve, and restore the community. I think that I have the discipline and sense of public responsibility to be a good prosecutor."

Related Fields: criminal defense, drunk-driving defense, federal defense, white-collar defense, public defender, license defense.

Reflect: Would you want to prosecute crime? If so, then what is your motivation? Do you identify with victims of crime, or is your concern more for protecting the community or saving the criminal? Or does crime itself, with all of its darkness, distortion, and savagery, simultaneously fascinate, repel, and attract you? Or are you simply attracted to the power, prestige, and public service of the prosecutor's position?

Engage: Rate each of the following conditions of much prosecution work as either +1 (like), 0 (neutral), or -1 (dislike): (a) public rather than private employee; (b) salary grades rather than incentive compensation; (c) step wage increases rather than bonus and merit raises; (d) no clients; (e) no billing; (f) no timekeeping; (g) no rainmaking; (h) politically elected or appointed supervision; (i) work most closely with detectives and police officers; (j) deal with matters in the media; (k) public criticism possible; (l) no law work on the side; (m) deal with violent individuals; (n) deal with abuse, serious injury, and death; (o) potential personal security risks; (p) reasonable job security; (q) substantial supervision; (r) limited innovation. Total your plusses against your minuses.

Dear J.D.

If you scored five or higher, then consider prosecution work. If you scored zero or lower, then consider not pursuing prosecution work, or consider your answers more closely.

91 Public Defender

Courts must appoint at public expense a lawyer to represent indigent defendants facing incarceration in criminal cases. Some jurisdictions do so through a public defender's office that employs criminal-defense lawyers full time. Full-time public-defender work can be either a satisfying career position or important experience preparing you for private practice in criminal defense or other areas. Public-defender offices can be more than a place employing assigned counsel. Public-defender offices can become repositories from which local lawyers draw for the most insightful subject-matter knowledge and masterful expertise. Public-defender offices can also be effective advocates for criminal-justice-system reform. "Public Defenders ('PDs') have often been called 'the frontline of the Bill of Rights.' They provide legal services for indigent clients. They are often overworked and underpaid. They don't have the luxury afforded to private attorneys of picking their own clients. Often, their clients are less than appealing. It's only with their great sense of advocacy and belief in the system that they are able to defend some of the people that they are ordered to represent." WALTON, AMERICA'S GREATEST PLACES TO WORK WITH A LAW DEGREE, at 773.

Larger-population counties inclusive of a metropolitan area often form public-defender offices. Smaller-population counties will often instead contract with a local lawyer or law firm for indigent-defense services. Courts also maintain lists of lawyers interested in taking indigent-defense assignments, with the county then paying those lawyers modest fixed fees. The federal government also funds federal-defender offices providing indigent federal defendants with representation.

When defender offices have conflicts of interest in representing two indigent defendants in the same case at once, then they typically refer one defendant to assigned counsel who will receive a modest public fee for the representation. "As a public defender, Timijanel Boyd Odom finds her work with her indigent clients immensely rewarding. 'I provide people who can't afford a private lawyer the best defense possible. Just being a good defense attorney is a reward in itself,' she says. Timijanel also says that her love of people makes being a public defender the perfect job for her." ABRAMS, THE OFFICIAL GUIDE TO LEGAL SPECIALTIES, at 121.

Takeaway: **Consider public-defender work, either as a career or for substantial trial and client experience on which to build a private practice.**

Response: "I look forward to public-defense work, whether I work for a public-defender office, or my firm gets a contract for indigent defense, or simply take assignments off a court list."

Related Fields: prosecution, criminal defense, drunk-driving defense, federal defense, white-collar defense, license defense.

Reflect: What is your impression of public defenders? Where did you gain that impression? Do you believe that it is accurate? How much do you value the work that public defenders do? Would you prefer that government pay you to defend clients charged with crime or that clients charged with crime pay you themselves? How efficient can you be in providing indigent-defense services? How well do you think you could manage a large case load? How badly would it frustrate you to have less time than you want to represent a client charged with crime?

Engage: Rate each of the following common conditions of public-defense work as either +1 (like this condition), 0 (neutral), or -1 (do not like this condition): (a) courts assign clients rather than clients choosing you; (b) you represent the assigned client whether you would prefer to or not; (c) clients question whether you work for them or the court; (d) the clients are all indigent; (e) the clients are all charged with crimes; (f) some clients are former clients and may be future clients; (g) modest pay unaffected by outcomes; (h) substantial client interaction; (i) substantial court time; (j) frequent negotiations with prosecutors. If your plusses and minuses total four or more, then consider public defense. If your plusses and minuses total zero or less, then consider a different field, or re-examine your answers.

92 Public Interest

In a sense, a private civil-rights practice is public-interest work, although on behalf of private parties. Yet lawyers think of public-interest practice as a different activity, either one explicitly devoted not to individual clients as much as to systemic change or to working for a single nonprofit employer representing clients who would otherwise have no representation. Public-interest lawyers step in where the private market for law services does not meet client and public needs. Lawyers form and operate nonprofit public-interest law firms and other organizations devoted to specific causes such as environmental litigation, wildlife-and-resource protection, fair-housing litigation, voting-rights litigation, and other national causes. Lawyers work as employees of those firms and organizations, devoting their full time to advancing the public-interest cause. They also work for legal-services organizations providing direct representation to indigent clients in landlord-tenant, welfare-benefits, and family law matters. "Legal services programs have existed for decades in every jurisdiction throughout the United States. Many programs are a part of the Legal Services Corporation funded by Congress." MUNNEKE, THE LEGAL CAREER GUIDE, at 255.

Public-interest firms and organizations may depend in part on public grants and private contributions but may also collect substantial prevailing-party fees in successful cause litigation. Public-interest lawyers will identify individual clients or organizations who have standing relating to the firm's mission cause, to represent pro bono, but will undertake the litigation with the prospect of recovering those substantial prevailing-party fees. Public-interest lawyers naturally may face public opposition given the sometimes-controversial and usually unsettled nature of their causes and so must maintain the courage and confidence of their convictions. "People in public interest find that the meaningfulness of their work is its most obvious virtue. You'll hear them say 'Without me, these people would be *lost.*'" WALTON, AMERICA'S GREATEST PLACES TO WORK WITH A LAW DEGREE, at 16.

Takeaway: Consider public-interest work on behalf of your favorite cause if you prefer nonprofit employment over private practice and have strong litigation skills and convictions.

Response: "I want to work for a public-interest law firm on environmental causes to ensure a safe and healthy environment for generations to come."

Related Fields: civil litigation, appellate advocacy, civil rights, legislative work.

Reflect: For what public causes do you have the greatest sympathy? If you could change one thing with the world, then what would that one thing be? Do you believe that small numbers of courageous individuals can make the world a better place through law reform? What law reforms would you adopt if you had the authority? Are you good at public debate? Can you articulate, rationalize, and justify your positions on political, ideological, policy, and social issues?

Engage: Which, if any, of the following public-interest causes might you be willing to support with at least some of your time using your law skills? (a) Minority housing rights with respect to apartment access, mortgage availability, and predatory lending. (b) Public health and safety with respect to toxic-waste disposal. (c) Environmental protection from fracking and other carbon-based energy development. (d) Eagle and other bird protection and preserving rural property values from green-energy wind farms. (e) Ocean fish-stock protection from over-fishing. (f) Open-borders initiatives supporting human migration. (g) Personal-privacy advocacy from government and technological intrusion. (h) Domestic-violence advocacy for battered women. (i) Anti-human-trafficking initiatives worldwide. (j) Preserving net neutrality for the internet. If you selected at least one of the above, then consider public-interest work as at least part of your practice mix.

Snapshot: After more than a decade litigating civil cases for a large law firm, she knew that she and her family needed something different. The travel to depositions and the intense preparation for trials did not give her the flexibility and consistency that her family needed. She also had the strong sense that she wanted to make a broader impact in one specific area, which had been her dream going to law school. Thus although she loved the litigation work and her colleagues and firm, when a position opened to become the executive director of a public-interest nonprofit on the board of which she had long served, she jumped at the chance. Nonprofit leadership gave her everything including a consistent but flexible schedule and a powerful cause to pursue drawing on her law and other professional skills. Ten years later, she was still passionately engaged in the work, as effective and resourceful as ever.

93 Legislative Work

Lawyers are prevalent in Congress and the state legislatures, and in private government-affairs, public-affairs, and lobbying positions working with legislators, making for significant career opportunities in legislative work. Lawyers not only serve as elected representatives but also as legislative analysts and chiefs of staff, and in similar roles. After all, legislatures draft, consider, and adopt laws. Lawyers have the peculiar education, training, and experience to both do the work and support the work of legislators. That work includes not only drafting proposed legislation but also analyzing, summarizing, editing, and revising legislation proposed by others. "Several thousand legislative assistants work on Capitol Hill and in state legislatures. The positions are relatively low-paying, but ideal for young lawyers just beginning their careers. They can also be excellent 'career builders,' stepping-stones to good jobs after a few years in the halls of a legislative body." HERMANN, FROM LEMONS TO LEMONADE IN THE NEW LEGAL JOB MARKET, at 117.

Lawyers doing legislative work also canvas legislators and analysts for views on proposed legislation, survey constituents for views, and summarize and report on responses. They also evaluate the effect of adopted legislation to consider amendment. Lawyer legislators and analysts also speak publicly about proposed legislation, both for public education and as advocates, and write and do other media work for the same public purposes. Legislative staff attorneys may also investigate constituent complaints and requests, particularly as they relate to law and legislation. Lawyers in staff positions in the legislature often use those positions as preparation for other work, whether to run for public office or join a law firm to support lobbying, public-policy work, or research, writing, and advocacy for which the legislative career prepared them. "Many areas of corporate activity involve meeting the requirements of various laws and regulations issued by governmental agencies and departments. In the government relations area, the industry seeks to bring its influence to bear upon pending legislation." MUNNEKE, NONLEGAL CAREERS, at 73.

Takeaway: **Consider legislative positions if your commitment is for policy work and skills are for drafting, analysis, communication, and strategy.**

Response: "I am networking to take a position as a legislative analyst or staff attorney so that I can put my drafting and communication skills to work on policy issues affecting our region."

Related Fields: administrative law, public interest.

Reflect: What public issues have engaged you in the past? Do you have current views that you like to share on public-policy issues? Are you skilled at drafting and communication? Are you effective at networking and learning the views of others?

Engage: How many of the following policy issues would you like to address in these varying legislative activities? (a) Summarizing citizens' views on campaign financing expressed at a community-center public forum. (b) Speaking at a public forum on proposed animal-abuse-registry legislation. (c) Researching other state laws on Social Security-number privacy for proposed legislation. (d) Drafting a bill on local authority to regulate wind turbines and solar panels. (e) Reviewing and editing a draft bill on minimum wages at big-box retailers. (f) Summarizing key points of dispute from a massive proposed bill rewriting the state's judicature act. (g) Canvassing other legislators and analysts for views on your legislator's proposed bill to expand charter-school authorizations. (h) Reviewing and summarizing citizen response to your legislator's proposed bill amending the state's no-fault act. If you counted five or more, then consider legislative work for a career.

94 Judicial Positions

Judges are lawyers, as are the judicial clerks and career staff attorneys who serve judges. Most judicial positions require a law license, and no wonder, given the distinct quality of the role that judges must know and apply law correctly, consistently, and predictably in all matters that parties bring to them. Doing so requires a special temperament. Judges do not choose their matters. Parties choose what judges decide, meaning that judges must often decide disputes that they would not have brought or would not have brought in that fashion. The bane of judging is having to decide disputes that the judge feels have no real place in court. Litigation can be a proxy for anything including mental illness, revenge or vendetta, and economic leverage or oppression. "[J]udges must find enough value in the adversarial system to tolerate sitting in the middle of argument and hostility. And they must learn to endure constant public scrutiny, second-guessing and criticism." ARRON, RUNNING FROM THE LAW, at 126.

Judges face challenges even when the role is as simple as deciding clear and credible disputes. Law is vast and complex. Judges whose dockets are of general jurisdiction face formidable intellectual challenges knowing and applying as much law as they must. New judges with specialized dockets such as criminal law, family law, probate, and business court will soon develop specialized knowledge and expertise, yet even senior judges with general dockets constantly see new matters involving unfamiliar or changing law. Judging carries prestige, security (at least until the next election or appointment round), fair compensation, and reasonable benefits, but its constraints are significant. The work can isolate and frustrate, meaning that one must possess peculiar judicial temperament. While many lawyers make judging a career or significant part of a career, many other lawyers serve as judicial law clerks for one or two years typically after law school graduation, or as career clerks or staff attorneys. "A judicial clerkship is an *excellent* credential, perhaps the best all-purpose credential you can get. Whether you want to go to a corporation, government agency, public interest organization, or become a law professor—no matter what you want to do next—judicial clerkships are the 'universal solvent.'" WALTON, AMERICA'S GREATEST PLACES TO WORK WITH A LAW DEGREE, at 916.

Takeaway: **Consider running for or seeking appoint as a judge if you seek a position of influence from which to resolve disputes while shaping law for others, particularly if you have judicial patience and discernment. Also consider judicial clerkships if you have the research, writing, and analytic skills of a judge.**

Response: "I want first to clerk for a judge for a year or two and then run for local judge as soon as I have the minimum required experience. I have always had discerning insight into dispute resolution."

Reflect: What aspects of judging would attract you? What aspects of judging would repel you? Do you have judicial temperament? Do you have judicial insight and discernment? How strong is your law knowledge? How strong are your research and writing skills?

Engage: Rate each of the following common conditions of judging as a +1 (like), 0 (neutral), or -1 (dislike): (a) wear a black robe; (b) sit behind a bench all day; (c) listen a lot, speak seldom; (d) choose no matters, instead handling what others bring to you; (e) read a lot; (f) research and write orders and opinions; (g) have appellate judges review, critique, overturn, and send back your work; (h) job security until the next election or appointment; (i) steady fair compensation; (j) reasonable benefits. If your plusses and minuses total eight or more, then consider seeking a judicial career. If anything less than eight, then consider other careers, not judging.

Snapshot: The trial lawyer smiled as he walked through the Y's shower room on his way to the lap pool for his lunchtime exercise. The judge stood leaning heavily against the tiled wall, his weary head planted firmly under the shower nozzle, hot water pouring through his thinning hair, steam rising from his aching back. Must have been another difficult motion docket this morning, the trial lawyer thought as he chuckled at the judge's familiar position. The lawyer swam a few short laps, climbed out of the pool, and headed back to the shower room, where sure enough, the judge still stood with his head planted firmly under the soaking nozzle.

95 Corporate Counsel

Some organizations, whether for-profit, government agency, or nonprofit, are large and complex enough to be able to have their own in-house lawyer. For a lawyer to be *in-house* means that the lawyer is an employee of the organization. The in-house counsel effectively has only one client, the counsel's employer. Organizations call their chief lawyer employee their general counsel, corporate counsel, or in-house counsel. If the organization is large enough to have more than one lawyer employee doing legal work for the organization, then the organization may have a corporate-counsel office led by a general counsel supervising associate or assistant corporate counsel. "Because corporate attorneys often have to consult with accountants, bankers and various employees of the companies they represent, they also have to be able to communicate well with non-lawyers." KOURI, VAULT GUIDE TO CORPORATE LAW CAREERS, at 16.

Large-enough organizations may develop a corporate-counsel office sophisticated enough to look and function like a captive law firm. A captive law firm is one that works solely for and within a large organization but that maintains a law-firm like structure, even bearing its own name, to facilitate its law-service function. Captive law firms are typically found within insurance companies that require representation of the insurer and insureds. Corporate counsel, though, serve only the employer organization. "Ask an in-house lawyer what she does for a living and you will get answers ranging from the serious 'we do everything' to the not-so-serious 'saying "no" and "I don't think you can do that" as often as possible.' The reality is that, a description of an in-house counsel's duties depends on the size and structure of the legal department, the prevailing corporate culture, and the legal and business roles held by the lawyer." CAREY, FULL DISCLOSURE, at 274.

Corporate counsel may retain outside lawyers who work for independent law firms, to gain required special expertise that corporate counsel does not possess and to ensure objective evaluation of critical matters. Corporate-counsel work can attract private practitioners who struggle managing relationships and finances with multiple clients. Corporate-counsel positions are the long-term goal of some practitioners once they gain requisite private-practice experience. Although some lawyers devote their full careers to corporate-counsel work from right out of law school, many employers prefer to hire corporate counsel only once they have some years of experience. "[M]any law students regard corporate jobs as real plums. And there's a good reason for that. No billable hours, no need to generate business—qualities like that are attractive to many of us. Not only that, working in a corporation's Legal Department gives you an excellent jumping-off point for other kinds of corporate work that you also might enjoy...." WALTON, AMERICA'S GREATEST PLACES TO WORK WITH A LAW DEGREE, at 712.

Takeaway: **Consider a corporate-counsel position if you prefer employer loyalty over individual client service and want to build an institutional culture of compliance.**

Response: "I plan to look for a corporate-counsel position as soon as employers feel that I have acquired the necessary experience. I want to use my law knowledge and skills to help my employer organization and co-workers long term to build a strong organization and institutional culture."

Reflect: Have you worked for a business large enough to employ its own in-house lawyer or lawyers? If so, then what work did the in-house counsel seem to be doing? Would you like to do that work? Do you like constantly meeting new people, or do you prefer to work long term with the same people to build something of integrity? If you were in-house counsel, would you miss the entrepreneurial nature of law practice that you get to do some picking and choosing of clients and matters?

Engage: How many of the following common features of in-house counsel work would you like and appreciate? (a) One client—your employer. (b) You work with and for the same people every day rather than a stream of new clients. (c) You handle the matters that your employer needs you to handle, not what matters you choose to handle. (d) Your fortunes rise and fall with your employer's fortunes, not with the success or failure of your own work. (e) You may retain and supervise outside lawyers for litigation and other matters. (f) Your employer client has a non-law mission, of which your law services are only a supporter. (g) You may work directly with few or no lawyers, having little interaction with others knowledgeable in law. (h) You may know most of what you will do in a day, which may not change that much. If you counted six or more, then consider a corporate-counsel position for a career.

96 Judge Advocate General Corps

Military forces and actions raise law issues, requiring that the military have lawyers. Military bases in their myriad functions must comply with law, rule, and regulation. Military servicemembers also need lawyers who are familiar with the peculiar terms, requirements, and benefits of military service, and who can counsel and represent them in both military matters and in civilian matters that military service affects. The military provides for these law services through the Judge Advocates General Corps also known as the JAG Corps. Each branch of the military commissions lawyer officers to serve in the Judge Advocates General Corps. To be a military lawyer in the Corps, you must join a service branch, whether Army, Navy, Air Force, Marines, as a candidate for the Corps. "Upon becoming an officer, JAG attorneys attend a training program emphasizing courtroom skills and includes classroom instruction on the Uniform Code of Military Justice, which is the military's own criminal code." ABRAMS, THE OFFICIAL GUIDE TO LEGAL SPECIALTIES, at 320.

Once in the Corps, military lawyers perform a range of law services involving everything from international law, treaty, and convention, to rules of engagement, foreign law, court-martial law and procedure, law, rule, and regulation having to do with the terms of military service, veterans-benefits law, federal and state criminal law for servicemembers performing domestic base operations, and civil law of all kinds from family law to estate planning, real-property law, and simple contract obligations. Military bases are like small cities with all of their law issues and problems. Life goes on while servicemembers are in the military. JAG Corps lawyers may find themselves assisting servicemembers with many matters that lawyers in a civilian general practice also handle. JAC Corps service in effect combines two noble careers, military service and law, in one. "To perform well at their job, Judge Advocates need excellent writing, communication, interpersonal, teamwork, organizational, and self-management skills. Being courageous, honest, respectful, flexible, resourceful, and disciplined are personality traits that successful Judge Advocates share." ECHAORE-MCDAVID, CAREER OPPORTUNITIES IN LAW, at 21.

Takeaway: **Consider service in the judge advocate general corps if you share a strong commitment to the support of the nation's military and its servicemembers, desire to use your law knowledge and skills to address their issues, and have the character and fitness for military service.**

Response: "I plan to apply for service in the Judge Advocates General Corps to help the nation's military and its servicemembers address their many significant law issues. I have the commitment, character, fitness, and skills to be a military lawyer."

Reflect: Do you have prior military service or close family members who do? If not, then what experiences have you had and commitments do you hold that interest you in military service? What character, skills, and fitness do you have that would qualify you for military service? Do you know some of the law issues that the military and its servicemembers face? Do you have the law knowledge and skills to address those issues effectively?

Engage: How many of the following military-law matters would you be interested in handling as a member of the Judge Advocates General Corps? (a) Researching and writing memoranda for military generals on rules of engagement, treaties, and conventions. (b) Advising base commanders on environmental law and land-use issues. (c) Advising servicemembers regarding mortgage, lease, credit-card, and other obligations when they depart for active duty. (d) Assisting servicemembers with wills and powers of attorney when they depart for active duty. (e) Representing servicemembers in defense of local criminal charges. (f) Counseling servicemembers on separation, divorce, child-custody, child-support, and other family law matters. (g) Assisting servicemembers returning from active duty with enforcing federal laws guaranteeing re-employment in private positions. (h) Counseling servicemembers on terms of service and discharge from service. (i) Prosecuting and defending servicemembers in military court martials. (j) Assisting veterans with military-benefits issues. If you counted six or more and have the character and fitness for military service, then consider pursuing a career in the Judge Advocates General Corps.

Snapshot: The Christmas card showed the gorgeous couple standing arm in arm at a dress ball in a fabulously festooned hall. She wore a white gown with her hair piled regally atop her head. He wore his military officer's parade-dress uniform, cap, sword, and all. Her accompanying note glowed in pride at his JAG service, while describing her satisfying work as a staff attorney at an appellate court. They had graduated together several years earlier. He had gone immediately to officers training and then to his first assignment at one of the nation's largest domestic military bases. There, he had handled *everything*, he would say later, that lawyers in a general practice handle. He had thought he would practice military law but had instead represented servicemembers in all manner of civil and criminal matters. Although the general practice was not at all what he had expected, he had loved every minute of it.

Only after a couple of years had the Corps transferred him to another base where he began what seemed much more like the work of a military lawyer. And from the Christmas card, it sounded like he was loving every minute of that law practice, too.

97 Legal Education

Consider then just a few of the many other ways that lawyers use their legal education beyond law practice or employment requiring the direct practice of law. Legal education is one such field. In a sense, all lawyers teach law, some in undergraduate programs, others at law schools, still others in other graduate programs, but the rest in daily law practice. "One of the least recognized types of legal work is education. The most obvious example would be a law school teacher, followed by a lawyer teaching at some other level of school or college. In fact, a substantial number of lawyers are employed in the educational field. But many practicing lawyers engage in teaching through client seminars, newsletters, public speaking engagements, and educating clients how to utilize self-help remedies to legal problems." MUNNEKE, CAREERS IN LAW, at 24-25.

While teaching law does not involve directly providing law services, many lawyers who teach law also practice law. Adjunct law professors in particular may still be in full-time law practice or be judges or corporate counsel dealing daily with substantial law matters. Adjunct law teaching can help full-time practitioners confirm and update current knowledge and skills, deepen and broaden knowledge while honing skills, and teach the adjunct professor new practice knowledge and skills. Many lawyers teach as adjunct faculty in law schools, other graduate programs such as medicine and business, and undergraduate programs. "Many lawyers, examining their own careers, discover that they missed a calling when they failed to pursue a life in academia. Their concern is that they had hoped to make a larger contribution to the life of lawyers generally." CAIN, TURNING POINTS VOL. II, at 46.

Full-time law professors at accredited law schools may also still practice law, such as performing substantial pro bono service or even occasional compensated service. Full-time law professors also serve as expert witnesses on law matters and as consultants to lawyers and law firms facing complex law matters. They also publish practical books and articles for practitioners to read and follow, conduct seminars and speak at conferences for practitioners, teach in continuing-legal-education programs for lawyers, and of course teach law students. Law teaching can be a rewarding supplement to a practice field or a rewarding full-time career. "Law teaching also takes place far beyond just law schools. In fact, there are now more positions teaching law outside of law schools than within them, and the gap in favor of non-law school positions is growing rapidly. These jobs do not require that you meet the same very rigorous qualifications criteria that you must to teach at the law school level." HERMANN, FROM LEMONS TO LEMONADE IN THE NEW LEGAL JOB MARKET, at 83.

"One of the least recognized types of legal work is education. The most obvious example would be a law school teacher, followed by a lawyer teaching at some other level of school or college. In fact, a substantial number of lawyers are employed in the educational field. But many practicing lawyers engage in teaching through client seminars, newsletters, public speaking engagements, and educating clients how to utilize self-help remedies to legal problems." MUNNEKE, CAREERS IN LAW, at 24-25.

Takeaway: **Consider pursuing a career teaching law, after you have the experience to make your instruction practical, if you have the skill and calling to help others become committed and effective lawyers.**

Response: "As soon as I have valuable experience, I would like to teach law either at a law school or in undergraduate programs or other graduate programs, where I can convey to others the value of law and beneficial purpose of law services."

Reflect: What education, skill, or experience do you have in teaching? Do you have an interest in helping others learn?

Engage: Rank in order of your preference the following whom you would most like to teach about law: (a) law students; (b) paralegal students; (c) graduate students in business; (d) undergraduate students in business; (e) medical students; (f) physicians in a continuing-medical-education program; (g) nursing students; (h) nurses in a continuing-medical-education program; (i) education students; (j) teachers in a continuing-education program.

98 Human Resources

Human resources and personnel management is another area where lawyers sometimes work outside of direct law practice. Employment involves so many law issues that human-resources managers and experts often deal with lawyers and constantly deal with law issues. Human-resources managers negotiate labor agreements, implement evaluation and discipline systems, investigate harassment and discrimination complaints, support workplace-safety programs, negotiate benefits packages, and perform many similar activities each replete with law issues. A law degree gives a human-resources manager deep, reliable, and comprehensive knowledge of tax, worker's compensation, unemployment-benefits, contract, privacy, defamation, and other law issues directly affecting employment. "Depending on the corporation, this function may also be called industrial relations, labor relations, human resources, or personnel administration. ... The desirability of having law school-trained personnel employed in these activities is evident in the substantial number of lawyers now occupying these positions." MUNNEKE, NONLEGAL CAREERS, at 69.

Human-resources educational programs provide substantial law training but cannot do so to the depth and in the comprehensive quality of a law degree. Human-resources managers with a law degree also have a broader understanding of business planning and governance, sales and other commercial transactions, regulatory compliance, and similar law concerns that business leaders face, making those law-degreed human-resources managers key contributors to a business's leadership team.

Dear J.D.

Takeaway: **Consider human resources as an alternative field to law.**

Response: "I am pursuing a law degree in order to be more effective in my human-resources field, where I work all the time with lawyers and legal issues."

Reflect: Are you currently in human resources? Do you have education or experience in human resources? Do you like managing people? Are you effective at counseling others in ways that help them improve and perform?

Engage: In how many of the following human-resources issues would you like to be involved in trying to fashion a resolution? (a) Developing job descriptions and qualifications. (b) Establishing and updating compensation structures. (c) Reviewing online job applications and resumes. (d) Helping job applicants with criminal convictions find employment. (e) Recommending final decisions among equally qualified job candidates. (f) Developing and implementing an employee evaluation system. (g) Maintaining personnel record systems. (h) Working with a business office to ensure timely and accurate payroll. (i) Evaluating and negotiating benefits packages. (j) Terminating non-performing employees including providing severance. (k) Helping the company's board develop an executive-compensation framework. (l) Investigating and evaluating discrimination and retaliation complaints. If you counted eight or more, then consider human-resources work as alternative employment.

99 Business Management

Many lawyers pursue alternative careers managing businesses rather than practicing law. Some of those lawyers work their way up to chief executive officer of major corporations through the general counsel's office or simply through other non-law management positions. Lawyers manage at high levels within Fortune 500 companies including chief-executive positions. Other lawyers start their own businesses or join the management teams of existing small or large businesses, either from the ranks of law practice or corporate-counsel positions, or again simply out of other management positions in which law is not the focus. Lawyers make good business managers in part because of their law knowledge of significant business issues like formation, governance, contracts, liability, intellectual property, employment, finance, taxation, succession, and compliance. Yet lawyers also make good managers because of their logic, reasoning, research, investigation, writing, communication, and advocacy skills. "Many lawyers decide to make use of the business and management skills they have developed. Bolling ... accepted an offer to assume the managing directorship of an international manufacturing company ... after realizing that 'law is a business, and I am basically a business person who has developed some valuable entrepreneurial and managerial skills.'" ARRON, RUNNING FROM THE LAW, at 106.

Lawyers know how to frame business issues, collect data around those issues, and make rational decisions based on data rather than emotion or conjecture. They understand how to challenge premises and examine evidence. Business management is so much about identifying the goal, discerning and implementing the strategies to accomplish it, and assessing plan progress, all professional skills that lawyers learn early and exercise daily. Lawyers also have the training in interviewing, counseling, confrontation, and negotiation skills through which to manage the people and relationships critical to any business's success. Business management is an exciting and rewarding non-law field closely related to law and well suited for lawyers. "If you have a hard time seeing yourself as anything other than a lawyer, think about the dreams you had before law school. A few lawyers we know decided not to pursue their entrepreneurial dreams because of family considerations. When they finally got too dissatisfied with law, they left and proceeded to thrive in business." SCHNEIDER, SHOULD YOU REALLY BE A LAWYER? at 183.

Takeaway: **Consider owning or running a business using your law degree if you prefer to use your law knowledge and skills to develop business value.**

Response: "I am earning a law degree to make me a better business manager and leader. Law knowledge and skills should make me a much better business manager in regulated environments."

Reflect: What business education or experience do you have? Are you presently employed in managing a business? If not, then do you have close contacts that could gain you employment managing a business? Are you interested in business ownership? In what field of business would you manage if given the opportunity? What most qualifies you for that field? How strong are your management skills? What evidence do you have of their strength?

Engage: Choose and rank in order of preference your most-desired three of the following ten business-management opportunities: (a) be the sole proprietor of a tech startup; (b) be one of five founders and a co-manager of a craft-beer brewery; (c) manage a regional chain of ten restaurants for its wealthy but aging owner; (d) join the management team of a national seating-manufacturing business; (e) be a division manager of a multinational family owned direct-sales company; (f) manage overseas operations of a U.S.-based tier-one automotive supplier; (g) become the second-in-command executing the directives of a charismatic chief executive officer of a studio in the film industry; (h) accept board appointment to be chief executive officer of a national transport logistics company; (i) accept a hedge fund's retainer as a turn-around expert to save a nearly bankrupt energy-services company through severe cost-cutting; and (j) serve as president of a private nonprofit university during a time of program and enrollment growth.

100 Risk Management

Risk management is a broad and important field applying across many other fields, industries, and sectors. Every enterprise entails at least some risk. Indeed, risk is a necessary condition to reward. Nothing ventured, nothing gained. Risk management relates closely to regulatory compliance but goes beyond ensuring the lawfulness of activities to include measuring the size and probability of success against loss. Risk managers attempt to measure the positive and negative effects of uncertainty on various enterprises. That additional aspect of risk management, measuring positive and negative effects beyond law compliance, is what makes the field a good one for lawyers but one that simultaneously goes beyond law. "Risk management involves analysis of all corporate risks of accidental occurrences, both actual and potential, in the areas of property loss, loss of income, worker's compensation, and liability." MUNNEKE, NONLEGAL CAREERS, at 79.

Will the business or other activity succeed financially, socially, environmentally, and in other ways, or will it fail along one or more of those same measures? Risk inheres in every activity. Risk managers attempt to measure it against recognized or emerging standards, meaning attempt to predict its incidence while quantifying its effects. Risk managers obtain education and certification in those standards and measurement processes. Yet the processes of identifying, avoiding or accepting, controlling, and transferring risk are processes in which lawyers engage constantly in practice. Law school effectively educates lawyers in the fundamentals of risk management, making lawyers natural risk managers. "A growing number of corporations have risk management offices that attempt to evaluate financial and other risks companies face and minimize them through insurance purchases and other risk-avoidance measures. Attorneys are taught to evaluate and temper risk every day, and the risk management industry recognizes that: approximately 20 percent of the risk managers in the U.S. have law degrees." HERMANN, FROM LEMONS TO LEMONADE IN THE NEW LEGAL JOB MARKET, at 48.

Takeaway: **Consider risk management as a law-related career if you have the foresight to predict positive and negative outcomes of business and social enterprises.**

Response: "I want to work in risk management so as to help businesses and other enterprises evaluate activities proactively to reduce the harm and maximum the advantage in each case."

Reflect: Do you have consequential awareness? Do you see things before they happen? Are you constantly warning family, friends, and acquaintances of things that might happen if they continue in a certain course, or even if you do not actually warn others, then do you want to often? Do you have any education, skill, experience, or interest in statistics and probability? Are you reasonably good at quantitative reasoning? Do you prefer protecting things to fixing things, preventing events to cleaning up after events?

Engage: Count the number of the following common conditions of risk management that you would appreciate and would be good at doing: (a) interdisciplinary work learning about other fields than your own; (b) using formulas, statistics, probabilities, and quantitative reasoning; (c) financial-risk evaluation; (d) legal-risk evaluation; (e) social and reputational-risk evaluation; (f) preparing written recommendation, reports, and evaluations for others; (g) preparing risk-management and loss-prevention initiatives and programs; (h) investigating property, financial, and human

Dear J.D.

losses for cause and prevention; (i) quoting, evaluating, and negotiating insurance coverage; (j) reviewing and revising insurance agreements. If your count was five or more, then consider risk management as an alternative career.

Conclusion

Well then, you have one last lawyer role to encounter, my role as that of your law school campus dean. A law dean sees the extraordinary social ambition you bring to law school, social in the sense that you have gone to law school to learn to affect relationships among people, and extraordinary in consistency, diversity, and uniqueness. I once surveyed law-student core commitments, thinking that students would share a half dozen to one dozen common items. Instead, the 100 survey respondents disclosed well over 200 *different* core commitments. Despite the items' extraordinary breadth, reasonable minds would have endorsed every single one of them as socially constructive and highly appropriate for professionals. Many commitments were beyond laudatory into the profound. They were not some odd collection of eccentric values. Their breadth and large number suggested strongly your unique character, experience, and perspective, that which makes you unique.

Thus while you will pursue some work that others recognize as a law field, you will pursue that work in your own fashion, bringing your own qualities, merits, skill, insights, and commitments. Nothing, I feel, could be better for you to do so, and nothing could be better for your clients. You are your unique you, made in God's exquisitely varied and never-ending image.

You are thus capable of acts and counsel so startlingly sound, restorative, and generous that legions of clients should follow you. Those legions should be your professional legacy, that when you look back on your career, you will not see fields in which you engaged, events you influenced, and fees you earned but instead a parade of redeemed, restored, and regenerated souls. Such is the power of law practice to guide on a path of personal, social, economic, and eternal prosperity.

As a law dean, I have this immense privilege of orienting students as they enter law school each with their unique character and commitments. I then share with my professor colleagues the immense privilege of learning law with you, of allowing law to enliven and engage us while together we help you discern your unique path into this noble profession. I also have the extraordinary pleasure of seeing and hearing from law graduates each of whom have found their practice niche, perhaps traditional or at least recognizable as a law field but nonetheless unique in its full character. I get to share their excitement, engagement, challenges, and successes as if in very small part they were my own. You will be one of those graduates soon. Having read this book and completed some of its exercises, you may not be that much clearer on exactly what kind of law you want to practice. Yet you now understand much more about your opportunities and how they may or may not be your unique path. May God bless you richly as you walk, run, and exult along that path. You are already choosing well.

About the Author

Nelson Miller is a professor and associate dean at Thomas M. Cooley Law School. Before joining Cooley, Dean Miller practiced civil litigation for 16 years in a small-firm setting, representing individuals, corporations, agencies, and public and private universities. He has published 20 books and dozens of book chapters and articles on law, legal education, and law practice. The Harvard University Press book *What the Best Law Teachers Do* included him among the couple of dozen law professors that it studied, while the State Bar of Michigan honored him with the John W. Cummiskey Award for pro-bono service. He earned his law degree at the University of Michigan before joining the firm that later became Fajen and Miller, PLLC, his practice base before moving full-time into law teaching.

Bibliography

ABRAMS, LISA L., THE OFFICIAL GUIDE TO LEGAL SPECIALTIES: AN INSIDER'S GUIDE TO EVERY MAJOR PRACTICE AREA (The BarBri Group 2000);

ARRON, DEBORAH, RUNNING FROM THE LAW: WHY GOOD LAWYERS ARE GETTING OUT OF THE LEGAL PROFESSION (DecisionBooks 2004);

ARRON, DEBORAH, WHAT CAN YOU DO WITH A LAW DEGREE? A LAWYER'S GUIDE TO CAREER ALTERNATIVES INSIDE, OUTSIDE, & AROUND THE LAW (DecisionBooks 2004);

ARTHUR, JAMES, & KAREN BOHLIN, EDS., CITIZENSHIP AND HIGHER EDUCATION: THE ROLE OF UNIVERSITIES IN COMMUNITIES AND SOCIETY (Routledge 2009);

BATTISTONI, RICHARD, & WILLIAM E. HUDSON, EDS., EXPERIENCING CITIZENSHIP: CONCEPTS AND MODELS FOR SERVICE LEARNING (Stylus 1997);

BEAN, JOHN C., & MARYELLEN WEIMER, ENGAGING IDEAS: THE PROFESSOR'S GUIDE TO INTEGRATING WRITING, CRITICAL LEARNING, AND ACTIVE LEARNING IN THE CLASSROOM (Jossey-Bass 2011);

BEAN, LAUREN, ED., CAREERS IN NATIONAL SECURITY LAW (American Bar Association 2009);

BERG, GARY A., LOW-INCOME STUDENTS AND THE PERPETUATION OF INEQUALITY (Ashgate 2010);

BLAKELY, SUSAN SMITH, BEST FRIENDS AT THE BAR: WHAT WOMEN NEED TO KNOW ABOUT A CAREER IN THE LAW (Aspen Pubs. 2009);

BRUNER, JEROME, THE CULTURE OF EDUCATION (Harvard Univ. Press 1996);

BROOKFIELD, STEPHEN D., TEACHING FOR CRITICAL THINKING: TOOLS AND TECHNIQUES TO HELP STUDENTS QUESTION THEIR ASSUMPTIONS (Jossey-Bass 2011);

BUDD, JOHN M., HIGHER EDUCATION'S PURPOSE: INTELLECTUAL AND SOCIAL PROGRESS (University Press of America 2008);

BUTIN, DAN W., SERVICE-LEARNING IN HIGHER EDUCATION: CRITICAL ISSUES AND DIRECTIONS (Palgrave Macmillan 2005);

CAIN, GEORGE H., TURNING POINTS: NEW PATHS & SECOND CAREERS FOR LAWYERS VOL. II (American Bar Association 2009);

CAMENSON, BLYTHE, CAREERS FOR LEGAL EAGLES & OTHER LAW-AND-ORDER TYPES (McGraw-Hill 2d ed. 2005);

CAREY, CHRISTEN CIVILETTO, FULL DISCLOSURE: THE NEW LAWYER'S MUST-READ CAREER GUIDE (ALM Publishing 2001);

CHAN, ADRIENNE S., & DONALD FISHER, EDS., THE EXCHANGE UNIVERSITY: THE CORPORATIZATION OF ACADEMIC CULTURE (UBC Press 2009);

CHRISTENSEN, CLAYTON M., & HENRY J. EHRING, THE INNOVATIVE UNIVERSITY: CHANGING THE DNA OF HIGHER EDUCATION FROM THE INSIDE OUT (Jossey-Bass 2011);

CURRY, LYNN, & JOHN F. WERGIN, EDUCATING PROFESSIONALS: RESPONDING TO NEW EXPECTATIONS FOR COMPETENCE AND ACCOUNTABILITY (Jossey-Bass 1993);

DEWEY, JOHN, EXPERIENCE AND EDUCATION (Free Press 1997);

DEWEY, JOHN, HOW WE THINK (FQ Books 2010);

EADES, RONALD W., HOW TO BE A LAW PROFESSOR GUIDE (Vandeplas 2008);

FALLOWS, STEPHEN, & STEVEN CHRISTINE, INTEGRATING KEY SKILLS IN HIGHER EDUCATION: EMPLOYABILITY, TRANSFERRABLE SKILLS, AND LEARNING FOR LIFE (Routledge 2000);

FARNSWORTH, KENT A., LEADERSHIP AS SERVICE: A NEW MODEL FOR HIGHER EDUCATION IN A NEW CENTURY (Rowman & Littlefield Pubs. 2006);

FRIEDLAND, STEVEN, & GERALD HESS, TEACHING THE LAW SCHOOL CURRICULUM (Carolina Academic Press 2004);

FURI-PERRY, URSULA, FIFTY UNIQUE LEGAL PATHS: HOW TO FIND THE RIGHT JOB (American Bar Association 2008);

GAMINO, JOHN, ROBB A. LONGMAN, & MATTHEW R. SONTAG, EDS., CAREERS IN TAX LAW: PERSPECTIVES ON THE TAX PROFESSION AND WHAT IT HOLDS FOR YOU (American Bar Association 2009);

GARDINER, LION F., REDESIGNING HIGHER EDUCATION: PRODUCING DRAMATIC GAINS IN STUDENT LEARNING (Jossey-Bass 1994);

GERSON, DONNA, CHOOSING SMALL, CHOOSING SMART: THE JOB SEEKER'S GUIDE TO SMALL LAW FIRMS (NALP Revd. 3rd ed. 2012);

GEYH, CHARLES, WHAT'S LAW GOT TO DO WITH IT? (Stanford Univ. Press 2011);

GITLOW, ABRAHAM, AMERICA'S RESEARCH UNIVERSITIES: THE CHALLENGES AHEAD (Univ. Press of America 2011);

GOTTLIEB, KARLA, & GAIL ROBINSON, A PRACTICAL GUIDE TO INTEGRATING CIVIL RESPONSIBILITY INTO THE CURRICULUM (Community College Press 2007);

GRUBB, TIMOTHY, VAULT GUIDE TO LABOR AND EMPLOYMENT LAW CAREERS: AN INDISPENSABLE GUIDE TO THE FAST-GROWING FIELD OF LABOR AND EMPLOYMENT LAW (Vault 2003);

HAHN, IRENE, ED., BUILDING A BETTER LEGAL PROFESSION'S GUIDE TO LAW FIRMS: THE LAW STUDENT'S GUIDE TO FINDING THE PERFECT LAW JOB (Kaplan Pub. 2009);

HENSLEE, WILLIAMS D., ENTERTAINMENT CAREERS FOR LAWYERS (American Bar Association 2014);

HERMANN, RICHARD L., FROM LEMONS TO LEMONADE IN THE NEW LEGAL JOB MARKET: WINNING JOB SEARCH STRATEGIES FOR ENTRY-LEVEL ATTORNEYS (DecisionBooks 2012);

HERMANN, RICHARD L., MANAGING YOUR LEGAL CAREER: BEST PRACTICES FOR CREATING THE CAREER YOU WANT (American Bar Association 2010);

HERMANN, RICHARD L., PRACTICING LAW IN SMALL-TOWN AMERICA (American Bar Association 2012);

HORN, CARL, III, LAWYERLIFE: FINDING A LIFE AND A HIGHER CALLING IN THE PRACTICE OF LAW (American Bar Association 2003);

HOUCHIN, KEVIN E., FUEL THE SPARK: 5 GUIDING VALUES FOR SUCCESS IN LAW & LIFE (MadeEasy Pub. 2009);

JOHNSON, BRIAN T., & CAROLYN R. O'GRADY, EDS., THE SPIRIT OF SERVICE: EXPLORING FAITH, SERVICE, AND SOCIAL JUSTICE IN HIGHER EDUCATION (Anker Pub. Co. 2006);

JUNCO, REYNOL, & JEANNA MASTRODICASA, CONNECTING TO THE NET.GENERATION: WHAT HIGHER EDUCATIONAL PROFESSIONALS NEED TO KNOW ABOUT TODAY'S STUDENTS (National Assn. of Student Personnel Admins. 2007);

KAHLENBERG, RICHARD D., REWARDING STRIVERS: HELPING LOW-INCOME STUDENTS SUCCEED IN COLLEGE (The Century Foundation 2010);

KOURI, ZAHIE EL, VAULT GUIDE TO CORPORATE LAW CAREERS: INVESTIGATE THE PRESTIGIOUS AND LUCRATIVE FIELD OF CORPORATE LAW (Vault 2003);

LASSON, KENNETH, TREMBLING IN THE IVORY TOWER: EXCESSES IN THE PURSUIT OF TRUTH AND TENURE (Bancroft 2003);

LE BRUN, M., & R. JOHNSTONE, THE QUIET (R)EVOLUTION: IMPROVING STUDENT LEARNING IN LAW (Law Book Co. 1995);

LEE, KEITH, THE MARBLE AND THE SCULPTOR: FROM LAW SCHOOL TO LAW PRACTICE (American Bar Assn. 2013);

LISMAN, C. DAVID, & IRENE E. HARVEY, BEYOND THE TOWER: CONCEPTS AND MODELS FOR SERVICE LEARNING (Stylus 2000);

LITOWITZ, DOUGLAS E., THE DESTRUCTION OF YOUNG LAWYERS: BEYOND ONE L (Univ. of Akron Press 2005);

MACFARLANE, BRUCE, THE ACADEMIC CITIZEN: THE VIRTUE OF SERVICE IN UNIVERSITY LIFE (Routledge 2006);

MAHARG, PAUL, TRANSFORMING LEGAL EDUCATION (Ashgate 2007);

MARTIN, JAMES, & JAMES E. SAMELS, TURNAROUND: LEADING STRESSED COLLEGES AND UNIVERSITIES TO EXCELLENCE (Johns Hopkins Univ. Press 2008);

MARTIN, RANDY, UNDER NEW MANAGEMENT: UNIVERSITIES, ADMINISTRATORS, AND THE PROFESSIONAL TURN (Temple Univ. Press 2011);

MERRIAM, SHARAN B., & ANDRE P. GRACE, THE JOSSEY-BASS READER ON CONTEMPORARY ISSUES IN ADULT EDUCATION (Jossey-Bass 2011);

MOORIS, KATHY, & JILL ECKERT, ASK THE CAREER COUNSELORS: ANSWERS FOR LAWYERS ON THEIR LIVES AND LIFE'S WORK (American Bar Association 2003);

MUETING, ANN M., STARTING AN IP LAW PRACTICE: CRITICAL QUESTIONS TO ASK YOURSELF (American Bar Association 2012);

MUNNEKE, GARY A., CAREERS IN LAW (McGraw-Hill 3d. ed. 2004);

MUNNEKE, GARY A., HOW TO SUCCEED IN LAW SCHOOL (Barron's Educ. Series 4th ed. 2008);

MUNNEKE, GARY A., NONLEGAL CAREERS FOR LAWYERS (5th ed. American Bar Association 2006);

MUNNEKE, GARY A., & ELLEN WAYNE, THE LEGAL CAREER GUIDE: FROM LAW STUDENT TO LAWYER (American Bar Association 5th ed. 2008);

NASH, SHANNON KING, VAULT GUIDE TO TAX LAW CAREERS: GET THE INSIDE SCOOP ON CAREERS IN TAX LAW (Vault 2004);

NIELSEN, SHEILA, JOB QUEST FOR LAWYERS: THE ESSENTIAL GUIDE TO FINDING AND LANDING THE JOB YOU WANT (American Bar Association 2011);

NODDINGS, NEIL, EDUCATING FOR INTELLIGENT BELIEF OR UNBELIEF (Teachers College Press 1993);

PARKS, SHARON DALOZ, BIG QUESTIONS, WORTHY DREAMS: MENTORING EMERGING ADULTS IN THEIR SEARCH FOR MEANING, PURPOSE, AND FAITH (Jossey-Bass 10th anniversary ed. 2011);

PFEIFER, WILLIAM L., JR., HOW TO START A SUCCESSFUL LAW PRACTICE: THE NEW LAWYER'S GUIDE TO OPENING AN OFFICE AS A SOLO OR SMALL FIRM ATTORNEY (Pipers Willow 2006);

POPHAM, W. JAMES, UNLEARNED LESSONS: SIX STUMBLING BLOCKS TO OUR SCHOOLS' SUCCESS (Harvard Educ. Press 2009);

RANDALL, VERNELIA, PLANNING FOR EFFECTIVE LEGAL INSTRUCTION: A WORKBOOK (Carolina Academic Press 2011);

REDFIELD, SARAH E., THINKING LIKE A LAWYER: AN EDUCATOR'S GUIDE TO LEGAL ANALYSIS AND RESEARCH (Carolina Academic Press 2d ed. 2011);

RESNICK, DANIEL P., & DANA S. SCOTT, THE INNOVATIVE UNIVERSITY (Carnegie Mellon Univ. Press 2004);

SALT, VULNERABLE POPULATIONS AND TRANSFORMATIVE LAW TEACHING: A READER (Carolina Academic Press 2011);

SALTMARSH, JOHN, & EDWARD ZLOTKOWSKI, EDS., HIGHER EDUCATION AND DEMOCRACY: ESSAYS ON SERVICE-LEARNING AND CIVIC ENGAGEMENT (Temple Univ. Press 2011);

SANDEEN, ARTHUR, ENHANCING LEADERSHIP IN COLLEGES AND UNIVERSITIES: A CASE APPROACH (Charles C. Thomas Pub. Ltd. 2011);

SCHACHTER, MADELEINE, THE LAW PROFESSOR'S HANDBOOK: A PRACTICAL GUIDE TO TEACHING LAW STUDENTS (Carolina Academic Press 2003);

SCHAUER, FREDERICK, THINKING LIKE A LAWYER: A NEW INTRODUCTION TO LEGAL REASONING (Harvard Univ. Press 2009);

SCHNEIDER, DEBORAH, & GARY BELSKY, SHOULD YOU REALLY BE A LAWYER? THE GUIDE TO SMART CAREER CHOICES BEFORE, DURING & AFTER LAW SCHOOL (DecisionBooks 2005);

SEDBERRY, STEVEN R., LAW SCHOOL LABYRINTH: A GUIDE TO MAKING THE MOST OF YOUR LEGAL EDUCATION (Kaplan Pub. 2009);

SHULMAN, LEE S., THE WISDOM OF PRACTICE: ESSAYS ON TEACHING, LEARNING, AND LEARNING TO TEACH (Jossey-Bass 2004);

SKEMP, RICHARD R., INTELLIGENCE, LEARNING, AND ACTION: FOUNDATION FOR THEORY AND PRACTICE IN EDUCATION (John Wiley & Sons 1979);

SLAUGHTER, SHEILA, & GARY RHOADES, ACADEMIC CAPITALISM AND THE NEW ECONOMY: MARKETS, STATE, AND HIGHER EDUCATION (Johns Hopkins Univ. Press 2009);

SMITH, BARBARA LEIGH, JOHN MCCANN, & ALEXANDER W. ASTIN, REINVENTING OURSELVES: INTERDISCIPLINARY EDUCATION, COLLABORATIVE LEARNING, AND EXPERIMENTATION IN HIGHER LEARNING (Jossey-Bass 2001);

SMITH, FRANK, THE BOOK OF LEARNING AND FORGETTING (Teachers College Press 1998);

SMITH, WILSON, & THOMAS BENDER, EDS., AMERICAN HIGHER EDUCATION TRANSFORMED, 1940-2005: DOCUMENTING THE NATIONAL DISCOURSE (Johns Hopkins Univ. Press 2008);

STAUDENMAIER, HEIDI MCNEIL, ED., CHANGING JOBS: A HANDBOOK FOR LAWYERS IN THE NEW MILLENIUM (American Bar Association 1999);

STELLJES, ANDREW D., SERVICE-LEARNING AND COMMUNITY ENGAGEMENT: COGNITIVE DEVELOPMENTAL LONG-TERM SOCIAL CONCERN (Cambria Press 2008);

STEVENS, DANNELLE D., & JOANNE E. COOPER, JOURNAL KEEPING: HOW TO USE REFLECTIVE WRITING FOR LEARNING, TEACHING, PROFESSIONAL INSIGHT AND POSITIVE CHANGE (Stylus Pub. 2009);

STEVENS, ROBERT BOCKING, LAW SCHOOL: LEGAL EDUCATION IN AMERICA FROM THE 1850S TO THE 1980S (Lawbook Exchange 2001);

STUHL, SETH, VAULT GUIDE TO BANKRUPTCY LAW CAREERS: GET THE INSIDE SCOOP ON THE BOOMING FIELD OF BANKRUPTCY LAW (Vault 2003);

SULLIVAN, WILLIAM M., ANNE COLBY, JUDITH WELCH WEGNER, LLOYD BOND, & LEE S. SHULMAN, EDUCATING LAWYERS: PREPARATION FOR THE PROFESSION OF LAW (Jossey-Bass 2007);

TALASKA, RICHARD A., ED., CRITICAL REASONING IN CONTEMPORARY CULTURE (State Univ. of New York Press 1992);

TANAKA, GREG, THE INTERCULTURAL CAMPUS: TRANSCENDING CULTURE AND POWER IN AMERICAN HIGHER EDUCATION (Peter Lang Pub. 2007);

TAYLOR, MARK C., CRISIS ON CAMPUS: A BOLD PLAN FOR REFORMING OUR COLLEGES AND UNIVERSITIES (Knopf 2010);

Thelin, A History of American Higher Education (Johns Hopkins Univ. Press 2d ed. 2011);

Thomson, David I.C., Law School 2.0: Legal Education for a Digital Age (LexisNexis 2009);

Viswanathan, Neeraja, Vault Guide to Litigation Law Careers: Get a Step Up in the Fast-Paced and Challenging Field of Litigation Law (Vault 2003);

Vogt, M. Diane, Preparing for Reentry: What Lawyers Need to Know to Navigate the Road Ahead After a Career Break (American Bar Association 2009);

Walton, Kimm Alayne, America's Greatest Places to Work with a Law Degree — and How to Make the Most of Any Job, No Matter Where It Is! (Harcourt Brace 1999);

Ward, Kelly, Faculty Service Roles and the Scholarship of Engagement: ASHE-ERIC Higher Education Report (Jossey-Bass 2003);

Wildavsky, Ben, The Great Brain Race: How Global Universities Are Reshaping the World (Princeton Univ. Press 2d ed. 2010);

Zachary, Lois J., The Mentor's Guide: Facilitating Effective Learning Relationships (Wiley 2000).

Index

Administrative Law 262
Affinities 39
Appellate Advocacy 178
Bankruptcy 218
Boutique Practice 127
Business Management 298
Business Planning 231
Calling 52
Care 4
Choices 26
Choosing Sides 87
Civil Litigation 165
Civil Rights 200
Class Actions 175
Collections 222
Commercial Litigation 169
Confrontation 84
Constraints 23
Conversation 1
Corporate Counsel 286
Courage 58
Criminal Defense 148
Criminal Justice 145
Criminal or Civil 142
Direct Pursuit 34
Dispute Resolution 139
Drunk-Driving Defense 152
Economics 15
Effectiveness 18

Employment Law	212
Employment or Practice	68
Estate Planning	225
Faith	50
Family Law	203
Federal Defense	155
Federal Litigation	172
Firm Finances	112
Firm Size	92
Forums	90
Full Time	71
General Practice	121
Good Decisions	29
Happiness	32
Health Law	255
Human Resources	296
Immigration Law	266
Insurance Defense	186
Insurance Law	252
Intellectual Property Law	238
Intrinsic Value	11
Judicial Positions	283
Judge Advocate General Corps	289
Juvenile Law	206
Labor Law	215
Large Firms	95
Legal Education	293
Legacy	55
Legislative Work	280
License Defense	162
Licensure	63
Listening	61
Litigation	136
Making a Living	66
Malpractice	196
Management	106

Master or Servant?	20
Meaning	42
Mid-Size Firms	97
Municipal Law	259
Natural Resources Law	249
Part Time	74
Personal Finances	77
Personal Injury	182
Persons	48
Philosophy	45
Practice Fields	115
Practice Mix	118
Probate Practice	228
Prosecution	270
Public Defender	274
Public Interest	277
Risk Management	165
Question	6
Rainmaking	109
Real Property	245
Risk Management	301
Rule of Law	13
School Law	209
Securities Law	235
Skill Building	80
Small Firms	100
Social Security Disability	193
Solo Practice	103
Specializing	125
Stress	9
Taxation	242
Transactional Practice	133
Transactions or Litigation	130
Virtue	37
White-Collar Defense	159
Worker's Compensation	189

www.ingramcontent.com/pod-product-compliance
Lightning Source LLC
Chambersburg PA
CBHW071856290426
44110CB00013B/1167